THE CARE
OF PRINTS AND DRAWINGS

The Care of Prints and Drawings

MARGARET HOLBEN ELLIS

AASLH Press • Nashville, Tennessee
The American Association for State and Local History

*Published with the assistance
of the J. Paul Getty Trust*

Author and publisher make grateful acknowledgment to the Grant Program of the J. Paul Getty Trust, which provided the funds that made possible the publication of this book.

Some of the material in this book has appeared in print before, in different form, in *Drawing,* a publication of the Drawing Society, and is published in revised form here by permission.

Library of Congress Cataloging-in-Publication Data

Ellis, Margaret Holben.
  The care of prints and drawings.

  Bibliography: p.
  Includes index.
  1. Prints—Conservation and restoration.
  2. Drawing—Conservation and restoration. I. Title.
NE380.E45   1987   760′.028′8   86-7962
ISBN 0-910050-79-1

Designed by Gillian Murrey

*This book
is dedicated
to M. M. E.*

As publisher of this book, the American Association for State and Local History expresses full confidence in the professional judgment and expertise of Author Margaret Holben Ellis, Chairman of the Conservation Center, Institute of Fine Arts, New York University and Consulting Conservator at the Metropolitan Museum of Art, where she was formerly Associate Conservator of Prints and Drawings.

Ms. Ellis emphasizes that the advice she offers here on conservation procedures for works of art on paper "is meant to be useful. My purpose . . . is to offer information that may be helpful to anyone responsible for providing good care and a safe environment for prints and drawings . . . It is my hope that [these] pages . . . can help to fill a critical need for practical, straightforward information on the general care of such artifacts." In view of the fact that the desired results to be obtained by following the suggestions offered will depend, however, to a great extent, upon the reader's individual judgment, skill, accuracy, and caution, the Association cannot guarantee results and will not accept responsibility for any damage or injury to property or person arising from the use of any information in this book.

—The Editors, AASLH Press

Contents

Acknowledgments

I AM DEEPLY appreciative of the continuing support of my colleagues in the Department of Paper Conservation of the Metropolitan Museum of Art, beginning with Merritt Safford—now retired—who initially approved this project, and Helen K. Otis, Marjorie N. Shelley, Betty Fiske, and Margaret Lawson. All gave freely of their knowledge and expertise; but of more personal significance, all expressed confidence in the worthiness of this endeavor. I hope that the result lives up to their high standards. Lindsey Fisher provided the matting and hinging diagrams and Vivienne Valentine helped enormously in compiling Appendix I.

Colta Ives, Curator of Prints and Photographs; Jacob Bean, Curator of Drawings; William S. Lieberman, Chairman of Twentieth-Century Art; George Szabo, Curator of the Robert Lehman Collection; John K. Howat, Lawrence A. Fleischman Chairman of the Departments of American Art; and William D. Wixom, Chairman of Medieval Art, have generously allowed me to study and use items in their collections to illustrate various conservation problems. Staff members of these departments have been most co-operative, as have the dedicated members of the Thomas J. Watson Library and the Photograph and Slide Library.

The owners of the privately held prints and drawings were, without exception, willing to have their pieces illustrated, since their use in this book might lead to the recognition and prevention of conservation problems in other collections. I thank them all, especially Dr. and Mrs. Ronald E. Ohl, for their selflessness. Providing these illustrations would have been impossible without the help of my friend Sheldan Collins, who, despite his own publishing deadlines, managed to accommodate mine with a smile.

Conservators from other institutions and in private practice gave forthright, often differing, opinions on sections of this book. Records were opened and information given without hesitation or thought of recompense. I recognize the level of trust involved in these gestures. It is difficult to express my gratitude adequately to the many extraordinary conservators who have helped me.

Caroline K. Keck, Executive Director of the Foundation of the American Institute for Conservation, deserves special mention for introducing me to the American Association for State and Local History, and furthermore, for putting in some good words on my behalf.

I must add that both the AASLH, as my publisher, and Betty Doak Elder, as Director of the AASLH Press when this book was being prepared, dealt admirably with the conservation controversies that invariably arise over this kind of publication. Both the Association and its press director trod the fine line between allegiance to the author and responsibility as publishers always with patience and diplomacy. Above all, we were concerned that information about the conservation of prints and drawings be presented with the utmost caution and clarity.

This book grew from a series of articles originally commissioned by the Drawing Society and published in *Drawing*. I am grateful to them for allowing me to use material from those essays.

The ideas expressed herein are those of the author and do not necessarily represent those of the Metropolitan Museum of Art.

THE CARE
OF PRINTS AND DRAWINGS

Introduction

*T*HE PURPOSE OF this book is to give practical, straightforward advice to those responsible for the care of prints and drawings, works of art traditionally made on paper or— though much less often, nowadays—on parchment. The book grew and took shape in response to many inquiries that indicated, by the repetition of certain questions, a critical need for this information.

The objects I speak of caring for and preserving need not belong to a museum, although this book tends to address such institutions. My suggestions here might apply equally to the care of a priceless Renaissance ink drawing prized by connoisseurs, a twentieth-century superstar's striking graphic, purchased for its investment potential, or to a fragile, handmade valentine, of incalculable value to its owner as a sentimental keepsake. *All are irreplaceable, and all need—and deserve—care of the highest quality.*

Prints and drawings vary in kind, according to differences in the type of background material—usually called *support*—on which they appear, and to differences in the medium used to put them there. All of them, however, share certain common characteristics, and they are susceptible to common problems, defects, injuries, and disfigurements.

Good maintenance for them is based on the ability to recognize their common characteristics and to cope with the common conservation problems they can be heir to. Many of the things that can go wrong with prints and drawings can be detected, in good time, if the signals of trouble developing are recognized. Some apparently negligible symptoms are, in fact, early warning signs of a major threat to their well-being. Some conservation ailments, such as *buckling*—the wrinkling, warping, or distorting of paper—are quite general and can affect almost any type of print or drawing. Others, such as flaking paint, are restricted to works in a much narrower range.

To devise appropriate protective procedures to counteract problems that beset these works of art, therefore, it is helpful to have a clear idea of what prints and drawings are, the ways in which they are similar or

3

different, the ways they are made, and the reasons their composition and construction can make them vulnerable to the kinds of problems they often develop.

Some general comments on the nature of prints and drawings follow, here, with directions to that area of the text where more detailed information on various points can be found.

The creative beginning of the kinds of art we call *prints* and *drawings* is much the same: they came into being when some human hand made visible marks—or caused them to be made—on a piece of background material. The marks might be made with any number of substances; and the background material could also vary—though, from the beginning, the support had a number of consistent characteristics: it was some substance comparatively thin, flat, portable, capable of being folded or rolled, and capable of retaining the artist's marks on its surface.

Over the years, different areas of the world have devised varied kinds of materials on which to write and draw. Some of these substances were a bit esoteric, and some were used in circumscribed areas, for rather limited purposes; and because of the way they were made, they have radically different characteristics from those of parchment or paper—which, since medieval times, have been the two kinds of support used most extensively for prints and drawings. Anthropological or ethnographic collections today may include documents or drawings on such variants as bark, palm leaves, Pacific Islands tapa cloth, Mexican amatl, or Chinese rice paper—which is not made from rice at all, but from the pith of a Chinese plant, *Tetrapanax papyriferus,* called "the rice paper plant." Such collections may even include works on papyrus, which was made thousands of years before the birth of Christ and used throughout the Mediterranean world for centuries as a material for writing and drawing.[1] Close relatives of paper, in that they all have vegetal origins and can be formed into flat, foldable, rollable, portable sheets of material capable of retaining marks put on their surfaces, these substances are mentioned only briefly, here, and in chapter 1, and are not further discussed in the book. Major museums whose holdings include these paperlike substances often can provide helpful information on their care.

Chapter 1, "Parchment and Paper: Supports for Prints and Drawings," discusses parchment and paper in detail and introduces discussion of general conservation problems shared by all works of art on paper, regardless of their media. *It should be noted here that, in this book, the discussion of paper is confined to kinds of paper made from organic substances, omitting those that include mineral and synthetic fibers; and that not all of the pliable organic substances for writing or drawing that may be found in a collection are discussed.*

Conspicuously absent from this work is discussion of photographs and photographic papers. Over the years, it has become apparent to conservators of paper that the conservation of photographs differs vastly from that of prints and drawings. Standard conservation procedures for photographs also require modifications in procedures for matting, framing, storage, and exhibition—matters well covered in specialized literature readily available and heartily recommended to the interested reader.[2]

Chapter 2, "The Media of Prints and Drawings," deals both with the varied kinds of art that may appear on paper and the varied media used to produce it. Here the reader will find descriptions of those conservation problems that affect specific artistic materials. It should be mentioned that the category of drawings has been expanded to include pastels, watercolors, gouaches, and oil paintings made on paper.

Chapter 3 discusses matting, hinging, and framing—the necessary preparation of a work of art on paper so that it can be more readily protected from the ordinary rigors of handling, examination, exhibition, environmental fluctuations, and general wear and tear.

This is my first opportunity—and I seize it eagerly—to say that *the careful matting, hinging, and framing of prints and drawings according to conservation standards is one of the most effective ways to provide a longer life for these works of art.*

Chapter 4, "Storage and Environment," considers the almost universal quandary of so many of us who have fragile works of art to protect and must achieve that despite such common hazards as leaky basements, sun-filled galleries, ovenlike attics, insect and animal pests, skimpy shelving, shallow storage bins, make-do materials, atmospheric pollution, inadequate humidity control—and chronic shortages of both space and money. Chapter 4 suggests some workable ways around such obstacles to providing a safe environment for art on paper.

Chapter 5, "Basic Conservation Procedures," outlines a number of things that can be done to reclaim damaged or disfigured prints and drawings and help to prevent further damage.

At the end of each chapter is a list of reading material that can provide additional information on various topics discussed in that chapter.

And I close this introduction by restating something I've already said, so important to remember that it bears repeating: The human element, unfortunately, is often the cause of the most irreparable damage, often brought about with the best of intentions but a lack of reliable information. If the reader comes away from this book with only one firm resolve in mind, I hope that resolve will be to treat all prints and drawings with the respect that they deserve, as irreplaceable pieces of our artistic heritage.

NOTES

1. For a description of these paperlike materials, see Lilian A. Bell, *Papyrus, Tapa, Amatl, and Rice Paper: Papermaking in Africa, the Pacific, Latin America, and Southeast Asia* (McMinnville, Ore.: Liliacae Press, 1983), and Victor von Hagen, *The Aztec and Maya Papermakers* (New York: Hacker, 1977).

2. The following works describe the proper care of photographs: Doris Bry, *An Approach to the Care of Photographs* (New York: Sotheby Parke Bernet, 1976); Eastman Kodak Company, *Preservation of Photographs*, Publication F–30 (Rochester, N.Y.: 1979); Debbie Hess Norris, "The Proper Storage and Display of a Photographic Collection," *Book and Paper Group Annual* 2 (1983): 66–81; Laurence E. Keefe, Jr., and Dennis Inch, *The Life of a Photograph: Archival Processing, Matting, Framing, and Storage* (London: Butterworth, 1983); Alice Swan, "Conservation of Photographic Print Collections," *Library Trends* 30:2 (Fall 1981); 267–295; Robert Weinstein and Larry Booth, *Collection, Use, and Care of Historical Photographs* (Nashville: American Association for State and Local History, 1977); Eastman Kodak Company, *Conservation of Photographs* (Rochester, N.Y.: 1985).

[*The Book and Paper Group Annual*, noted above, is not sold by subscription; it is published by the American Institute for Conservation of Historic and Artistic Works and should be available in a good library.]

1

Parchment and Paper: Supports for Prints and Drawings

EGINNING A BOOK on the care of prints and drawings with a first chapter on the materials that prints and drawings *appear* on, without first discussing these works of art themselves, may seem to be putting the cart before the horse. Actually, it follows the soundest of logic, from both the artist's and the conservator's point of view; this is the way prints and drawings come into being, to begin with: before there can be prints or drawings, there must be something to put them on; and the best materials ever yet found to carry the work of the artist, the printmaker, the calligrapher, and the record-keeper, the world over, have traditionally tended to be the more vulnerable part of the completed work, the part needing the greatest care for the whole to endure. That is why we begin this book by saying that *the first step in caring for prints and drawings is to learn something about the material on which they appear. Learn something about its physical makeup, the way it behaves, and learn how best to protect and preserve it.*

Begin with a quick inventory of the prints and drawings in your collection and list them according to the material on which they have been made. Depending on their age and place of origin, these works of art may be found on a variety of materials.

The majority, of course, will be on paper. Some may quite likely be on parchment, which was expertly made in Asia Minor two hundred years before Christ's time and extensively used throughout the Western world for centuries. If truly ancient documents or drawings appear among your holdings, or if your collection is highly specialized, papyrus may be found as the support for some items.

7

Papyrus antedates both parchment and paper. The oldest known manuscripts, found in Egyptian tombs, were written on papyrus, the earliest dating from before 3000 B.C.; and the extensive body of Greek literature housed in the ancient world's greatest library, at Alexandria, was written on large sheets of papyrus, glued together, end to end, and rolled on wooden rods to form manuscripts cylindrical in shape. Papyrus was made from an Egyptian sedge of the same name. The sedge was an extremely useful plant, providing not only the substances needed to make writing material, but also food, fuel, and material to make sails and sandals, boats and boxes, mats, twine, and cloth. It was valued most highly, however for the writing material made from it, which was used sporadically in the Mediterranean world until the tenth century A.D. Popular though papyrus was, by the tenth century, it had been gradually superseded by parchment.

Old records, documents, and drawings originating before the invention of paper, or in areas where neither parchment nor paper was easy to obtain, may appear on one or another of the various paperlike substances mentioned in the introduction: tapa cloth, amatl, papyrus, rice paper, or materials made of bark or palm leaves.

Amatl, a primitive, feltlike sheet, was made in Mexico and Central America, in pre-Columbian times; tapa cloth, made from the soft inner bark of trees, substituted for paper in the Pacific Islands; many tropical and subtropical countries used palm fronds; and a popular Oriental paper substitute was called *rice paper*, which is somewhat misleading, since it has nothing at all to do with rice, but was—and still is—made from the inner core, or pith, of a Chinese plant, *Tetrapanax papyriferus*, called "the rice paper plant." The term *rice paper*, incidentally, is frequently—but inaccurately—used as a generic term for Oriental papers.

As a base for old documents and drawings, these materials are sometimes mistaken for paper, and they *are* related to paper—at least, in having vegetal origins. Manufacturing processes for each differ greatly from those for manufacturing paper, however; they exhibit a galaxy of different properties and characteristics among themselves, and all differ variously from paper.

These materials are mentioned here a second time, briefly, as interesting sidelights on humanity's long history of making marks on something thin, strong, portable, and foldable, and details of their manufacture and preservation are not a part of this book. If, in inventorying your collection, you find prints and drawings on support material that you believe to be neither paper nor parchment, but one of these paperlike substances, the best way to find out what sort of treatment may be suitable for it is to ask advice of the conservator of a major museum likely to include similar materials among its holdings.

Unless a collection is highly specialized or is chiefly anthropological or ethnographic in nature, however, most of the prints and drawings in it are likely to be on one of the two kinds of supports that grew into extensive use in the Western hemisphere during and following the Middle Ages: parchment and paper. Of the two, paper gradually became by far the more extensively used, especially after the invention of movable type and the printing press, which created a sudden and almost unquenchable demand for material to print on.

As they are the two substances we find prints and drawings on most often, parchment and paper are the support materials we concern ourselves with, here.

Parchment

A superb material for writing and drawing, parchment is made of the untanned skins of animals, especially the sheep, calf, and goat. It has been used for manuscripts, legal documents, public records, and works of art since before the birth of Christ—and still is, though much less frequently now than it was in earlier times. Works of art and historical documents on parchment—drawings, folk art, deeds, wills, diplomas, legal papers—abound in all types of collections; and any notion that the care and preservation of parchment can be a headache for only those of us who happen to be medievalists, rare-book librarians, or the keepers of the Dead Sea Scrolls is—a mistaken notion.

A call to any major artists' supply house today will confirm that parchment is still in demand. Because of its artistically appealing surface and its great durability, it has remained a popular working material for artists and calligraphers through the ages, its devotees ranging from the ranks of medieval monks who used it to create countless superbly lettered and illuminated manuscripts, to the sixteenth century's Albrecht Dürer and the seventeenth century's Rembrandt van Rijn, to Winslow Homer and Picasso of our own times.

As is often true, an economic crisis hastened the commercial production of parchment and its eventual ascendancy over papyrus as a more readily available writing and drawing surface. In the second century before Christ, a ban on Egypt's exportation of papyrus meant that parchment had to be used, instead, to meet the needs of the growing library of Pergamum, in Asia Minor. The library at Pergamum gradually grew to rival those of Alexandria, site of the most famous libraries of antiquity. In fact, it is thought that the word *parchment* is derived from the word *Pergamum*, where the demand for a good, readily available writing surface became so intense that Pergamum was the place where the development of parchment attained top priority. More durable than papyrus, parchment could also be folded into book form, and it gradually superseded papyrus. Four hundred years later, parchment was available throughout Europe. During parchment's heyday, it was used in the codex form, as the carrier of illuminations, in a single-sheet form, as the surface for pen, brush, and ink drawings, and as the support for metalpoints and tempera paintings. In the fourteenth century, however, paper began to appear in Europe. Then, in the fifteenth century, the printing press was invented, and the demand for large, consistent supplies of material on which to print skyrocketed. Parchment could be printed on, but it was tedious and time-consuming to produce and there were constant labor problems, which were not helped by the social stigma associated with working with the foul-smelling materials from which parchment was made. In the end, economics once again played a role in determining parchment's future, and it could not compete with paper, which gradually displaced it.

Both ordinary parchment and an especially fine grade of it called *vellum* remain classic materials for works of art and documents of state. Vellum was the name applied, in the Middle Ages, to any fine parchment used in working with manuscripts. Its exceptionally fine quality is sometimes attributed to its having been made from the skin of the unborn calf or kid. For important manuscripts, vellum could be—and often was— dyed a rich purple color.

Characteristics of Parchment

The great durability of parchment has been recognized and highly valued for centuries: in 1494, a certain Abbot Johann Tritheim is said to have exhorted his hardworking scribes to choose parchment over paper, with this reminder: "Truly if writing is set down on vellum, it will last a millennium. When writing is on paper, however, how long will it last?"[1]

Often the same color as paper, often very thin and flexible, though with a "solid" feel and a tough "body," parchment can easily be mistaken for the sturdy paper that items in many collections appear on. Parchment's behavior and recommended care, however, are radically different from that of paper, because of the great differences in basic natural materials from which each is made. *When parchment is mistaken for paper and subjected to certain paper conservation procedures, the results are disastrous.*

How Parchment Is Made

The manufacturing process that produces parchment endows this product with its special properties, both good and bad; and that process has changed only slightly, over the years.

Parchment-making begins when the untanned animal skins of which it is formed are soaked in water and treated with lime to loosen the hair. The skins are then scraped repeatedly with a sharp, crescent-shaped knife, to remove the loosened hair and skim away surface irregularities. They are then washed, stretched on a rectangular frame, dried, and again scraped with the knife, for additional thinning and leveling. A final rubbing with pumice and chalk completes the preparation. Sometimes various finishing substances may be applied to a parchment surface, to give it a glossy appearance.

A finished piece of parchment is the result of the simple cleaning and drying of animal skin under tension. It is this simultaneous action of stretching and drying that causes parchment to react differently from leather, which is made from animal skins that have been *tanned*—a quite different treatment.

Problems to Watch for in Parchment

The foremost conservation problem associated with parchment is *buckling*—the drastic dimensional reaction of parchment to changes in humidity. Buckling—distortion of form, bulging, warping—in a piece of parchment is the first sign that this material is being subjected to stress by high humidity levels or that there have been wide—and recurrent—fluctuations in the relative humidity of the place where it is kept. The undulations in a piece of buckling parchment may form random patterns or may follow only the contours of an affected area. Buckling comes about as the fibers of the parchment's organic base—the animal skin—begin to lose the directional orientation imposed on them as they dried under tension: high humidity causes the skin tissues to relax and go slack, in partial reversion to their original configuration.

A cautionary note should be inserted, here: *some degree of buckling may be expected to occur naturally in parchment*. In fact, that natural manifestation should not be a cause for alarm and should not be prevented by overzealous or overconstraining mounting procedures—parchment has sometimes been glued to stiff cardboard or pressed against glass to keep it flat, which is not a good idea.

In general, works of art and documents on parchment should be matted in the same way as they would be if they appeared on paper; but sometimes deeper mats might be a wise preventive measure if some buckling already exists, or if the artifact is to be stored in an area where maintaining constant levels of humidity might be a problem.

If buckling worsens more than is to be normally expected, however, not only is the result displeasing (see figure 1.1), but the medium with which the parchment support is decorated is likewise threatened (see

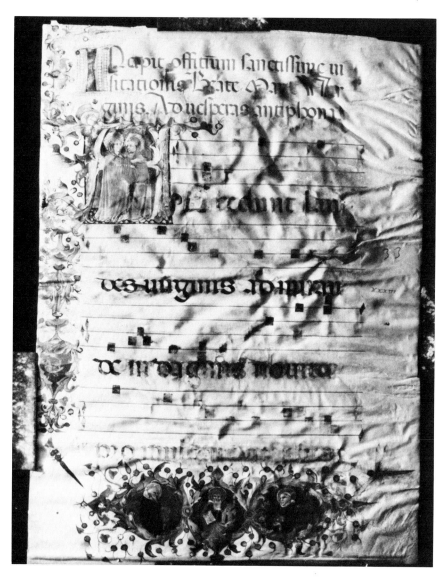

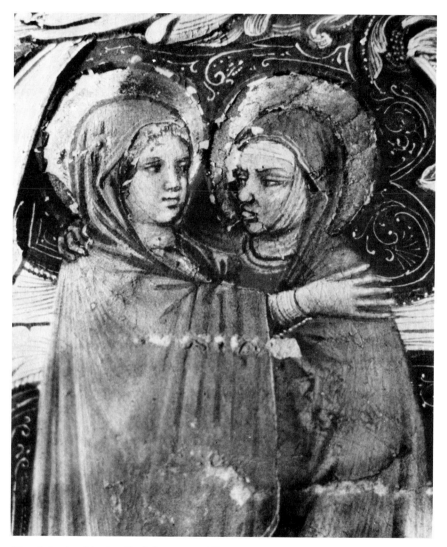

Fig. 1.2. As this detail of figure 1.1 illustrates, buckling of parchment can also disrupt paint layers.

OPPOSITE PAGE: *Fig. 1.1. Buckling of parchment can interfere with the enjoyment of a work of art. In this* Page from an Antiphonal with the Visitation and Three Saints, *the three saints pictured are,* left to right, *a Dominican saint (unidentified), Saint Jerome, and Saint Dominic.* —Anonymous; North Italian, ca. 1400; the Metropolitan Museum of Art: bequest of Mrs. A. M. Minturn (90.61.3) figures 1.2 and 1.3); if the parchment buckles, the paint on it may simply crack and flake off. Figures 1.2 and 1.3 illustrate the extreme degree of flaking of the tempera on the buckled surfaces of the paintings shown. The exaggerated, harmful buckling of a parchment support can cause powdery paints and grounds to be lost by the shifting and changing in form of the support under them.

Any instance of extreme buckling in parchment should be taken to a qualified conservator for treatment. If the damage is recent, the buckling can sometimes be arrested and the parchment coaxed back into something nearer its original flat state, by use of traditional flattening procedures. If extreme buckling is the result of the parchment's being improperly stored or from having been kept folded for a very long time—which happens, with many documents—the deformation that may have taken place is much more difficult to correct. In such instances, more elaborate treatments—again, by a qualified conservator—will be necessary.

Storage for Parchment: Temperature, Humidity

In storing parchment, close attention should be paid to both temperature and humidity levels. A range of 60 degrees to 70 degrees Fahrenheit in temperature and 45 percent to 55 percent relative humidity is ideal. Both paper and parchment can adapt to *gradual* shifts of either temperature or relative humidity (RH) in either direction, but it must be remembered that above 68 to 70 percent RH, the danger of mold growth is great. At 65 percent RH, the intake of moisture by parchment rapidly increases.[2]

Stains and Routine Cleaning

Stain removal, cleaning, the repairing of torn places, and other conservation procedures involving parchment are complicated by this product's natural sensitivity to water. Consultation with a conservator is, therefore, highly recommended, any time an artifact on parchment must be cleaned or repaired.

Despite its natural vulnerability to its surroundings, parchment, because of its basic composition, is a strong, resilient material that can withstand much manipulation. It provides marvelous surface texture and color for drawing and painting. The alkaline substances used in its manufacture render it naturally resistant to acid deterioration from poor-quality framing materials and insidious air pollution. *If it is properly*

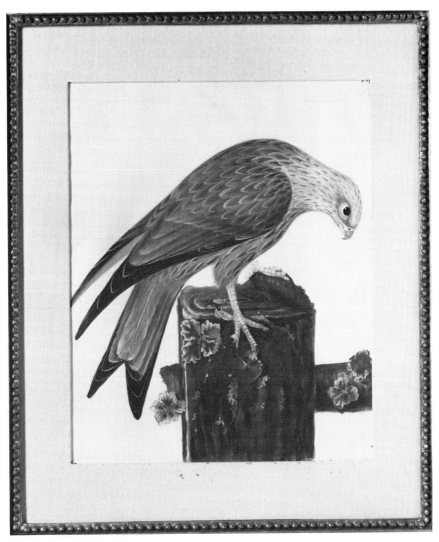

Fig. 1.3. Flakes of tempera have fallen away from the parchment of this piece and are trapped between the mat and the glass.—Anonymous; English, Study of Bird; *private collection; photograph by Sheldan Collins*

cared for, a piece of parchment will last for a thousand years or more. The task of providing conditions that will enable it to do that is far easier, once we understand its basic nature.

Paper

Paper, which came to supplant parchment as the substance most often used as a support for prints and drawings, was invented by the Chinese, before the second century A.D. It has been phenomenally useful to humanity in uncountable ways from that time to the present.

A.D. 105 is the official date for the invention of paper, although today it is commonly believed that paper is a good bit older than that. A Chinese dictionary dated A.D. 69 contains a character for paper; and samples of earlier papers have been excavated at burial sites predating the life of Ts'ai Lun, long held to be the inventor of paper.[3]

Certain it is that the substance we now call paper was first *known* to have made its appearance in the Hunan Province of China somewhere near that time and that the Chinese kept the method for making this useful material a closely guarded secret as they developed it to an advanced state and became expert at its production.

The earliest form of paper made by the Chinese appears to have been a mixture of bark and hemp. Later, as the papermakers learned more about their product, bits of silk and other fibers were suspended in water and formed into a sheet that, upon drying, would accept writing or drawing better than the first bark-and-hemp paper and the bulky, inflexible bamboo strips and fabric that had previously been used to write or draw upon.

For six hundred years, the art of making paper remained an exclusively Far Eastern enterprise—until the jealously guarded secret of its making fell into the hands of the Persians, who conquered the Chinese in A.D. 751 and established, in fabled Samarkand, the first paper mill to be built outside China.

Once the knowledge of papermaking reached the Middle East, it spread rapidly to the eastern Mediterranean countries—to Egypt with the Arab traders, to Spain with the Moors, and gradually over the rest of Europe. Late in the thirteenth century, paper mills had been established in Italy; by the end of the fourteenth, in France and Germany; and by 1495, paper was being made in England and was well on its way to superseding parchment as an excellent surface on which to draw pictures and inscribe legal records and public documents.

With the invention of movable type and the great upsurge of printed material that took place after the 1450s, paper was recognized as a first-rate printing surface, as well, capable of satisfying the sudden enormous need for something on which to print the scores of books now made possible by the newly available printing presses.

Paper Composition and Inherent Problems

Any discussion of the way paper is made and the reasons that can lead to problems should include a very general statement about what paper is and does, and gradually refine that to focus on the substance that supports so many prints and drawings.

The word *paper*—derived from *papyrus*—applies to such a wide, varied range of materials that it almost seems, sometimes, as if this useful product is the one marketable item that comes closest to being all things to all people. Paper is—grocery bags, newsprint, gift wrapping, cigarette papers, toweling, magazines, cleansing tissues, book pages, book covers, book jackets, cardboard, wallboard, wallpaper, drawing paper, fine stationery—and a thousand other things, in addition to being the frail-but-durable support for prints and drawings.

For our working purposes, here, paper is defined (in *Webster's Third New International Dictionary*) as "a felted sheet of usu. vegetable but sometimes mineral or synthetic fibers laid down on a fine screen from a water suspension." As mentioned earlier, this book deals only with the types of paper made from organic substances and does not comment on those that include mineral and synthetic fibers.

Figure 1.4 shows, magnified five hundred times, a sample of "Whatman," an English paper very popular with artists, including John James Audubon. Widely distributed in the eighteenth, nineteenth, and twentieth centuries, Whatman is found in many collections and is, as the photograph makes plain, representative of paper generally: it is a densely matted sheet of long, intertwining fibers deposited evenly on a porous surface by the action of water.

The method of manufacturing paper has changed remarkably little, through the years, and throughout its long odyssey from East to West. Even in today's awesomely fast-running, highly automated commercial paper mills, the process remains basically the same as it was in the Hunan Province, where it all began.

Paper begins with fiber. In the East, in centuries past, plant fibers from the inner bark of native shrubs were preferred as the basic raw material for paper. For economic reasons today, however, wood pulp is used more and more frequently in the East.

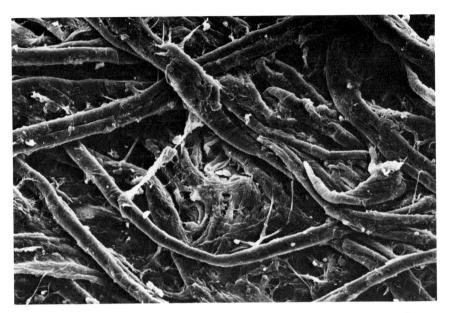

Fig. 1.4. The nature of paper is dependent upon both its method of manufacture and the chemistry of its fibers. This is a scanning electron micrograph of Whatman paper, magnified 500 times.—Photograph by Robert Koestler

In the West, since the late 1800s, most of the plant fiber needed has come from wood. In the early years of papermaking, however, linen and, later, cotton rags, then fairly easily obtained, were initially used and became the traditional source of fibers for making paper. Before rags could be used for paper pulp, however, they had to be broken down into their original plant fibers by a cumbersome, time-consuming process. As the years passed and the demands for paper skyrocketed, the supply of rags grew smaller and scarcer and could not keep pace with the burgeoning demands of the paper mills. In America, where thrifty housewives since the time of the Puritans traditionally kept ragbags for the necessary mending of clothes and piecing of quilts, the rag shortage threatened even those small repositories; and by the nineteenth century, rags had become so scarce in the Western World that Egyptian mummy wrappings were being scavenged to make paper. Regulations stipulated that corpses be entombed in shrouds of wool, rather than linen. Spurred on by the prospect of great financial reward, venturesome nineteenth-century papermakers began grinding up every kind of plant in sight—

and learned a worthwhile lesson from a lowly source: the American paper wasp and his cousins the hornet and the yellow jacket, which all quite skillfully use chewed-up wood mixed with saliva to build strong, durable nests of a substance remarkably like paper. Wood pulp is an ingredient in more than 90 percent of the paper produced in America today; and thanks to the work of conservationists generally, a respectable amount of new paper in this country is now being made by recycling waste paper.

It is still true that, to make paper, as the Chinese discovered, eighteen centuries ago, one must collect a great lot of material and—soak it, cook it, beat it, clean it—break it down into its component parts, because what is needed from the plant are its long, stringy, threadlike strands of fiber. *There is something magical in that fiber that makes the substance obtained, at the very end of the process, a very fine material to write or draw on.* Early papermakers didn't know what the mysterious vital ingredient was, in plant fiber—they knew only that certain fibers made the best paper, in terms of strength, appearance, and longevity. It wasn't given a name until modern times, was not even isolated as a chemical until 1838, and was not identified by a chemical formula until 1913.[4] *It was—and is— cellulose, the chief constituent of the cell walls of plants.*

After the essential fibers (refined from plants or rags) are cleaned, cooked, and macerated, the pulpy mass is mixed with a great deal of water, thinning it to liquid consistency, mixing it well, allowing the long strands of fiber to distribute themselves uniformly throughout the pulp. Then a very finely meshed flat sieve, or screen, held level, horizontally, is sunk down into the pulp and lifted, bringing out a thin, dripping layer. The water drains off, across the top and through the bottom of the screen, and the residue—a flat, even layer of intertwined strands of fiber—will be a primitive sheet of paper, if it's merely set aside and allowed to dry.

Why and how does the greatly simplified procedure just described make paper?

Cellulose is what makes the whole thing work. Chemically speaking, cellulose exists as thousands of atoms of carbon, hydrogen, and oxygen joined together to form long chain molecules called *polymers*. The molecular structure of cellulose makes it ideal for papermaking, since a mass of long, intertwining fibers composed of an orderly parallel arrangement of cellulose polymers has great strength and flexibility. The long, wavy polymers are hygroscopic—that is, they attract and absorb moisture. Early Western papermakers never knew, precisely, why their mixtures of water and plant fiber—mainly obtained from cotton or linen rags—made a surface one could write on; but their experiments did tell them that some plants with apparently more of some necessary substance worked better than others that had less. Raw cotton, they found, had a lot of it; flax was good, too; hemp, jute, straw, manila rope, bamboo, sugar cane, and various grasses carried it, to varying degrees, and were—and still are—used to make paper pulp.

When cellulose was eventually isolated and identified, modern-day chemists found that raw cotton is 91 percent cellulose, which explains its efficacy in papermaking and the high preference for cotton rags in making stationery and other fine papers. Linen rags were also highly valued, because flax, from which linen is made, also is high in cellulose content.

The Four Steps in Papermaking

Once the raw material is assembled, then, the papermaking process can be roughly divided into four steps: *preparation of the pulp, formation of the sheets, pressing and drying,* and *sizing and finishing.*

These four steps apply to paper made in both the Eastern and the Western world, whether by hand or by machine; machines for making paper had been perfected by 1850.

To make the pulp, as roughly outlined above, the fibers selected are first cleaned, cooked, macerated, and suspended in water.

Enough of the suspended fibers to make a single sheet of paper are then brought up out of the mass on a·screen, which allows the water to drain away, leaving behind an even layer of pulp. The device used for this dipping up of the fibers, layer by layer, is called a *mold.* The designs of Eastern and Western molds vary, but their function remains the same. In industrial papermaking machines, an endlessly moving screen replaces the individual molds.

Figures 1.5 and 1.6 illustrate the formation of a homemade sheet of paper. The *vatman*—handling the mold—dips it horizontally into the pulp, brings it straight up, and gently rocks it from side to side, to distribute the pulp evenly and drain off any excess. In some primitive papermaking processes, pulp is poured directly onto the molds.

In figure 1.6, the pulp can be seen evenly deposited across the screen. The sheet of paper-in-the-making at this point is very thick and more than 90 percent water. The rectangular frame seen floating in the vat is the *deckle,* attached to the mold, when it is dipped, to prevent the dipped-up pulp from running off the surface of the mold entirely. The deckle must be removed before the paper can be taken from the mold for pressing.

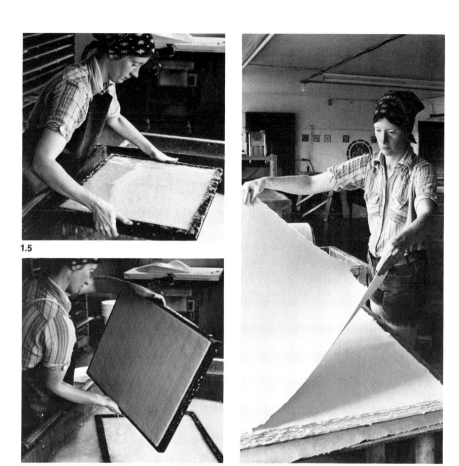

1.5

1.6 **1.7**

Fig. 1.5. In the papermaking process, the vatman dips the sheet mold into the pulp soaking in the vat, then lifts and shakes the mold from side to side to form an even layer of pulp — the beginnings of a finished sheet of paper. Cotton rag pulp is used here. — Courtesy of Kathryn Clark, Twinrocker Handmade Paper, Inc.; photograph by John Dumont

Fig. 1.6. The mold is drained, after the deckle — the mold's removable frame, now floating in the vat — has been taken off. The sheet just lifted from the vat is about to be couched, or transferred from the mold onto felts, to build up a post for pressing. — Courtesy of Kathryn Clark, Twinrocker Handmade Paper, Inc.; photograph by John Dumont

Fig. 1.7. After its initial pressing, which removes most of the water, the sheet of damp paper is laid in the pack for further pressing. — Courtesy of Kathryn Clark, Twinrocker Handmade Paper, Inc.; photograph by John Dumont

Transferral of the newly formed paper sheet from the mold onto *felts*—the Western fashion—or placement directly on another sheet of damp paper—customary in the East—is necessary before the paper can be *pressed*. The transfer is accomplished by *couching*—inverting the mold and rocking it from one side to the other, while firmly pressing against the wet, pulpy paper. In one even movement, the paper is released from the mold and attached to the felt below. This step is repeated until enough alternating felts and papers have accumulated to form a *post*. A press is then used to squeeze out the tremendous amount of water remaining in the layers that make up the post.

In the East, where felts are not used, the molds are flexible and can simply be rolled off the paper; as in the West, a post is formed and is placed in a press.

Presses vary in sophistication, from primitive stone contraptions to carefully controlled hydraulic machines. In figure 1.7, the *layman* separates the paper after the post's first pressing, to form a *pack*. This step may involve many pressings, until the paper has lost most of its water. The sheets are finally hung in ventilated drying rooms for a curing period of varying length, depending upon the type of paper to be produced, the season of the year, subsequent finishing procedures, and the properties the end product is intended to have.

Imparting to the paper various specific properties such as water resistance or a smooth surface suitable for printing is the final step in making paper, and usually involves *sizing*, a water-resistant substance introduced before or after the pulp is formed into a sheet of paper. All writing papers are "sized," to prevent the spreading of the ink used in writing. Sizing—or, as it is usually referred to, *size*—may be mixed directly into the pulp, as is usually done with rosin-sized papers, producing a paper that is "internally sized." If the pulp has been formed into sheets of paper without size, the size can be added by bathing the paper sheets in a sizing solution, such as dilute gelatin. Like wood pulp, the particular size used may, owing to its chemical properties, shorten the life of the paper.

Other forms of finishing include burnishing the surface with smooth stones, an Eastern practice; or *glazing*, in the West. Papers intended for specific uses, such as photography, are often coated or otherwise processed in special ways.

Ask papermakers about the nature of the substance they create, and—if they trust you enough—the philosophers among them will give you answers bordering on the mystical. And for good reason: any material that has borne the history, philosophy, art, literature, music, and drama of nation after nation, transmitting them to succeeding generations, year after year, must be tinged with magic. The origins of all the substances on which we write and draw are humble; but their inherent beauty and strength and their services to humanity in carrying its story from age to age must surely place these materials among the more significant achievements of civilization.

Contrary to popular belief, paper is not necessarily short-lived. Western papers made in the fifteenth century may often be seen today in excellent condition. Samples of still-flexible paper fifteen hundred years old have been excavated in China. As to the early question of its durability, the life span of a piece of paper is determined by the way it is made and by its subsequent handling, factors identified in Table 1.1 as internal and external sources influencing deterioration in paper.

As shown in Table 1.1, internal sources of paper deterioration include poor-quality pulp, bleaching residues, and unstable sizings, which result from the papermaking process.

Internal Sources of Paper Deterioration

Pulp. Cellulose is essential for making paper. Cellulose itself is almost neutral (pH 6.6) and is very stable, when kept in a neutral environment. Once exposed to acid, however, the cellulose polymer begins to break down. The more acidity present, the faster the scission (or separation) of

TABLE 1.1
Sources of Deterioration in Paper

Internal Sources	External Sources
Poor-quality pulp	Contact with acidic materials
Bleaching residues	Air pollution
Unstable sizings	High temperatures, fluctuations in temperature
	High and fluctuating levels of relative humidity
	Light
	Insects and rodents
	Careless handling
	Natural disasters (fire, flood, etc.)

The listing of internal causes of deterioration in paper given here result from the paper-making process. Proper framing, storage, and exhibition can lessen the damage they may cause, to some extent.

These listed external causes of deterioration in paper result from improper storage, framing, and exhibition. They can be counteracted by establishing and maintaining proper conservation procedures.

the cellulose bonds; that long polymer of cellulose so vital to the health of a sheet of paper is reduced to shorter and shorter brittle segments, its side-to-side, layer-by-layer arrangement disrupted. And the paper begins to disintegrate.

Always destructive to paper, acid can enter paper in several ways. First, it may be present in the fiber used to make the paper. Wood pulp, while a good papermaking material in some respects, contains *lignin*, the amorphous cement that binds together the long cellulose molecules in the wood. Lignin is chemically unstable; becoming acidic as it breaks down, it attacks the cellulose around it. For this reason, unrefined wood pulp is used only to make papers for which a long life is not required. Newsprint, for example, may contain 80 percent unrefined wood pulp by weight. Because many artists have used newsprint and similar papers to produce art of lasting value—ranging from Winslow Homer's wood engravings reproduced in *Harper's Weekly* to Pablo Picasso's Cubist collages—we need to understand the conservation problems associated with papers of this sort, made of ground-up wood that has not been chemically treated to dissolve the lignin in it.

It should also be noted, however, that not all wood pulp papers are necessarily bad, from a conservation standpoint; the industry has developed refining techniques for wood pulp that yield pure alpha cellulose suitable for making archival papers.

Bleaching. Chemicals left over from the bleach sometimes used on low-grade rags and nonrag fibers used for pulp may also be a built-in hazard to paper. Almost all the traditional bleaches developed at the turn of the century contained chlorine, which often remained within the paper as residue. Even *traces* of a chlorine bleach are highly reactive and can form hydrochloric acid. Once again, the long cellulose polymer is attacked from acidity generated within the paper itself.

Sizings. Rosin sizing, developed in the nineteenth century to give paper a better printing surface, required a precipitating agent to disperse the solution evenly over the paper. Alum used for this purpose can produce sulfuric acid within the paper. Alum is not new to papermakers; it may have been used as early as the fifteenth century. The combination of unrefined wood pulp, bleaching residues, and large amounts of alum particularly threatens paper's longevity.

External Sources of Paper Deterioration

The life span of a piece of paper is also affected by conditions to which it is exposed after manufacture. Table 1.1 lists, as external sources of paper deterioration, contact with acidic materials, air pollution, high temperatures and fluctuations in temperature, high and fluctuating levels of relative humidity, light, insects and rodents, careless handling, and natural disasters such as fire and flood.

Acid. Acid appears at the top of the list of external sources of paper deterioration, as it did for internal sources. This time, it is shown as an attacker from the outside, through a process called *acid migration*. Cellulose, because it is highly absorbent, takes in any liquid or gas that surrounds it. As a result of simple contact, acid can travel from a source, usually poor-quality framing materials, into the paper of a print or drawing. This acid migration, like internally generated acidity, leads to discoloration and embrittlement of paper.

Air pollution. Acidic gases often reach paper in the form of air pollution. The bad effects of air pollution on paper and pigments have been known for some time; we know, for example, that books in urban libraries deteriorate faster than their counterparts stored in the country. Gaseous pollutants such as sulfur dioxide are converted within the paper into sulfuric acid, with devastating results.

Temperature levels and fluctuations. The temperature in which it is kept is a vital factor in the overall conservation of paper. Although lower temperatures are ideal, a range of 60 degrees to 70 degrees Farenheit is the most practical temperature range for both paper and parchment. Both materials *can* adjust to minor temperature variations, so long as the change *is* minor—and is *gradual*. Ideally, however, both temperature and humidity levels in collections areas should vary as little as possible. Because of the effect on humidity, sudden, repeated episodes of fluctuating temperatures can cause serious damage to prints and drawings.

Humidity levels and fluctuations. When works of art on paper are exposed to high levels of humidity—above 68 to 70 percent RH—they quickly become vulnerable to harm from two prime sources: mold growth and buckling (see pages 41, 49-51, 53 below). As noted above, levels of both temperature and humidity should vary as little as possible in all areas where prints and drawings are kept. Since both paper and parchment readily absorb moisture from the atmosphere around them, high and fluctuating levels of relative humidity—perhaps as a result of mechanical difficulty or poor maintenance procedures—can be harmful to paper artifacts if it continues over a very long period of time. The *ideal* range of relative humidity for prints and drawings is 45 to 55 percent RH; if the area's equipment makes it impossible to maintain that ideal, it is wise to keep the moisture level attainable as close to that as possible, and it is *essential* to keep it *steady*, the year round, with as little daily or seasonal fluctuation as possible.

Light. Because light and heat are catalysts, papers exposed to daylight often discolor rapidly, as their dyes, sizings, and impurities absorb radiant energy. Similarly, when works of art on paper are stored in hot attics or hung over radiators, they become brittle rapidly. Light and heat artificially age paper—in fact, they are sometimes used specifically to hasten aging for purposes of analysis. Light can likewise cause alterations in light-sensitive or "fugitive" media.

Careless handling. Careless handling, perhaps the greatest cause of unnecessary damage to fragile works of art, is plainly the easiest threat to banish. More unnecessary damage is caused by impatience than by any other factor in Table 1.1. While we may have no control over the composition and manufacture of materials used to produce works of art, we *can* work toward proper storage, good framing materials, and careful procedures for exhibition that will help keep damage to a minimum.

Natural disasters. Although no one can prevent natural disasters, damage from such unfortunate events can be minimized by establishing a "conservation strategy" for your institution. Emergency preparedness need not apply only to major catastrophes—mini-disasters and minor calamities such as broken pipes or nonfunctioning dehumidifiers are much more likely to strike with unsettling suddenness, surprisingly often. Before predictable mischance can take place, prepare a list of the unfortunate events that *could* happen on your premises, with brief but *very* clear directions about what should be done in the event of each, and be certain that everyone on the staff not only has a copy, but is familiar with what it says. Maintaining good storage facilities will also go a long way in keeping damages to a minimum.

Recognizing Basic Paper Conservation Problems

Below are some signs and symptoms whose detection can indicate that the sources of deterioration of paper listed in Table 1.1 are at work: ways to recognize the consequences of poor-quality pulp, the action of high humidity, too much light, and other troubles. Quick recognition of a conservation problem can help in more quickly rectifying its causes.

Overall darkening and embrittlement of paper. General discoloration in a print or drawing on paper—often accompanied by a marked decrease in paper strength—is evidence that destructive internal sources, such as poor-quality pulp, bleaching residues, and unstable sizings, are breaking down the long cellulose molecules of the paper. With time, the paper becomes weaker and more brittle until it can hardly support its own weight. At that point, paper can rupture with even the slightest handling and cannot tolerate being curled or bent.

The deterioration of paper caused by internal chemical factors can be slowed by ensuring that mats are made of acid-free materials and that the prints are always exhibited and stored under proper conditions. What is sometimes euphemistically called "time toning" has almost always been caused or aggravated by poor-quality mats or overexposure to light. A print in the condition of the Jan Matulka lithograph shown in figures 1.8 and 1.9 should be examined by a conservator who can *re*-repair the torn areas properly or line the back of the print with a sheer Japanese tissue for additional support. Papers containing a high percentage of lignin (those with a base of unrefined wood pulp) should not be "deacidified"— a process also known as *acid neutralization* or *buffering*—(see below) because that process worsens the darkening. While *some* darkening may be acceptable in dealing with documents or archival material, many conservators do not consider it an acceptable side effect when treating unique and irreplaceable works of art.

Localized discoloration of paper. A work of art on paper darkens in one particular area almost certainly because that area is in contact with an external source of acidity, such as corrugated cardboard, newsprint, labels, tapes, glues, and other materials used in framing and repair. Acid generated by chemically unstable materials such as these migrates into the naturally absorbent paper of the art. Figure 1.10 illustrates one common form of localized discoloration. This print, after Audubon, was matted with cheap wood pulp mat board made by laminating a layer of unrefined wood pulp between two sheets of heavier paper. The *bevel,* or angled edge of the mat window exposes the compressed mass of wood pulp. Acid from the decomposing wood pulp sandwiched within the endpapers migrates from the bevel into the work of art, forming a continuous band of discoloration called *mat burn.* In this print, the acid traveled one-eighth of an inch into the print itself. The print is also darkened beyond the mat burn, simply through contact with the back of the window mat.

Poor-quality mat board can also discolor the reverse side of a print, when used behind it. The discoloration is accompanied by a general weakening of the paper that can lead to torn and tattered edges. Figure 1.11 shows more generalized staining around the edges of an etching by Andrew Karoly; here, also, the damage was caused by contact with poor-quality mat board. The damage to the face of the print is minor, com-

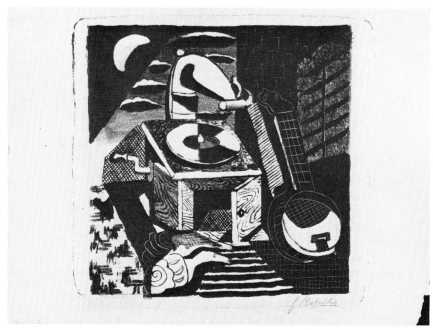

Fig. 1.8. The paper of this lithograph is deteriorating due to the unrefined wood pulp and chemicals used in the papermaking process.—Jan Matulka, Still Life; the Metropolitan Museum of Art: gift of Mr. and Mrs. Mark Jay Lerner (1981.1186); photograph by Sheldan Collins

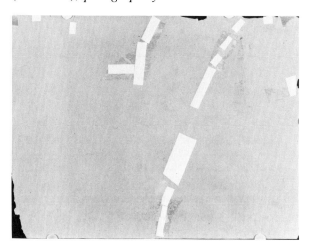

Fig. 1.9. Old repairs on the back of the lithograph shown in figure 1.8 indicate the extent of fracturing the print has undergone.—Photograph by Sheldan Collins

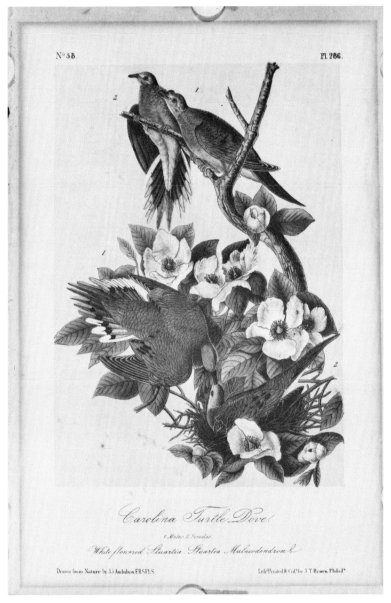

Fig. 1.10. *The rectangular stain following the contours of this print is called* mat burn. *It has been caused by acid traveling from the bevel of the window of a wood pulp mat.*—*J. T. Bowen, after John James Audubon,* Carolina Turtle Doves; *private collection; photograph by Sheldan Collins*

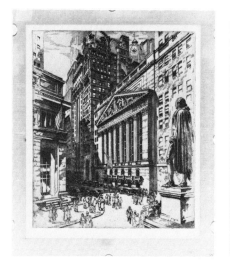

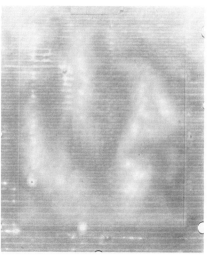

Fig. 1.11. The wide band of discoloration around the edges of this etching
was caused by contact with poor-quality
mat board.—Andrew Karoly, New
York Stock Exchange; private collection; photograph by Sheldan Collins

Fig. 1.12. Corrugated cardboard used
in framing caused the striped discoloration on the back of the etching in figure
1.11.—Photograph by Sheldan Collins

pared to that of the reverse side of the same print (figure 1.12). In this
example, corrugated cardboard used as a backboard in framing caused
severe darkening in a typical striated pattern.

Other materials used in mounting and framing prints can have
devastating effects. Adhesives such as rubber cement and white glue can
attack the paper and cause irreversible damage. Figure 1.13 shows the
reverse side of a drawing that was attached to a board with animal glue.
The glue used quickly discolored, stained the paper, dried out, and
eventually lost its tackiness, so that in addition to damaging the art, it
failed even to accomplish its original intended purpose. Paper can be
easily stained and damaged during the process of removing old adhesives; it is a procedure best left to a conservator.

If a drawing or print is glued to another piece of paper or cardboard,
never try to pry or peel them apart. Inevitably, much of the paper of the
drawing will be left behind—a disfigurement called skinning. Generally
speaking, if an unframed object cannot be easily disassembled from its
mat or mount, one should call a conservator and not try to remove it

Depression 1930

Fig. 1.13. The animal glue used on the back of this drawing darkened and stained the paper.—*Photograph by Sheldan Collins*

without qualified professional help, no matter how great the temptation is to do the job alone.

Pressure-sensitive and gummed tapes can also cause severe local discoloration. Figures 1.14 and 1.15, picturing a view of Minneapolis by Louis Lozowick and the print's reverse side, show the effects of masking tapes applied to the back side of a print to position it in its mat. A lithograph by Gordon Grant (figure 1.16) was similarly attached to a mat, with clear, pressure-sensitive Scotch tape. A detail of the Gordon Grant lithograph (figure 1.17) shows that damage from the tape has penetrated to the front from the back of the print. This print also shows mat burn, caused by use of poor-quality mat board. *No pressure-sensitive tapes now commercially available can be considered safe for hinging or repairing works of art*

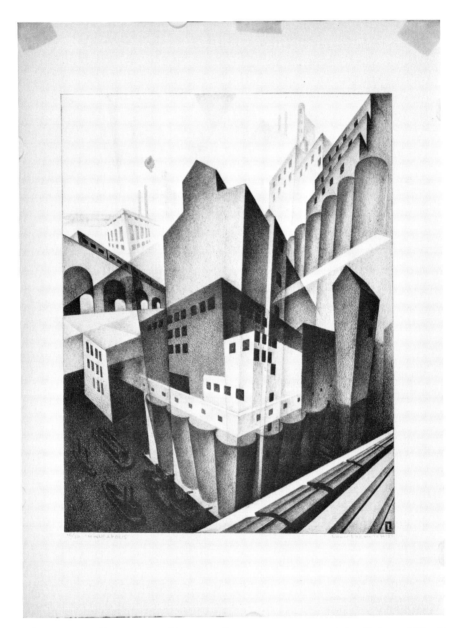

Fig. 1.14. Masking tape used in mounting can cause severe stains that are difficult to remove, which is what happened here—see figure 1.15.—Louis Lozowick, Minneapolis; *courtesy of Sylvan Cole Gallery; photograph by Sheldan Collins*

Fig. 1.15. Masking tape applied to the back of the print shown in figure 1.14 resulted in the penetration of the stain to the front.—Photograph by Sheldan Collins

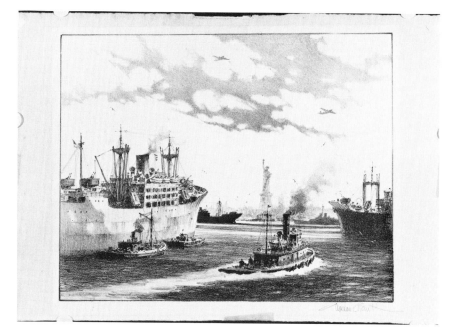

Fig. 1.16. The rectangular stains on the edges of this lithograph were caused by Scotch tape, which only strong solvents can remove. —Gordon Grant, The Upper Bay, New York; *private collection; photograph by Sheldan Collins*

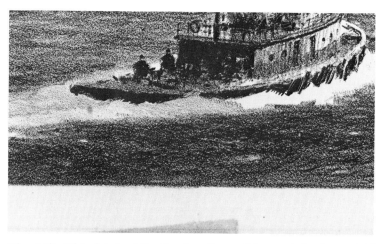

Fig. 1.17. This detail of the Gordon Grant lithograph in figure 1.16 shows the penetration of the adhesive in the Scotch tape used in mounting the work. —Photograph by Sheldan Collins

on paper; and the removal of those mistakenly applied to works of art should be treated only by a conservator. The solvents necessary for removing aged adhesives are very strong (polar); they can affect printing inks, and they are toxic.

A new family of pressure-sensitive cloth or paper tapes with a tacky, acrylic-based adhesive advertised as "archival" is quickly gaining popularity because of its convenience. A word of caution, however: while the chemical stability of this new adhesive has been significantly improved, these tapes cannot be removed with water, even a short time after application.[5] Without the use of solvents, their removal invariably results in "skinning." Water does not dissolve the adhesive; it merely "gels" it. As it is rolled along and off the paper, it takes with it paper fibers. The real problem, it seems to me, lies in the proper definition of *archival*, which should include the characteristic of *being reversible*.

Labels and other extraneous materials affixed to prints and drawings may also cause localized discoloration. The drawing by John Singer Sargent in figure 1.18 has a curious rectangular patch in the upper right corner. (The *circular* stains visible in figure 1.18—more clearly seen in figure 1.19, the reverse side of this work—are from an oily or waxy substance.) Examination of the reverse side of this print (figure 1.19) shows that a small sticker has caused the damage. Labels, seals, and stickers should not be used to identify prints and drawings.

Various methods of *safely* identifying works of art on paper, however, are discussed in *Marking Manuscripts*, a preservation leaflet available without charge from the Library of Congress Preservation Office. A two-ounce bottle of blue or black paper manuscript-marking ink is available, free of charge. Information on invisible inks, stamps, and pads can also be obtained from the Library. The decision to stamp works of art should be made carefully, since stamp marks are irreversible and stamping ink can penetrate *thinner* papers. The effectiveness of indelible ink identification numbers as a deterrent to theft is questionable; carefully planned, well-maintained security procedures provide the best assurance of safety from thievery or vandalism.

Damage can also result from incorrect placement of the stamping on prints and drawings—see figure 1.20. The inked stamp shown there has been badly placed, so that it interferes with the design; and the numbering was done with a ball-point pen. The pen's ink will eventually bleed through the paper.

From a conservation standpoint, the safest method of placing identification directly on prints and drawings—if that must be done—is to write it with a soft pencil. Identification marks in small letters may be made in a corner on the reverse of the artwork. Before writing these

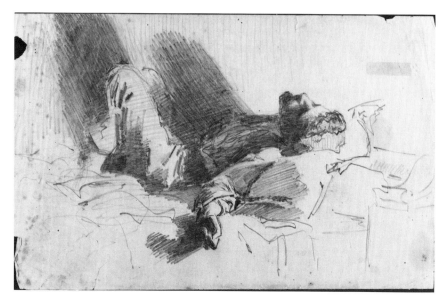

Fig. 1.18. *The cause for the rectangular stain in the upper right corner of this drawing is evident in figure 1.19.* —*John Singer Sargent,* Reclining Figure; *the Metropolitan Museum of Art: gift of Mrs. Francis Ormund (50.130.140r); photograph by Sheldan Collins*

Fig. 1.19. *Cause for the stain at upper right in figure 1.18 is the sticky label affixed to the back.* —*Photograph by Sheldan Collins*

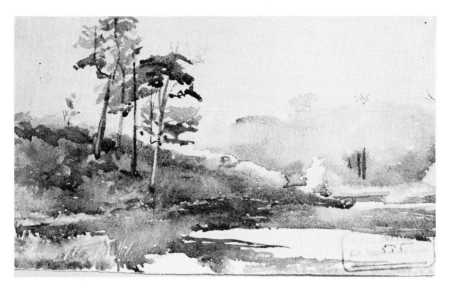

Fig. 1.20. This watercolor has been disfigured by the estate's inventory stamp in the lower right corner.—Turku Trajan, Untitled; *private collection; photograph by Sheldan Collins*

notations, always place the art face down on a hard surface, to avoid embossing the paper.

Other sources of localized discoloration may result from simple, ordinary accidents—spills and stains from water, oil, coffee, tea, and the like. Prevention of these kinds of mishaps is easier and cheaper than cure. Stains caused by wood pulp mats, adhesives, tapes, stickers, and accidents may often be lessened by a conservator; however, *any chemical treatment must be avoided if its use would jeopardize the well-being of the work of art in the long run.*

Darkening of paper exposed to light. Light catalyzes the breakdown of cellulose and aggravates the corrosive action of internal chemical residues found in some paper. Because it happens gradually, "light staining" of art on paper often escapes notice until the print or drawing is unmatted. Figure 1.21 illustrates light staining of a Whistler etching that had hung far too long in natural, unfiltered light. In the photograph, the mat has been lifted slightly, to reveal the way the contours of the mat window exactly follow the darkened area of the print. Anton Schutz's etching of a New York landmark (figure 1.22) suffers both from light staining and from corrugated cardboard stains penetrating from the print's back. The darkening of the paper in the two prints lessens the contrast of black and

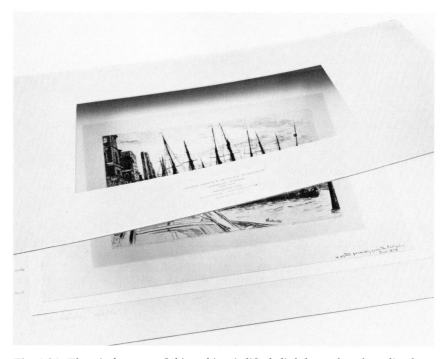

Fig. 1.21. The window mat of this etching is lifted slightly, to show how discoloration occurred only in the area exposed to light. —James Abbott McNeill Whistler, Billingsgate; *the Metropolitan Museum of Art: Harris Brisbane Dick Fund (17.3.41); photograph by Sheldan Collins*

white so important to etchings. Very simple precautions that will retard light damage can be taken when works of art are framed and exhibited. Damage from exposure to light is cumulative; each hour, day, and year takes its toll; placing the art in a dark storage place can neither reverse damage already done nor prevent further injury. For that reason, many museums deal with the problem of overexposure with established guidelines for the exhibition of prints and drawings.

Fading of colored papers. Like light staining, the fading of colored papers from exposure to light happens so slowy that it may pass undetected by the casual observer. With time, the rosy pink paper that Edgar Degas chose for the portrait of fellow artist Edouard Manet (figure 1.23) faded to a paler hue, undermining the lively tonal relationship that the artist originally intended. The edges of the drawing

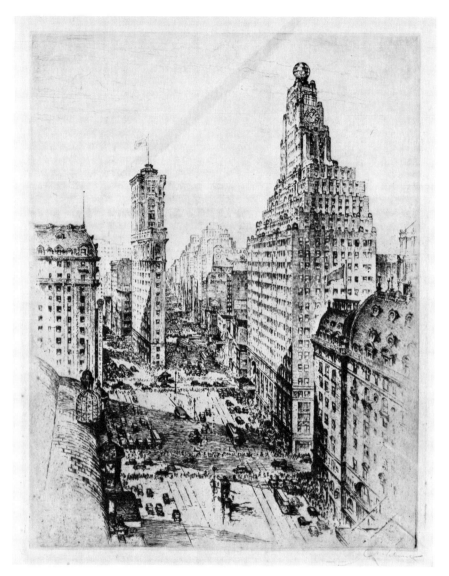

Fig. 1.22. Like Billingsgate *in figure 1.21, this etching also has been discolored by exposure to light. The darkening of the paper disrupts the contrasts of lights and darks so important in etchings.* —Anton Schutz, Hub of the World; *private collection; photograph by Sheldan Collins*

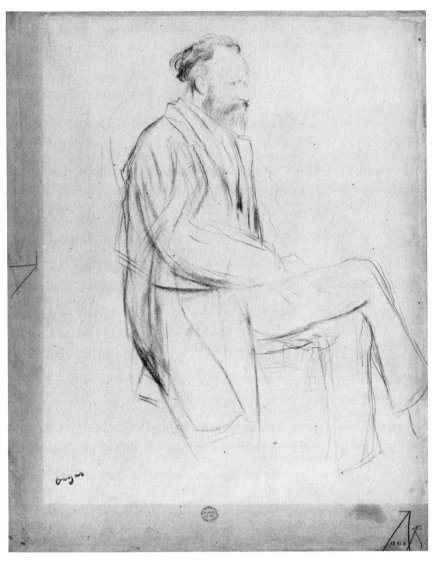

Fig. 1.23. The original color of the paper of this drawing was bright pink. The area exposed to light has faded, while the color around the edges, protected by the mat, remains intact.—Edgar Degas, Study for a Portrait of Edouard Manet; *the Metropolitan Museum of Art: Rogers Fund, 1919 (19.51.6); photograph by Sheldan Collins*

protected by the mat remain the original color. Such "fugitive" colors are not found in paper alone; they are also present in certain media. While the discoloration of light staining can sometimes be lessened by a conservator, there is no cure for fading. As always, prevention is preferable.

The color in most colored papers, especially modern ones, is caused by a dye, not by discrete pigment particles dispersed throughout the paper pulp. Because of their molecular structure, some dyes are extremely sensitive to light. Early synthetic dyes, developed after 1856, were made into printing and writing inks without special attention to the possibility of their fading, which occurred quickly after the inks were used. The "basic" family of dyes, one of the first to be formulated, is the brightest tinctorially and happens to have an affinity for groundwood and unbleached pulps, two quite common—and acidic—constituents of modern, inexpensive papers. The two types most familiar to us all, the telephone company's Yellow Pages and children's construction papers, are colored with basic dyes and, not surprisingly, they will fade very, very quickly.[6]

Mold growth and condensation. Mold spores are always present in the air. They remain dormant in drier environments, but with elevated humidity will readily attack sizings used in paper, surface coatings, various media, and even cellulose itself. Fingerprints may be invisible, but the oily residue from them can support mold growth. Using these substances as nutrients, mold will grow and spread, invading the paper and causing patchy discoloration. Eventually, the strong network of paper fibers is broken down, and the sheet becomes limp and pulpy. Their texture and the natural gums used as binders in them make pastels especially attractive to mold spores. Mold growth in pastels is often difficult to detect; the dappling caused by its growth pattern may resemble the artist's technique.

Mold growth is often difficult to detect early, because it appears in so many subtle forms and colors, including some lovely pastel shades. Fungus growing within a design area is often simply overlooked or mistaken for part of the image, as is true of the work seen in figure 1.24. At times, the mold itself may be invisible, but its musty odor indicates that the work of art has spent some time in a damp place. Figure 1.25, showing a drawing by Louis Comfort Tiffany, for one of his now-coveted stained-glass lampshades, shows how paper can be affected by long-term storage in a damp environment. In this instance, black and pink mold penetrated so deeply into the structure of the paper that complete removal of the fungus was impossible. In some cases (see figure 1.26), when mold growth has not progressed too far, a *soft* brush can be used to

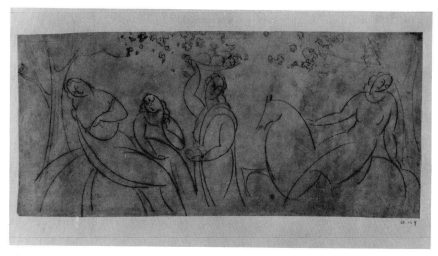

Fig. 1.24. What appears to be a bower of flowers above these frolicking nymphs is actually magenta-colored mold growth. Because it cannot be ascertained whether the mold grew after the drawing was done or whether the artist consciously incorporated it into the design, no attempt will be made to remove it.—Elie Nadelman, Study for Autumn; *the Metropolitan Museum of Art: gift of Lincoln Kirstein (65.12.4)*

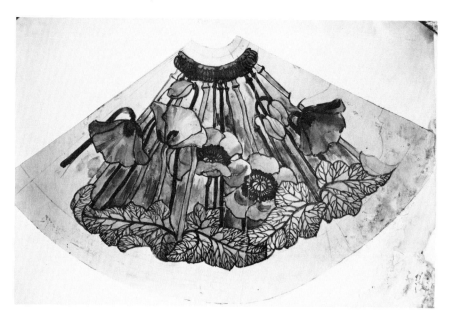

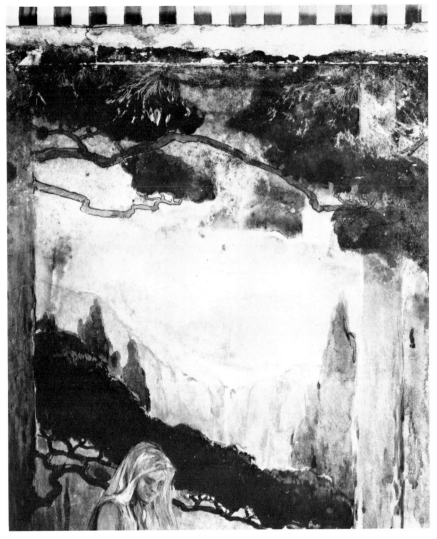

Fig. 1.26. The mold on this watercolor appears as white feathery strands along its upper edge.—Louis Comfort Tiffany, Study for a Stained Glass Window *(detail); the Metropolitan Museum of Art: gift of Julia Weld (67.653.4)*

OPPOSITE PAGE: *Fig. 1.25. Black mold growing within the paper itself disfigures the right side of this watercolor.—Louis Comfort Tiffany,* Poppy Shade; *the Metropolitan Museum of Art: William E. Dodge Fund (67.655.7)*

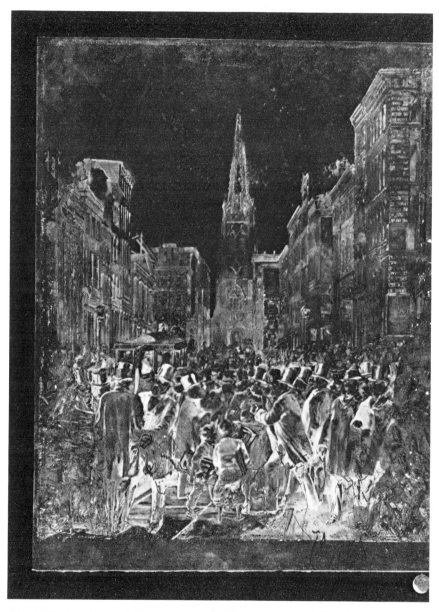

Fig. 1.27. The piece of glass photographed here was placed directly against an oil painting on paper during framing. The whitish haze is actually mold, which was sustained by the moisture trapped between the paint and the glass. The mold follows the contours of the design because the amount of condensation varied with the size of the air spaces created by the uneven layer of paint.—Photograph by Sheldan Collins

whisk the fungus away gently. This solution is obviously not prudent when the mold has attacked powdery media or when removal of the mold would otherwise disturb the image.

Mold can take a variety of forms, from the small black spots seen in figure 1.25 to the feathery white strands present in the upper right corner of figure 1.26, depicting a Louis Comfort Tiffany design for a stained-glass window.

In figure 1.27, we see a piece of glass incorrectly used in framing a drawing. The whitish haze visible is actually a fuzzy mold that has been sustained by humidity trapped between the drawing and the glass with which it was in direct contact. Note that the mold followed the contours of the drawing's image; the steeple of Trinity Church on Wall Street appears in the center of the design. This photograph graphically demonstrates the importance of leaving a breathing space between a print or drawing and the glass used in framing it.

At fairly frequent, regular intervals, prints and drawings must be inspected closely for mold growth, which can sometimes take the form of an inconspicuous haze. When mold growth is found or suspected in a framed print or drawing, the art should be unframed immediately, to dissipate any humidity that may be trapped inside. This is sufficient to stop or prevent mold growth, since mold simply cannot survive in 45-to-55 percent RH. Exposure of the art to thymol is indicated only in extreme conditions of long-term high humidity, such as during floods involving masses of water-logged paper. It is also a misconception to imagine that thymol fumes provide permanent protection against future mold growth. If the object is returned to a humid atmosphere, new mold spores will settle upon its surface and will soon grow.

It should be noted, here, that thymol fumes can attack and soften oil paints, varnishes, and some synthetic resins. They may also embrittle parchment. Works incorporating any of these materials must not be exposed to thymol fumes. Use of thymol in treating photographs should be undertaken only according to the directions of a conservator specializing in the care of photographs. Thymol crystals can also cause oily stains if they accidentally contact paper. Thymol should be used only with adequate ventilation, since the fumes are harmful (perhaps carcinogenic) to people. A design for a thymol chamber is given in Appendix 3; *thymol should not be used until all precautions mentioned in Appendix 3 have been thoroughly reviewed.* In the past, efforts to prevent mold from growing in framed prints and drawings have included inserting sheets of thymol-soaked papers behind the work of art. This should never be done, because of the danger of staining the art and because thymol fumes can soften Plexiglas, which may cause it to stick to the art. Further, it is doubtful that this precaution is actually effective, over time.

When mold growth occurs within the structure of the paper, when it interferes with a fragile medium, or when it leaves stains after having been brushed off, consultation with a conservator is necessary.

Foxing. The term *foxing* refers to the small circular patches of brownish discoloration that can mysteriously appear on both old and modern papers, for no apparent reason. The causes for this unsightly manifestation are still being investigated.[7] For some time, it was thought that iron particles deposited within the paper as it was made were rusting and that caused the brownish spots. Iron specks do indeed occasionally cause similar stains. *The most recent and generally accepted theory about the cause of foxing, however, identifies it as selective mold growth.* The particular kind of microorganism believed to cause foxing requires very specific conditions, yet to be fully identified, for its growth. It seems safe to conjecture that, had they remained in a nonhumid environment, prints and drawings marred by foxing would have been spared their disfigurement.

The theory that foxing is a special kind of mold growth is supported by the condition of a black-and-white chalk drawing (figure 1.28) by Charles Balthazar Julien Févret de Saint-Mémin, famous for his profile portraits of well-known Americans, drawn with the aid of a physiognotrace. Foxing is present all over the chalk drawing; the water stains along the right side are evidence of a damp environment.

Foxing may take place in all sorts of papers. Modern papers such as those used by Picasso and Chagall, as well as old papers, such as the sixteenth-century Albrecht Dürer drawing in figure 1.29 can be similarly affected. Except for the foxing, Dürer's intimate portrayal of the Holy Family is in otherwise perfect condition. Nothing about its physical condition hints at the cause of its disfigurement.

According to an ancillary theory, the fungus responsible for foxing is attracted to the sizing used in some papers. A drawing by Felicien Rops supports this theory; the foxing shown in figure 1.30 penetrates the paper and seems to have been nurtured by some substance found within it. Typical foxing is also present in the Sargent drawing (figure 1.18) and the print after Audubon, figure 1.10.

In addition to being inspected regularly for foxing, prints and drawings should also be checked for signs of any other mold growth (see above). When they are kept in safe surroundings, with stable relative humidity and temperature, foxing will not worsen. Sometimes other factors—such as animal glues or acidic cardboards in contact with the art—seem to aggravate the foxing. Foxing in or around these areas is sometimes more closely spaced or darker in color. The removal or reduction of foxing should be attempted only by a conservator who can

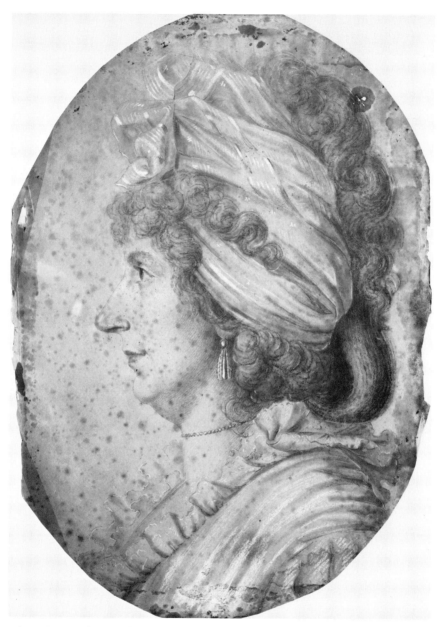

Fig. 1.28. Foxing—*the small dark spots seen throughout this drawing*—*is a form of mold growth. It most likely appeared on this portrait from prolonged storage in a damp environment.*—*Charles Balthazar Julien Févret de Saint-Mémin,* Profile of a Woman; *private collection*

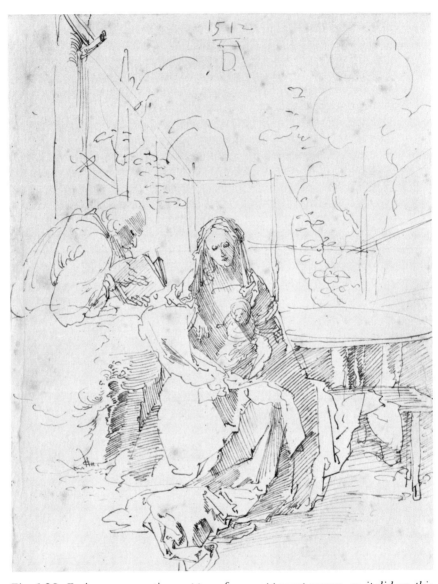

Fig. 1.29. Foxing can sometimes appear for no apparent reason, as it did on this otherwise pristine drawing. Scientists are still investigating the causes of foxing.—Albrecht Dürer, Holy Family in Trellis; *the Metropolitan Museum of Art: the Robert Lehman Collection (1975.1.860); photograph by Sheldan Collins, from George Szabo,* XV-XVI Century Northern Drawings from the Robert Lehman Collection *(New York: The Metropolitan Museum of Art, 1978), fig. 24*

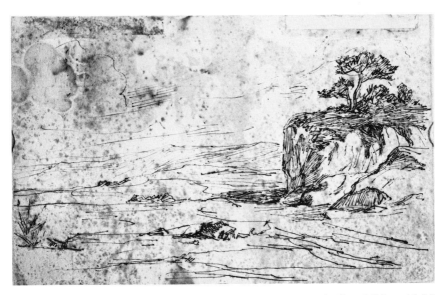

Fig. 1.30. A manifestation of foxing different from that seen in figs. 1.28 and 1.29 appears in this drawing. Sizing used in the manufacture of the paper seems to have provided the nutrients for mold growth here.—Felicien Rops, Landscape Study; *the Metropolitan Museum of Art: gift of Mr. and Mrs. Albert Broccoli (1979.668.6)*

determine the effect of the treatment on the medium and the paper of the print or drawing.

Extreme overall buckling of paper. As noted earlier, paper is a naturally hygroscopic substance—it loves water. And water, in the form of high humidity or fluctuating levels of humidity, can make paper buckle. The cellulose molecules of paper fibers will absorb water vapor until they reach equilibrium with the relative humidity of the surrounding environment. As the air around paper becomes less humid, the cellulose molecules likewise give up moisture. As can be expected, variations in moisture content are accompanied by dimensional changes—buckling. As the cellulose expands with an intake of water, the whole sheet of paper swells. When the paper dries out, the whole sheet shrinks. Different kinds of paper expand and contract at different rates and in different directions, depending on the characteristics of their fibers and the way the paper was formed.

Generally speaking, the movement of paper with environmental changes doesn't present a problem; it is a natural phenomenon, and should not be interfered with by its caretaker's squeezing the art in a heavy press, ironing it, or dry-mounting it to a stiff cardboard. Paper has a life of its own. Part of its beauty comes from this liveliness and "body."

Keep in mind that the artist chose a particular paper for working on, with its surface texture in mind. Drastic measures taken to stop buckling—ironing, dry-mounting, excessive pressing—usually alter the "personality" of the paper, resulting in a change of the look and feel of the work of art. Correctly hinged, matted, and framed, most works of art on paper will not seriously buckle if kept in a relatively stable environment.

Buckling is a serious conservation problem in several specific situations. Sometimes a general, overall "washboard" buckling takes place in a piece of art. Such an "all-out, all-over" attack may indicate drastic fluctuation in relative humidity and is often seen in prints hung in houses built near the sea. Such severe buckling should be regarded as a sign that humidity levels are unsafe, that mold growth may well occur as a result, and that appropriate measures need to be taken.

Buckling is especially dangerous when it warps the paper to such a degree that the art comes into contact with the glass of its frame. Condensation easily occurs when that happens, resulting in the kind of whitish haze seen in figure 1.27. Friable media are particularly threatened by extreme buckling. A layer of pigment *must* move if its support moves; a brittle pigment layer—pastel, desiccated tempera paint, or gouache—often flakes.

Finally, extreme buckling should be taken seriously when it interferes with the enjoyment of the art, as illustrated in figure 1.31. This Winslow Homer etching was kept in a damp environment for many years. If buckling becomes an aesthetic nuisance and proper precautions are taken, the print or drawing can be gently flattened. A reminder: parchment is particularly susceptible to dangerous buckling.

Localized buckling of paper. Localized buckling is the distortion of a sheet of paper in one particular area, as opposed to the overall buckling described above. Usually, localized buckling is caused by improper mounting of the print or drawing.

When a work of art is properly hinged into a mat, it is free to move with climatic changes. While it can exhibit severe overall buckling with fluctuations in humidity, under normal conditions no undue tension will be exerted by its hinges. Such is not the case with the Mary Cassatt drawing shown in figure 1.32. Because this work was glued down on all four sides, it could not move as the humidity rose and fell. Expansion and contraction led to terrible horizontal buckling. The result is not

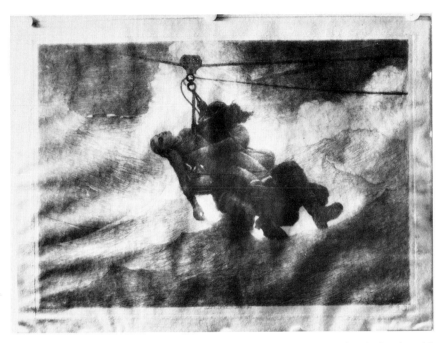

Fig. 1.31. Overall buckling of this print has resulted from high relative humidity.—*Winslow Homer,* The Lifeline; *private collection*

only aesthetically disturbing; it is also dangerous for the drawing. The paper will eventually rupture from being stretched so tightly. In many instances, the drawing is permanently warped from such long-term distortion.

Prints and drawings are often improperly mounted to paper or cardboard for framing, and the mount used may bear no relation to the artwork, either aesthetically or historically. In some instances, however, artists have mounted their works to secondary supports that they have dated, marked with a title, decorated, or signed. Drawings by Paul Klee and collages by Kurt Schwitters are examples, as is figure 2.5. Mounts so treated by the artist should never be taped, marked, trimmed, or otherwise altered. The same rule applies to mounts carrying information intimately related to the artwork—for example, the decorative mounts of eighteenth-century collectors, such as Pierre-Jean Mariette, which carry the collector's stamp or seal. Original or period mounts demand careful consideration before they are overzealously disposed of.

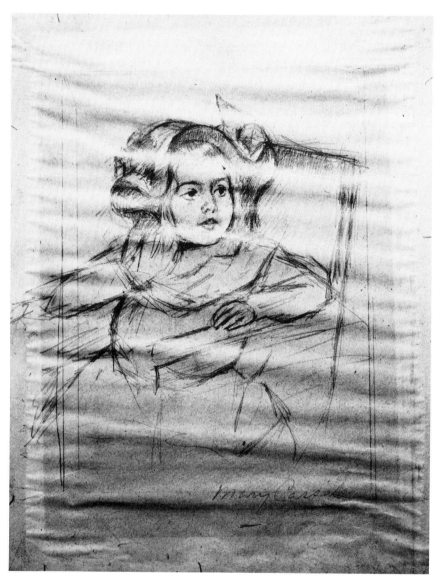

Fig. 1.32. All four edges of this drawing are pasted to a piece of cardboard. Because it is not free to expand and contract with changes in humidity, the paper has buckled horizontally. The thin paper is under extreme tension and may eventually rupture.—*Mary Cassatt,* Simone Wearing a Bonnet with a Wavy Brim; *the Metropolitan Museum of Art; gift of Mrs. Joseph du Vivier (54.97.2)*

Localized buckling can also result from the constrictions of a label, tape, hinge, or an old repair that restricts the natural movement of the paper of a print or drawing. The paper simply expands and contracts around the substance that impedes it. The etching shown in figure 1.33 exhibits localized buckling; its outside edges remain flat, while the design area and the area slightly beyond that are deformed. In prints, such buckling can reflect too much pressure brought to bear by the press. In this instance, however, the label on the reverse side of the print (figure 1.34) produced the buckling.

Extreme overall flatness of paper. It may seem paradoxical that, after the commentary on buckling given above, this author should now complain about a drawing or print looking too flat. My reason for it, however, is that when a print or drawing looks too flat, that is a good indication that it has probably been mounted on heavy cardboard, perhaps—ill-advisedly—to expedite framing or to eliminate buckling. The charcoal drawing in figure 1.35, by Josef Israels, illustrates such a problem. The mounting process is either done wet—using an aqueous starch paste or animal glue or a solvent-based adhesive such as rubber cement—or dry, using heat and a natural or synthetic resin. While mounting prints and drawings on cardboard seems to solve the problem of buckling, in reality, it poses many more serious threats to the art. First, the cardboard is often made of wood pulp and causes severe staining of the paper due to its acidity. Second, adhesives often discolor as they age, discoloring the work of art as well. Finally—and most important—cardboards become quite brittle with time. A sharp blow or sudden jolt, such as occurs when a framed piece falls from the wall, will snap the cardboard mount—and the art, as well—in two. From an aesthetic point of view, prints and drawings that have been mounted to cardboard often appear dull and lifeless, because the surface texture of their paper or design lines has been lessened.

The removal of mounted prints and drawings from cardboard should be attempted only by a conservator. This is a repetition of advice given earlier, but it is important enough to say again and again: *Never try to peel away a work of art on paper that has been firmly affixed to its mount,* even though a curled-up, lifting corner makes it look as if the whole piece would lift off at a touch. It won't; and before you know it, you'll have peeled away a hefty and irreplaceable layer from the art.

Overall mounting of intaglio prints to a solid support is also an aesthetic danger, as it alters the texture and body of the paper and inevitably flattens an intaglio print's "plate mark," an important attribute in the connoisseurship of fine prints.

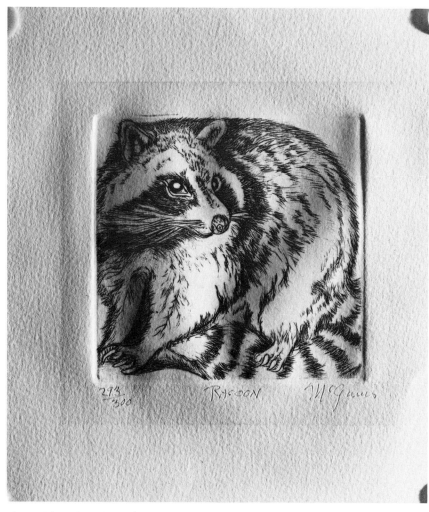

Fig. 1.33. Distortion of the paper is visible at the center of this etching.—
McGinnis, Raccoon; *private collection; photograph by Sheldan Collins*

Fig. 1.34. Cause of the distortion in Raccoon, *figure 1.33, is the label on the back, which is restricting the paper's natural movement in response to climatic changes.*—*Photograph by Sheldan Collins*

If a conservator removes a work of art from its mount, it should not be disposed of without consideration of its aesthetic and historic importance.

Insects and rodents. In addition to providing nutrients for fungal growth, paper is also attractive to hungry insects and rodents. Good housekeeping can help to prevent infestations. Pest infestation can be detected by that which the invaders take away (figure 1.36) and that which they leave (figure 1.37). Monitor housekeeping procedures rigorously, and at first hint of the presence of pests, take action to eliminate them. Insecticides must be carefully chosen and used with discrimination (see chapter 4). The unsightly damage that insects and rodents inflict on prints and drawings should be treated by a conservator.

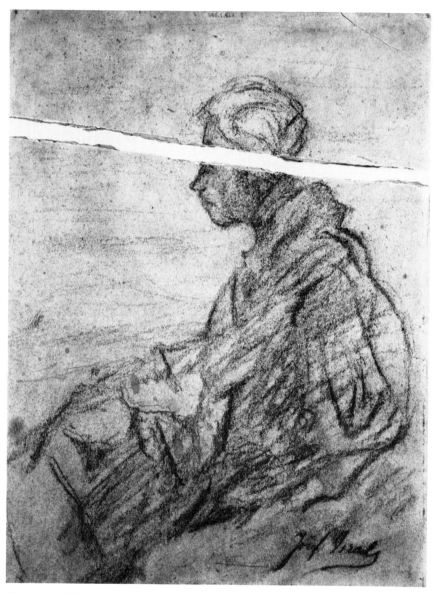

Fig. 1.35. This drawing was pasted to a piece of cardboard that became increasingly brittle as it aged. Boards in such condition readily snap in two.—
Josef Israels, **Profile of Seated Man;** *the Metropolitan Museum of Art: unaccessioned gift of H. G. Friedman, 1958*

Fig. 1.36. This paper shows erosion caused by insects.—Photograph by Sheldan Collins

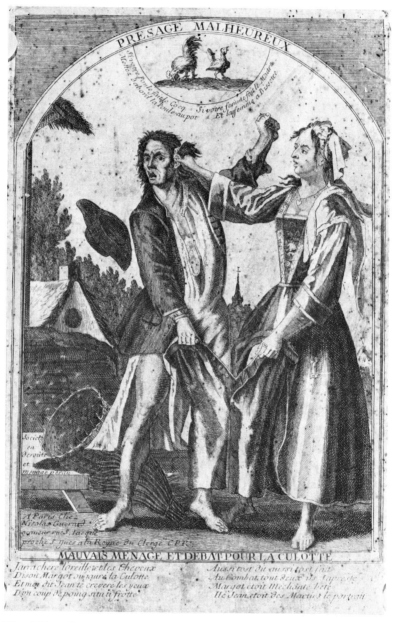

Fig. 1.37. The droppings of cockroaches disfigure this print.—N. Gué-rard, Moralities; *the Metropolitan Museum of Art: gift of Mrs. John H. Sichel (66.747.62); photograph by Sheldan Collins*

Tears, losses, and punctures. It hardly seems worthwhile to mention tears, losses, and punctures—usually avoidable instances of mishandling—in a listing of disfigurements caused by apparently less direct means. I do so only to illustrate that mechanical damages, such as tears, are often caused or aggravated by the factors discussed above. For instance, when incorrectly prying from its frame a drawing that has been pasted onto brittle cardboard, it is very easy to snap off a corner. Likewise, a print on nineteenth-century wood pulp paper can be fractured by the slightest curling. It is important, when handling prints and drawings, that one never assume that a remedy or a repair can be simple, easy, or done quickly, and that one never take *anything* for granted.

NOTES

1. Curt F. Buhler, *The Fifteenth-Century Book: The Scribes, the Printers, the Decorators* (Philadelphia: University of Pennsylvania Press, 1960), p. 35.

2. Stephen Weiner, et al., "Dead Sea Scroll Parchments: Unfolding of the Collagen Molecules and Racemization of Aspartic Acid," *Nature* 287 (October 30, 1980): 823.

3. Kiyofusa Narita, "A Life of Ts'ai Lun," *The Paper Maker* 24, No. 1 (1965):23.

4. The formula for cellulose is generally accepted to be $(C_6H_{10}O_5)x$ according to James P. Casey, in *Pulp and Paper Chemistry and Chemical Technology*, 3rd ed. (New York: John Wiley, 1980): 1:4–5.

5. For a history of the development of pressure-sensitive tapes and their conservation problems, see Merrily A. Smith, Norvell M. M. Jones, II, Susan L. Page, and Marian Peck Dirda, "Pressure-Sensitive Tape and Techniques for Its Removal from Paper," *Journal of the AIC* 23, No. 2 (Spring 1984): 101–113.

6. Thomas B. Brill, *Light: Its Interaction with Art and Antiquities* (New York: Plenum Press, 1980), p. 157.

7. See C. Eugene Cain and Barbara A. Miller, "Proposed Classification of Foxing," the American Institute for Conservation of Historic and Artistic Works, Book and Paper Group, Tenth Annual Meeting, Washington, D.C., 1982, *Postprints*, no pagination; C. Eugene Cain and Barbara A. Miller, "Photographic Spectral, and Chromatigraphic Searches into the Nature of Foxing" (Preprints of papers presented at the Tenth Annual Meeting, Book and Paper Group, the American Institute for Conservation of Historic and Artistic Works, Washington, D.C., 1982), pp. 54–66; G. G. Maynall and R. J. Newcombe, "Foxing: A Fungal Infection of Paper," *Nature* 274 (3 August 1978): 466–468; and Judith Walsh, "Selected Conservation Problems: Foxing in Papers," *Drawing* 7, No. 1 (May–June 1985): 5–8.

FURTHER READING

American Pulp and Paper Association. *The Dictionary of Paper.* 3d ed. New York: American Pulp and Paper Association, 1965.

Cain, C. Eugene. *The Chemistry of Paper.* Video cassette. Jackson: Society of Mississippi Archivists, n.d.

Farmer, Jane M. "Paper: The Technological and Spiritual Wonder of the Ancient World." In *New American Paperworks*, pp. 5–16. San Francisco: World Print Council, 1982.

Garlock, Trisha. *Glossary of Papermaking Terms.* San Francisco: World Print Council, 1983.

Heller, Jules. *Papermaking: The White Art.* Scotsdale, Ariz.: Scorpio Press, 1980.

Hunter, Dard. *Papermaking: The History and Technique of an Ancient Craft.* New York: Dover, 1978.

Labarré, E. J. *Dictionary and Encyclopedia of Paper and Papermaking.* 2d ed. Amsterdam: Swets and Zeitlinger, 1952.

Leif, Irving P. *An International Sourcebook of Paper History.* Hamden, Conn.: Archon, 1978.

Lewis, Naphtali. *Papyrus in Classical Antiquity.* Oxford: Clarendon Press, 1974.

Library of Congress. *Papermaking: Art and Craft.* Washington, D.C.: Library of Congress, 1968.

Plenderleith, H. J., and A. E. A. Werner. *The Conservation of Antiquities and Works of Art.* 2d rev. ed. London: Oxford University Press, 1971.

Reed, Donald. *Ancient Skins, Parchments, and Leathers.* London: Seminar Press, 1972.

Studley, Vance. *The Art and Craft of Handmade Paper.* New York: Van Nostrand Reinhold, 1977.

Sutermeister, Edwin. *The Story of Papermaking.* Boston: S. D. Warren, 1954.

Tschudin, Peter. "Papyrus." *The Paper Maker* 34, No. 1 (1965): 3–15.

Turner, Silvie, and Birgit Skiöld. *Handmade Paper Today: A Worldwide Survey of Mills, Papers, Techniques, and Uses.* New York: Frederic C. Beil, 1983.

Whitney, Roy P. *The Story of Paper.* Atlanta: Technical Association of the Pulp and Paper Industry, 1980.

2

The Media of Prints and Drawings

Prints

*C*ONSIDERED SOLELY IN terms of medium, prints are relatively trouble-free. The fact that a number of fifteenth-century specimens are in good condition today is evidence of their durable nature, especially when one considers that the earliest prints, many of which dealt with devotional subjects, were meant for everyday contemplation. Although most conservation problems associated with prints have to do with their paper support, a few problems arise solely from the way in which they are or were made.

Relief Prints

The most basic kind of print is the relief print. Examples include woodcuts, linoleum cuts, and wood engravings, and various less common types, such as metal cuts and relief etchings. The relief print began to appear in Europe during the fifteenth century, about the time when books began to be printed and when a reliable source of paper was established. The earliest Chinese relief print dates to the eighth century after Christ.

Relief prints were first used to make "exactly repeatable pictorial statements," in the words of William M. Ivins, Jr.[1] A design is drawn upon or transferred onto the surface to be carved—which, nowadays, is usually a linoleum block or a dense wood block sawed parallel to its grain. Practically any flat "carvable" surface can be used. The areas around the lines are carved away, so that the negative areas will receive no ink and thus will not print. A special sticky printing ink, viscous enough to sit on the surface of the raised parts of the block without running into the hollows, is necessary. Printing inks vary in composition and sometimes cause conservation problems.

Relief prints are fairly easy to print. Presses were not always utilized; many prints were made simply by placing the paper against the inked block and rubbing evenly by hand with a smooth tool, such as an agate burnisher or the back of a spoon. The shiny striations and indentations left by the tool are considered an important attribute of the print and are especially prized by collectors of Japanese *ukiyo-e* prints.

Woodcuts historically offered an advantage, in that they could be mounted in a press together with printing type, offering the possibility of illustrating written text. In contrast to engravings and etchings, however, woodcuts could reproduce an image in only rather limited detail. Perhaps that explains their decline in popularity after the sixteenth century. Later, artists such as Paul Gauguin and Edvard Munch explored the medium's expressionistic possibilities, and the 1980s have witnessed a sort of minirevival as artists discovered still other visual effects obtainable with woodcuts.

In the late eighteenth century, wood again began to be used in making prints. Printmakers discovered that fine detail could be achieved by carving a block that had been cut *across* the grain rather than *with* the grain of a plank. A block of boxwood, preferable because it is harder than copper engraving plates, could then be printed onto the newly available smooth-surfaced papers that reproduced images in greater detail. Wood engraving, as the new process came to be called, was used almost exclusively for commercial illustration. The blocks were made "type high" and were printed simultaneously with the text of books. John Tenniel made wood engravings to illustrate *Alice's Adventures in Wonderland;* Winslow Homer made countless wood engravings for *Harper's Weekly.*

Wood engravings such as that shown in figure 2.1 were frequently printed on extremely thin Japanese tissue paper, first imported into the United States in the 1880s, which showed the detailing of the design and the skill of the carver to greatest advantage. The fragile prints were then "tipped" into expensive books as illustrations. Etchings were often made on the same delicate sort of paper. Such wood engravings and etchings require special handling. In mistaken attempts to protect them, wood engravings and etchings have often been pasted down or otherwise improperly mounted, with disastrous results. The effort to achieve printing of high quality while at the same time lessening the fragility of the support led to the development of the *chine collé* print, discussed below.

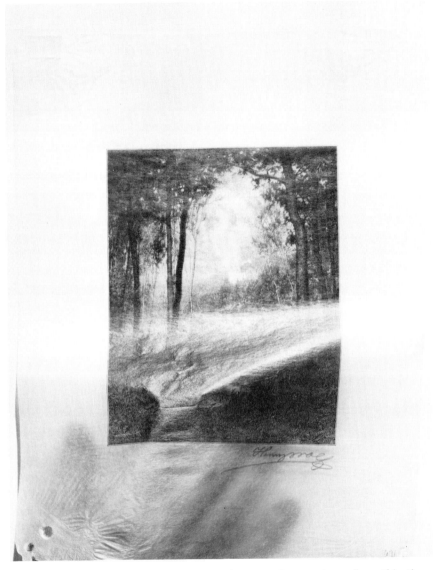

Fig. 2.1 In the late nineteenth century, prints were frequently made on thin tissue papers, which require careful handling. The wood engraving pictured here was previously glued onto a heavier paper at all four corners, resulting in cockling and losses. —Henry Wolf, after Alexander H. Wyant, In the Adirondacks; *private collection; photograph by Sheldan Collins*

Intaglio Prints

The category of intaglio prints includes engravings, etchings, dry points, mezzotints, stipple engravings, and aquatints, as well as photogravures, inkless intaglio (or embossing), and etchings done with various unusual grounds.

In the intaglio process, the lines to be printed are cut into a metal plate, usually copper or zinc, by means of a burin held in the hand (engraving) or through the corrosive action of acid (etching). When the plate is inked, the recessed lines fill with the ink, which is thinner than that used for woodcuts. The excess is wiped away, and the plate is then put on the moving bed of a intaglio press. A damp sheet of paper is positioned on top of it, followed by heavy felts. The plate, paper, and felts are then pulled between two rollers, which exert such tremendous pressure on the damp paper that it is forced into the grooves of the plate and absorbs the ink deposited in them. The paper is literally molded by the metal plate and bears its outline. The embossed line indicating the plate's border is known as a plate mark and is prized by collectors. Figure 2.2 shows how the texture of the paper of an etching has been pressed smooth by the plate. Beyond the plate mark, the paper remains rough. Notice the depth of the plate mark and the way it acts as a border between rough and smooth.

The history of engraving, the oldest intaglio process, goes back nearly as far as that of woodcuts. Etching followed soon after, in the sixteenth century. The etching process, like engraving, was used much earlier for decorating metal utensils and armor. Engraving and etching both afforded much greater detail than was possible by relief processes, and possibly for that reason intaglio prints were soon preferred to woodcuts. Other types of intaglio prints, such as aquatints, drypoints, stipple engravings, and mezzotints, are made following the same principle as engravings and etchings. They differ in the manner in which the image is incised into the metal plate.

In the intaglio process, because the paper is squeezed into the plate's grooves, its design lines stand in relief. In contrast, the lines of a woodcut design are sunk into the paper. Such relief prints were often printed upon moist paper, which further exaggerated their contours; and the indentations burnishers sometimes leave on the backs of relief prints have already been mentioned.

To a print connoisseur, the three-dimensionality of a printed line to a great extent determines the quality of the impression. In aesthetic terms, the height or depth of a printed line can make the difference between a design that is rich and vibrant and one that is faint and lifeless.

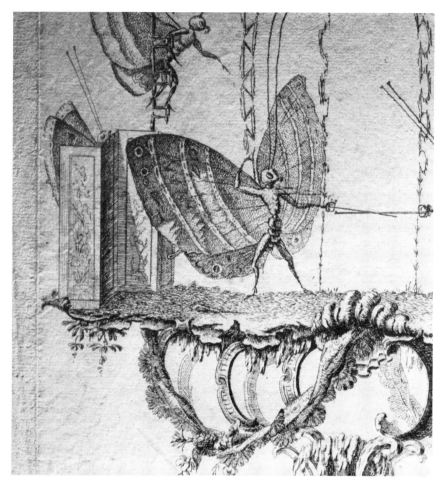

Fig. 2.2. The three-dimensionality of intaglio prints is evident in this etching.—Charles-Germain de Saint-Aubin, Papilloneries humaines *(detail); the Metropolitan Museum of Art: the Elisha Whittelsey Collection, the Elisha Whittelsey Fund, and Rogers Fund (1982.1101.5)*

People responsible for handling and preserving prints should respect the topography of these works of art; a print's texture can easily be destroyed by ironing, dry mounting, and other extreme flattening procedures. A heightened sensibility to the three-dimensionality of prints is a prerequisite to learning proper flattening techniques and is indispensable for the proper care and handling of all prints, even so-called planographic ones. The point is brought up here simply because the texture of both paper and ink is quite evident in intaglio prints.

The plate mark is one of the most noticeable and valued three-dimensional attributes of etchings and engravings and is also one of the most easily damaged. It is difficult to determine the reason for its importance, since in early intaglio prints the plate mark was carefully trimmed away. To some individuals, the plate mark is proof that the print is original—a misconception, inasmuch as plate marks are sometimes embossed upon photomechanical reproductions. In my opinion, the plate mark defines the area of the artist's design and must therefore be considered part of that design. Furthermore, the plate mark provides information about the print's creation—the paper used, its "body," its dampness when pressed, and the amount of pressure exerted. A plate mark can also indicate whether the print was correctly "pulled" and whether the printer was meticulous or careless. The plate mark manifests an action that requires both artistic skill and technical excellence. As such, it should remain unaltered.

Because of the tremendous pressure that produces plate marks, the resulting embossed line is usually weaker than the surrounding paper. The paper fibers along the plate mark may actually have been severed by the sharp metal edges of the plate. Fragile or cracked plate marks may indicate that printing pressure was incorrect or that the paper chosen cannot tolerate deformation. An etching by Anton Schutz (figure 2.3) shows a broken plate mark. In this case the damage resulted from dry mounting the print onto heavy cardboard; the plate mark, probably weak to begin with, was completely flattened by heat and pressure and, being inflexible responded to the tension by cracking. Possibly the print was dry mounted because the plate mark was already beginning to fracture, but rather than rectifying the problem, dry mounting only aggravated it.

Broken plate marks can be reinforced on the reverse side with thin strips of "feathered" Japanese tissue, preferably one that is extremely lightweight, such as *tengujo* or *chumino*, applied with starch paste. Such reinforcement will bring the cracked parts together and will add extra strength to the plate mark. Under no circumstances should a plate mark be lessened through conservation treatments or mounting procedures. Any flattening techniques used on the print overall must be executed with restraint and patience.

Despite the initial implication that a printed design is tough and durable, prints, in fact, can be easily damaged by rubbing or surface abrasion. Surface abrasion frequently goes unnoticed; however, it is

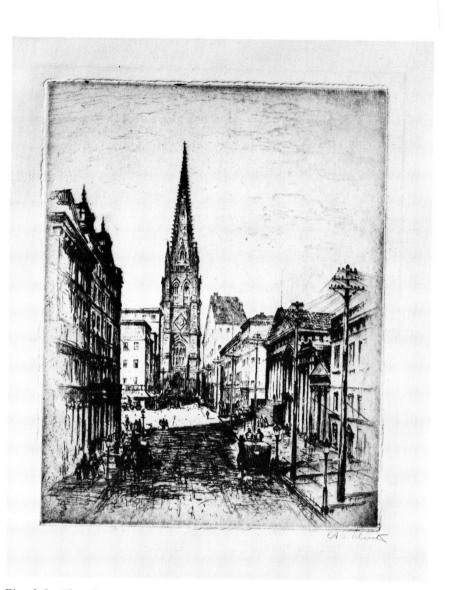

Fig. 2.3. *The plate mark of the etching shown here has ruptured because of improper mounting.*—Anton Schutz, Wall Street Fifty Years Ago; *private collection; photograph by Sheldan Collins*

particularly conspicuous on mezzotints, because of their method of manufacture. For mezzotints, thousands of densely packed, microscopic pits are first gouged into a metal plate by a "rocker." After the entire plate is covered with these tiny pits, the white highlights of the design are formed by burnishing, to create some smooth areas that will remain ink-free. The plate is inked and the excess rubbed away; each tiny pit remains filled with ink. Upon printing, a rich, velvety layer of ink is deposited across the surface of the paper. The design emerges from an inky black background. The unsized papers on which mezzotints are often printed are super-absorbent and soft-surfaced. Before printing is begun, the dampened paper may be lightly brushed, to make the paper fibers even fluffier and softer to the touch. Too often these inky shadows have been scratched or have paled from abrasion, as seen in Figure 2.4. Since the appeal of mezzotints depends upon the contrast of light and dark, the damage is distracting. Silk screen prints and *pochoir* prints, produced by a stenciling process, are similarly vulnerable; scratching of their ink layers is especially apparent in broad areas of flat color.

Obviously, the surface of all works of art on paper is fragile and must be continuously protected with either glass or clear acrylic when the art is framed or with neutral slip sheets when it is unframed, in storage. Unprotected prints and drawings should never be stacked and left to slide over each other; surface abrasion inevitably results in some degree of damage to the design.

Chine collé Prints

As previously noted, wood engravers frequently chose to print on thin tissues, because they gave the greatest detail. Other artists were attracted to these tissues by the clear, crisp effects they produced. Millet, Whistler, and Matisse all made etchings on thin Japanese tissues. The mounting of the resulting prints presented many difficulties, and many are in terrible condition today. *Chine collé,* a technique developed in the nineteenth century, simultaneously printed and mounted thin tissues, using the tremendous pressure exerted by the press. (Intaglio and lithographic presses can be used.) A tissue was dampened, its back was brushed with thin paste, and the sheet was positioned, pasted side up, over an inked metal plate or a lithographic stone. A heavier paper, also moistened, was placed over the pasted tissue. The whole package then passed through the intaglio or lithographic press, which both printed and adhered the tissue to the heavier paper. At one time, the process was so popular that prepasted tissue papers, which required only dampening, were commercially available.

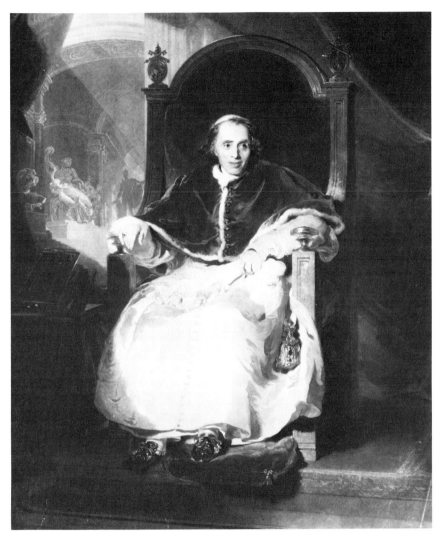

Fig. 2.4. Abrasion of the surface of this mezzotint is especially plain in the lower right corner. The damage detracts from the velvety blacks characteristic of mezzotints. — Samuel Cousins, after Sir Thomas Lawrence, Pius VII; *the Metropolitan Museum of Art: gift of Georgiana W. Sargent, in memory of John Osbourne Sargent (24.63.1888); photograph by Sheldan Collins*

Chine collé prints present unique conservation problems. They are frequently not recognized as consisting of two layers of paper and are treated as one sheet, with disastrous results, especially when moisture is applied to their surfaces. Chine collé prints can be difficult to recognize, because the tissue layer is normally the same color as the heavier paper below it. The tissue's smooth surface and fine edges make it easy to overlook. Sometimes air pockets form between the tissue and the paper on which it is mounted, probably a result of uneven pasting or a drying out of the paste as it ages. Often the tissue lifts at the edges, again a result of the paste's desiccation. The paste, probably starch or gum arabic, is often so thin and transparent as to be invisible. Nonetheless, chine collé prints seem to be particularly susceptible to foxing; possibly fungus uses the paste as a nutrient. Some unstable glues and tissue papers used for chine collé prints may yellow with aging and exposure to light.

In figure 2.5, a chine collé lithograph by Henri Matisse illustrates delamination of the thin tissue from the heavier paper to which it is mounted. In order to reattach the tissue, pieces of double-faced sticky tape were put in each corner. These subsequently darkened and stained the print. A strip of double-sided masking tape was also applied to the top of the heavier paper to attach it to the window mat. This secondary support, which carries the artist's signature, is just as much a part of the artwork as the tissue on which the image is printed. It should therefore never be taped, trimmed, written upon, or otherwise mutilated. Chine collé prints that have any of the problems discussed here should be treated only by a conservator.

Planographic Prints

Lithographs and monotypes are two products of the planographic printing process—that is, the design lines are not raised above or sunk below the printing surface. In the final print, the inked design is deposited across the surface of the paper. The paper is not deformed in the areas of the design lines, although the sheet may be indented from pressure against the lithographic stone or metal plate used in printing.

In this sense, lithographs and monotypes can have marks that correspond to the plate marks in intaglio prints. They are not nearly as sharp as intaglio plate marks, nor are they always distinguishable, but they usually appear as a smooth area where the paper has been pressed against the lithographic stone or plate.

Cliché verre prints are rare and are often classified as planographic prints. The image is produced when light passes through a design

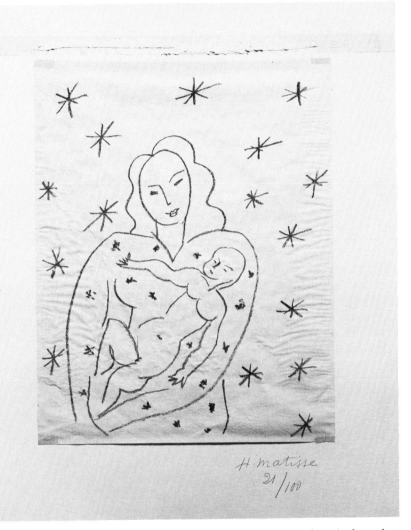

Fig. 2.5. The tissue in this chine collé lithograph is separating from its base sheet or secondary support. A poor attempt to reattach it was made by taping it at each corner.—*Henri Matisse,* Mother and Child; *private collection; photograph by Sheldan Collins*

scratched upon a coated glass, striking photosensitive paper. *From a conservation standpoint, cliché verre prints should be considered photographs.*

Lithographs. As an example of lithographic printing, consider the lithograph by George Bellows shown in figures 2.6 and 2.7. The pressure exerted during the printing process created a stone mark. The surrounding paper is in plane, while that within the mark is buckled. The paper was stretched so much that it could not return to its original shape. This example is an extreme case of a three-dimensional print made from a flat surface.

Lithography, which is based upon the principle that water and oil do not mix, was discovered in the late eighteenth century by Alois Senefelder, who as the story goes, jotted down his mother's laundry list on a slab of Bavarian limestone that he used to grind his printing inks. How it ever occurred to him to etch lightly and print the stone is not included in

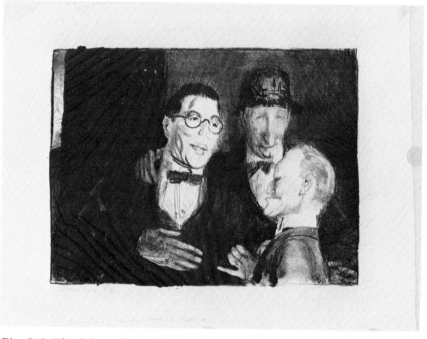

Fig. 2.6. The deformation of the paper of this George Bellows lithograph is not very apparent on the face of the work itself; but see figure 2.7. —*George Bellows,* Caricature of Speicher, Kroll, and Bellows; *the Metropolitan Museum of Art: gift of Gordon K. Allison (1982.1023)*

the story, but the Senefelder one reads of in the reference books was said to have been an ingenious fellow. The process, which was soon perfected to print sheet music, involves drawing a design on a clean, fine-grained lithographic stone with a greasy pencil or ink. Very light etching fixes the image and opens the stone's pores. Next, the entire surface is washed. Because the greasy lines have penetrated the stone, they are not removed, although the color may disappear. The porous stone is saturated with water. When it is subsequently inked, the ink is repelled by the water and adheres to the greasy areas. The stone is put onto the moving bed of a lithographic press, with a damp sheet of paper positioned over it and a flexible metal sheet above that. The ensemble passes under a scraper bar, which forces the ink from the stone onto the paper. Sheets of mechanically grained zinc and aluminum can be used instead of lithographic stone, which is often scarce and expensive.

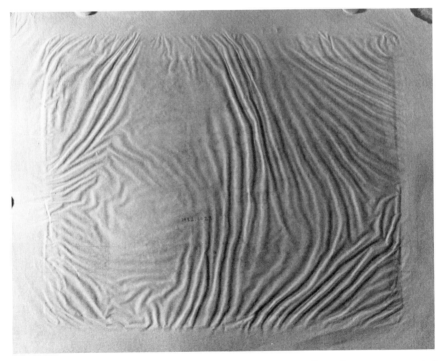

Fig. 2.7. The reverse side of the print in figure 2.6 shows how the paper expanded so much around the lithographic stone that it could not return to its original dimensions after printing.

The variety of lithographs is enormous, and the process is one of the most popular today. Perhaps the best-known and most loved lithographs are those by Currier and Ives. Conservation problems associated with them generally arise from three factors that are essentially unrelated to lithography. First, the paper on which Currier and Ives lithographs were printed is extremely unstable. It darkens when it is displayed in daylight, as almost all prints by Currier and Ives were, since they were intended for display. Second, in the nineteenth century, prints were frequently framed against wooden shingles, the acidity of which further darkened the paper. Finally, some of the colors applied to the prints after they were made are extremely light-sensitive. The greens, composed of Prussian blue and gamboge, two common nineteenth-century pigments, quickly fade to a pale blue; as a result, many of the deciduous trees in these prints now appear to be blue spruces. *From a conservation standpoint, hand-colored prints should be considered as sensitive to light as watercolors.*

Monotypes. In monotypes, the artist paints the image directly onto a glass or metal plate from which the print is made, with or without a press. Because most of the ink is transferred to the paper, usually only one or two prints can be made from any one plate. Monotypes were first made in the seventeenth century by artists such as Castiglione, who appreciated the spontaneity of this printing process. Degas will always be remembered for his mastery of the technique, which is again enjoying a revival. In the monotype shown in figure 2.8, Milton Avery brushed his design on the plate using an oily black ink. The oil, which has bled away from the design lines, was probably invisible at first, but has now darkened. Oxidized oil also causes paper to become brittle. Consequently, prints saturated with oily inks should be handled as little as possible. "Haloing," which occurs when excess oil wicks out into the surrounding paper, can also be seen in drawings made with oil paints or waxy crayons, media favored by Arshile Gorky and Jackson Pollock (and see figure 2.23).

Prints and colored printing inks. Since colored printing inks are frequently encountered in early lithographs, this is a good place to mention some of their properties and characteristics. The difference between *colored prints* and *color prints* is noteworthy, although the two are sometimes difficult to tell apart. A *color print* is one in which the colors have been printed using colored inks; printed colors appear flat and evenly deposited across the surface of the paper. Depending on the printing technique, a regular pattern of dots or specks of color will be apparent under magnification. Often one color will be uniformly out of register across the entire design. A *colored print*, on the other hand, shows color that has been applied by hand, usually with watercolor or gouache. The area to be colored was first coated with sizing. A man named Ackermann, a London purveyor of wildly popular prints in the early nineteenth century, used a sizing made from glue, soap, and alum, with some paper pulp added.[2] Watercolor washes are more translucent than printed colors and are not always evenly applied. Pools and tide lines form within the areas of color from uneven accumulation of pigment. Color in prints is often both printed and hand-painted, as is evident, for example, in some Currier and Ives lithographs.

Generally speaking, colored printing inks resist light more than watercolors applied to a print by hand, with the exception of two important families of prints—Japanese woodblock prints and nineteenth-century commercial lithographs (such as posters by Toulouse Lautrec.) In ukiyo-e prints, the printed colors are extremely sensitive to light and may quickly fade away entirely. Such fading is so common that many people expect Japanese prints to have pale tones. *Aigami* blue, from the dayflower, *ukon* yellow, from a vegetable root, and *beni*, a rose pink from the safflower, must all be protected from light.[3]

In 1856, William Perkin, then a young student, isolated aniline purple in an attempt to synthesize quinine for the treatment of malaria. By 1866, its popularity as an artist's color had spread throughout Europe and America. The French named the new purple *mauve* and enthusiastically greeted the other colors that quickly followed. Posters printed at about this time are particularly sensitive to light. Their blacks have frequently faded to a sickly green, while other colors have virtually disappeared, to the despair of collectors who have paid thousands for what was intended only as ephemera. Regardless of the inks used, these posters must be protected from the light because their paper is of horrendously poor quality and quickly darkens, further distorting the color balance. Generally speaking, a colored printing ink is only as resistant to light as the pigments or dyes contained in it.

Printing ink combines an oil, such as linseed oil, with finely ground pigment. The composition of inks differs, depending on the requirements of the process used. The viscosity, density, and tack of the ink are determined by the proportion of oil to pigment and by the presence or absence of additives. Excessive oil in an ink seeps into the surrounding paper and forms a halo around each printed line. As the print ages, the oil oxidizes and turns brown. Figure 2.8 shows a monotype that has been so affected.

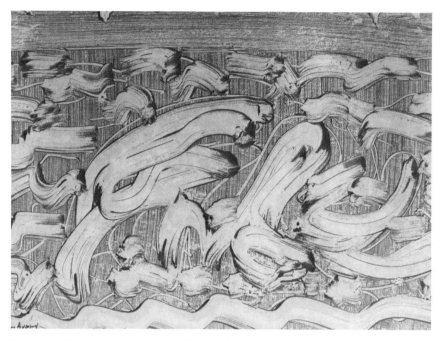

Fig. 2.8. Halos form around each line of this monotype, from an excess of oil in the ink. —Milton Avery, Birds and Ruffled Sea *(detail); the Metropolitan Museum of Art: the Elisha Whittelsey Collection, the Elisha Whittelsey Fund (1978.576); photograph by Sheldan Collins*

Some printing inks cause staining in paper because they are corrosive. The staining seems at present not to correlate with any date or locale and can be explained only as the result of different recipes or batches.

Figure 2.9 shows an engraving that was bound into a book as an illustration. It was folded down the center and inserted between two pages of text. The ink used in making the print seems to have been stable, while that used in printing the book must have been very acidic. The lines of text have burned so deeply into the back side of the page carrying the illustration that the discoloration penetrates through the paper to the obverse side where the print appears. Any librarian can attest that such acid migration is quite common in books. It is also frequently observed in prints, particularly on the reverse side if the print has been made with an unstable ink.

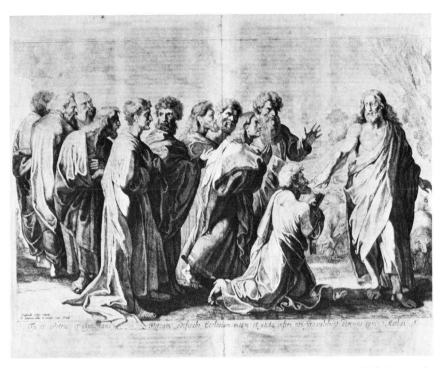

Fig. 2.9. This engraving was stained by the printed page with which it was in contact. The lines of printed text can be seen in the sky area.—Soutman, after Raphael, The Calling of Peter; *the Metropolitan Museum of Art: Dick Fund (47.100.421)*

Pen-and-Ink Drawings

Part of the difficulty of discussing pen-and-ink drawings relates to the problem of defining the term *ink*. We use the word here to mean *an aqueous suspension of ultrafine particles to which a binder, such as gum arabic, has been added to improve the flow.*

Inks are generally in liquid form, although Chinese and Japanese *sumi* inks come in solid bars that are wetted with each use. Uniformity and density of color are desirable in an ink, especially for writing purposes, although artists do not always require these properties.

Inks that artists have traditionally used alone or in combination include carbon black ink, iron gall ink, bistre, and sepia. Inks have also been made from berries, licorice, tobacco, and other, sometimes secret, ingredients. Inks in drawings have been identified incorrectly for centuries, each inaccuracy based upon another and passed along. Likewise, books on artists' materials have simply perpetuated the misinterpretation of old recipes, adding to the difficulty of identification. Consequently, we are left with volumes of conflicting descriptions of the inks used in Old Master drawings. Often the terms *sepia* and *bistre* are used to denote browns and not the actual composition of the inks used. The confusion does not stop with Old Master drawings. The works of one contemporary artist, generally thought to consist of ink washes, were actually made with hair dye. For greater understanding of inks as artistic media, we must systematically reconsider their uses and scientifically investigate their compositions.[4]

Generally, inks may be classified by color: black (carbon ink), blackish brown (iron gall ink), and brown (sepia and bistre). Carbon black ink, or lampblack, as it is sometimes called, is a truly black ink. One of the oldest of inks, carbon black ink was used by the ancient Egyptians in writing hieroglyphics on papyrus and also by the Chinese for calligraphy. It was historically made from candle soot or charcoal, which consists of almost pure carbon, mixed with water and a bit of gum arabic or other binder. Carbon black ink in solid form was available from the Far East and was always highly regarded by artists in the West. What we call *India ink* is a modern carbon black ink. In drawings, it can be recognized by its deep black color and by the slight sheen produced by the substances added to render it waterproof.

Drawings done in carbon black ink have few conservation problems specifically caused by the ink. Black carbon inks for drawing do not cause discoloration of the paper, as do some black printing inks. Because it is made from almost pure carbon particles, carbon black ink is not prone to fading. This can be misleading, however, since some modern inks, while appearing to be black carbon, are actually blue-black dyes. Their true color is usually visible under magnification along the edges of lines where the ink has bled into the paper fibers. True carbon black ink lines should appear uniformly black, rich, and opaque. Many drawings from the later half of the nineteenth century and the first half of the twentieth century were made with blue-black ink, a product resulting from the manufacture of aniline dyes. Because this ink is very sensitive to light, many of these artworks have faded to blue-gray or pale brown.

Occasionally, carbon black inks can have flaking problems, especially if they are thickly applied, are applied to a polished paper, or both.

Cracking and flaking of India ink has been observed on drawings by Jackson Pollock, who sometimes poured ink onto paper. Drawings on which the ink appears to have dried out or loosely adhered to the paper should be taken to a conservator for treatment.

The brown inks—iron gall, bistre, and sepia—are the most difficult to differentiate, because they can be similar in appearance. Of these three, iron gall ink is the most common. Its color, which was blackish brown when it was made, invariably lightens to brown or even to yellow. The name *iron gall* refers to its manufacture from ferrous sulphate, in the form of iron filings, combined with oak galls, which contain tannic and gallic acid. The color of iron gall ink is produced by the chemical reaction between these ingredients and oxygen. This ink was used in medieval scriptoria before the invention of paper. Although it is not specifically mentioned as an artists' material, its ready availability made it a natural choice for artists. It was cheap to manufacture in large quantities and could easily be made at home. In America, iron gall ink was used for documents, maps, and drawings until the nineteenth century, when carbon inks became more available, or later, when new dyes were introduced.

The problem most commonly encountered with iron gall inks seems to be fading. The writing on countless numbers of diplomas, deeds, and letters has lightened to the point of illegibility. For chemical reasons, iron gall inks will fade eventually, some more than others, but the reaction can be slowed considerably by protecting the ink from light. For that reason, strict measures should be taken when exhibiting documents bearing this type of ink. The Declaration of Independence, written in iron gall ink, is not only protected from light, but is also kept in an inert atmosphere of helium, which further retards fading.

The chemistry of iron gall ink gives it another bothersome characteristic—production of sulfuric acid. Figure 2.10 illustrates the interaction of iron gall ink with the paper of a drawing. In the areas where the ink concentrated, the paper has completely disintegrated. When this type of ink is used for writing, whole letters can sometimes fall away. The backs of drawings and documents made with iron gall ink should be inspected to locate any cracked or weakened areas. These areas can be reinforced with tiny strips of lightweight Japanese tissue for added strength. Occasionally, if the entire sheet of paper has been affected, a lining with Japanese tissue may be advisable. Consultation with a conservator will determine the extent of the treatment necessary for drawings damaged by iron gall ink. Many factors influence the extent of damage caused by this phenomenon—the exact formula used for the ink, the

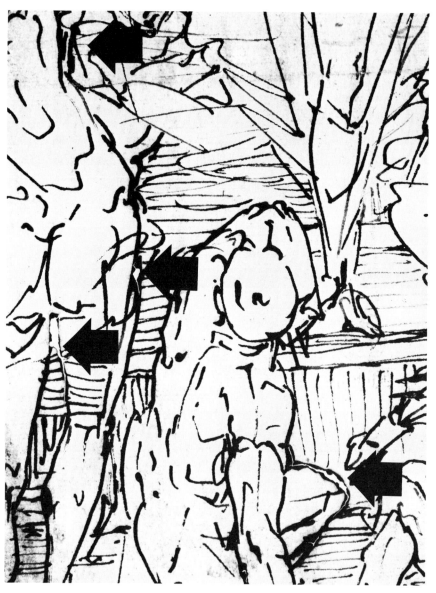

Fig. 2.10. Areas where iron gall ink was concentrated (crouching figure's knee, standing figure's hip and inner thigh) have completely fallen away from this drawing.—School of Cambiaso, Resurrection *(detail); the Metropolitan Museum of Art: gift of Mrs. John H. Wright (49.116.14)*

ink's concentration, the type of paper the ink is used on, and variations in environmental conditions over the lifetime of the drawing. Research is under way to determine whether there is any means of arresting the corrosive action. No "neutralizer" exists now, but the mechanism of the reaction is better understood. There is no method of restoring faded inks.

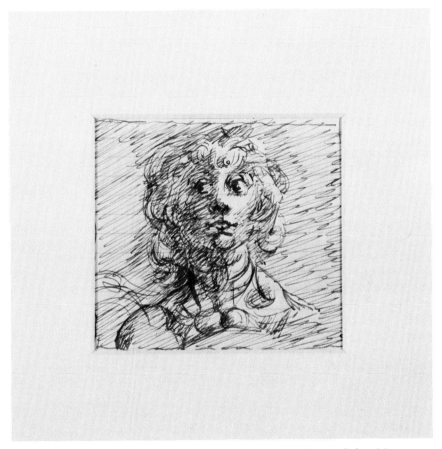

Fig. 2.11. This drawing, done with red fountain-pen ink on ruled writing paper, is particularly light-sensitive.—Peter Agostini, Untitled, 1947; *the Metropolitan Museum of Art: purchase, Friends of the Department, gifts, and matching funds from the National Endowment for the Arts (1978.186.3)*

Bistre and sepia, the brown inks, are so frequently confused that it is difficult to identify them positively without comparative material. Often, the two terms are simply used to describe brown colors. Bistre derives its rich brown color from the resins contained in the tarry chimney soot from which it is made. Bistre has been used by artists since the fourteenth century and is still sold as a watercolor.

The original sepia was made from the ink sac of cuttlefish and is relatively rare. Like bistre, sepia is also still sold as a watercolor, although its origins are no longer marine. Sepia and bistre do not share the acidic nature of iron gall ink. Of the two, sepia seems to be more sensitive to light. Since these inks cannot be readily identified and are similar in appearance to light-sensitive iron gall inks, they should likewise be protected from light.

Many new varieties of inks are available to today's artists, some based on the centuries-old recipes discussed here. We have mentioned the problems of inks made with aniline dyes. Their modern-day counterparts, marketed mostly for commercial purposes, are only slightly more light stable. Prudent measures are called for to protect the 1947 drawing shown in figure 2.11, which uses red fountain-pen ink on blue-ruled writing paper.

Pencil, Charcoal, Chalk, and Pastel

The four drawing media grouped together here have similar conservation problems. Many works of art done with pencil, charcoal, chalk, and pastel have been irreparably damaged by careless handling, improper framing, and inept restoration efforts, chiefly because the nature of these media is not appreciated and because suitable conservation methods are not fully understood. Such drawings constitute a major portion of many collections and include some of the most important works from every artistic era. It is therefore worthwhile to consider their particular conservation problems.

All four media can easily be smudged and abraded, characteristics causing the most consternation among collectors. Graphite pencil, charcoal, and chalk, being inorganic minerals, are not attacked by insects or fungi. The binder used in pastel, however, will sustain mold growth. Also, because many of the colors used in pastels are produced from organic substances, they are quite sensitive to light.[5] For these reasons, and because clear acrylic sheets, commonly used in frames, cannot be placed near powdery pigments, drawings made in these four media present special framing and exhibition problems.

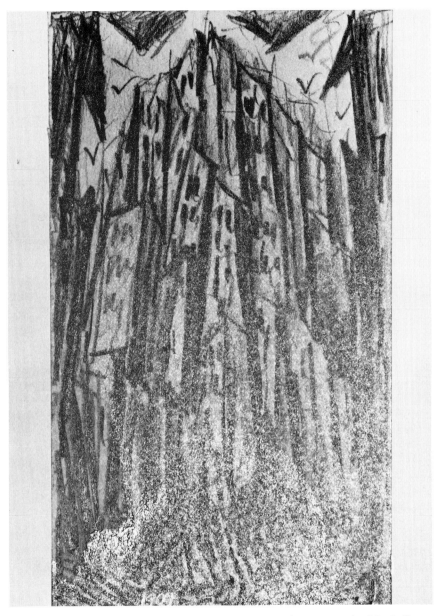

Fig. 2.12. This drawing done in soft graphite pencil was coated with shellac to keep it from smudging. —Abraham Walkowitz, City Abstraction; *private collection; photograph by Sheldan Collins*

Graphite Pencil

Graphite pencils, as we know them, are of fairly recent vintage. They were not officially invented until 1794 by Nicolas Jacques Conté, who blended clays and powdered graphite into a cylindrical mass that could then be fired and encased in wood. Until that time, the metal lead or crude sticks of natural graphite were used in special holders. Graphite is composed of pure carbon and therefore has the same composition as a diamond, but the carbon is not locked into place as it is in a diamond. When we write or draw, the graphite particles slide over each other and are deposited onto the paper by friction, producing a characteristic metallic sheen. Not all drawings done with graphite pencil are subject to the restrictions outlined here. In fact, the majority of designs drawn in graphite pencil are quite stable. Drawings made in softer grades of graphite or with heavy applications of graphite, such as those by Brice Marden, are as vulnerable as charcoal drawings and should be treated accordingly. (See *Matting, Framing, and Display,* below.) Figure 2.12 shows a drawing in soft graphite pencil that has been shellacked in an effort to keep it from smudging.

Charcoal

As might be expected, charcoal sticks made from twigs heated slowly in airless ovens were among the earliest drawing materials. Pliny is the first writer to mention them, and designs using charcoal have been found on the walls of Pompeian houses. On paper, charcoal sticks produce dry black lines that can easily be wiped away with traditional erasers such as chamois cloth, a feather, or bread crumbs. The medium's paleness and the tendency to smudge led artists to search for ways to improve charcoal's working properties. One method called for soaking the sticks in linseed oil. As we know today, charcoal can produce powerful and expressive drawings with a wide range of effects. Degas and Millet were masters of this use of charcoal.

Chalk

Like charcoal, natural chalks are ancient drawing materials first used for the humble task of outlining or transferring wall designs. Throughout Europe and the Middle East, mineral deposits supplied natural carbon (black), iron oxides (reds, umbers, ochres), and calcium carbonate and talc (white). Because they contain varying amounts of clay, natural chalks produce denser, softer lines that are less likely to smudge. The clay acts as a binder, improving the malleability of the chalk while adhering the pigment particles to each other and also to the paper. Lines drawn with natural chalk are more cohesive than dusty charcoal lines, which, under magnification, carry shards of distinct carbon particles. Like charcoal, natural chalks were superseded in the eighteenth century by commercially manufactured sticks of color, known today as *conté* crayons. These man-made materials were preferred by artists as being of more consistent quality.

Pastel

Pastels and their derivatives, formulated from natural—and, later, synthetic—dyes or minerals combined with fillers and binders, seemed not to have the shortcomings of charcoal and natural chalks. The degree of hardness and softness could be controlled in their production; more or less binding medium could result in a denser or fluffier line; and an infinite variety of hues could easily be obtained by combining several pigments. Pastels as we know them had their heyday in the eighteenth and nineteenth centuries, although crudely processed sticks of compressed pigments were used somewhat earlier.

Because of its tendency to smudge, pastel has suffered from the popular misconception that it is not permanent. The fresh, velvety colors of an eighteenth-century portrait or a Degas ballerina should dispel this belief. Although some unusual binders (sugar, whey, beer, and oatmeal) have tended to deteriorate, and certain organic dyes tend to fade, pastels are intrinsically no less permanent than oils or watercolors. Once again, the care that they receive after creation determines their longevity.

The binders historically used in manufacturing pastels have, however, proved attractive to mold. Gum tragacanth, the traditional binder, provides nutrients for mold spores that will grow within the pastel layer when relative humidity is higher than 68 to 70 percent. Proper levels of temperature and humidity will prevent mold from growing. In addition, pastels are made today with fungicides and contain more resistant binders (methyl cellulose or similar cellulose ethers). If growth is detected, the drawing should immediately be unframed and aired in a drier environment. Thymol fumigation, *to be carried out only under the conditions described in Appendix 3,* will destroy active mold spores. Removal of the fungus should be left to a conservator, as it may have disturbed the design layer by penetrating through to the paper support.

It is especially important in the case of powdery media to eliminate excessive movement of the paper support. Pastels should therefore be hinged to sturdy 100-percent rag or conservation mat board—a four-ply, six-ply, or even heavier panel, which can be made or purchased.

Like oil paintings, pastels have often been backed with canvas and stretched around strainers, a typical eighteenth-century framing method. They have also frequently been "tipped"—pasted down around all four edges—onto cardboard. In either case, a conservator should examine the mount to determine whether it is exerting too much tension on the piece and whether unmounting is feasible or even desirable. If the mount is original, it may be such an important component of the work of art as a whole that its removal is not warranted unless keeping it would be of high risk to the art. The danger of buckling as well as that of mold growth makes control of temperature and humidity particularly important for pastels.

Fixatives

Many people spray pencil, charcoal, chalk, and pastel drawings with fixatives, believing that they will both prevent and cure smudging, and the practice is not new. European academies in the eighteenth century taught artists to apply fixatives repeatedly, using mouth blowers, to charcoal designs as they were drawn. Degas, Cassatt, and other nineteenth-century artists specializing in pastels each had favorite formulas. Today, artists use fixatives with similar frequency and, because of the large size of some contemporary works, are virtually forced to do so in the course of packing, transporting, and exhibiting their work. The decision to apply a fixative in such cases is made by the artist and must therefore be respected. The artist should, furthermore, be presumed to be well aware of the fixative's aesthetic effects.

Throughout history, artists have warned that fixatives cause colors to become unevenly saturated and dull. Calcium carbonate whites become transparent and disappear, while titanium whites retain their opaqueness. The delicate matte surface of soft pastels is made shiny, and the fine blending of colors is muddied. The color and the texture of the paper also change as the fixative is absorbed. In short, fixatives alter the character of media and can destroy the essence of the art itself. Even manufacturers of pastels have cautioned against spraying fixatives on their products.[6] The uneven application of fixative to the charcoal drawing shown in figure 2.13 caused droplets of pigment to form around the head. Another Walkowitz drawing coated with shellac appears in figure 2.12.

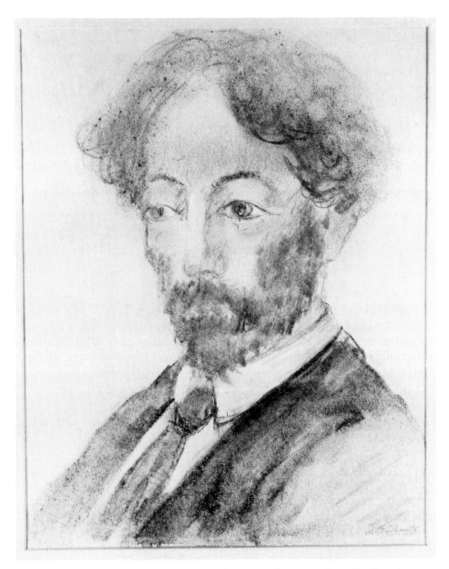

Fig. 2.13. Small pools of pigment formed around the head when this drawing was sprayed with fixative. —Abraham Walkowitz, The Poet, 1906; the Metropolitan Museum of Art: the Alfred Stieglitz Collection (49.70.160)

The long-term conservation consequences of fixatives are no more reassuring. Simply stated, chemical instability, color changes, low pH, tackiness, and other unsatisfactory aging properties make most commercially available fixatives unsafe, from a conservation point of view. While some acrylic-based fixatives theoretically should have better aging properties than so-called "workable" fixatives, which usually contain cellulose nitrate, it should be pointed out that no brand has been specifically tested. Our predictions are based upon conjecture, and, in light of what has been observed in the past, are not reassuring. Halos of yellow fixative may surround chalked lines. A cloud of yellow fog may blur an entire image. Even worse, an entire sheet of paper may turn an unnatural slick beige from fixatives. How can anyone responsibly apply a fixative, given that its ingredients are unknown, its future life uncertain, and its aesthetic effects irreversible? Ironically, even today several spray fixatives are not only called archival by their manufacturers, but are said to prolong the life of the paper itself by protecting it from aging and air pollution. Such a claim might be construed as meaning that we should spray every drawing, regardless of its medium.[7]

Advertising hyperbole notwithstanding, fixatives do not prevent papers from aging, and they should not be considered the answer to smudging problems. We should search instead for safer solutions. Does the problem result from improper storage or handling? Do vibrations from passing traffic or air forced through ventilation ducts contribute to it? Could reframing or rematting in a different way prevent smudging? Is the damage continuing, or does pigment loss indicate a past accident? Such questions often suggest simpler solutions to old problems while preventing new ones from occurring.

Matting, Framing, and Display

After proper hinging and matting, charcoal, chalk, and pastel drawings should be framed behind glass, with a small space left between the art and the glass to dissipate trapped moisture. This breathing space should routinely be provided for all framed works of art, but it is especially vital for drawings done with powdery media, which tend to stick to the glass, particularly when it is moist. Figure 2.14 shows pastel that transferred to the glass with which it was in direct contact. Ideally, drawings made with powdery pigments—particularly pastels—should be stored horizontally in frames. If framed storage is not feasible, drawings with a fragile surface should at least be matted with extra deep "sink" mats with sturdy covers, to prevent them from rubbing against

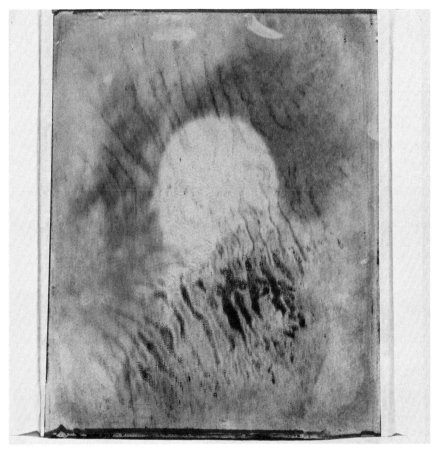

Fig. 2.14. The pastel of this portrait has been transferred to the glass with which it was in direct contact. Mold growth also occurred because of excessive humidity. — Photograph by Sheldan Collins

other surfaces. When stored in mats, such drawings should have slip sheets made only of neutral glassine, the least abrasive type of paper for this purpose. Unframed pastels should have nothing on their surfaces and can be so stored, alone, in solander boxes. Common sense should dictate whether the medium can withstand any slip sheet at all. Slip sheets of polyester film (Mylar) must *never* be used on or placed near drawings done in charcoal, chalk, pencil, or pastels, because of its static charge, which attracts loose pigment particles.

Acrylic sheeting (Plexiglas) should never be used as a glazing material for drawings done in a powdery medium. The action of wiping the sheet clean creates a static charge that pulls the particles from the paper, so that the drawing may eventually transfer to the plastic. The sensitivity of pastel to electrostatic charges was recently converted into an advantage by the Los Angeles Museum of Art, working in cooperation with the Hughes Aircraft Corporation to develop a new framing technique for powdery media. The new method employs an electrostatic stabilizing plate to create an attraction between the pastel particles and the paper support. The drawing is placed against the charged plate, which is connected to a power source. The plate, with the pastel electrically adhered to it, is then framed in a traditional manner. Batteries provide provisional energy in the event that electricity fails. It was found, however, that the pastel particles remained charged and attracted to their support even when the power was discontinued for five weeks. The technique remains too complicated for use by most owners at the present time, but it offers hope for the future and may prove to have many applications.[8]

The need for glass in framing pastels means that extra care must be taken when the art travels or is exhibited. The glass can be taped when traveling (see figure 3.15) or covered with clear contact paper to provide protection in the event of breakage. The contact paper is clear or translucent, so that the drawing can be readily identified without unframing it. Contact paper also leaves less sticky residue than adhesive tape, eliminating the need to scrape the glass with razor blades or to apply solvents, which agitate the fragile drawing and invite damage from slips or spills. Great care must obviously be taken in crate construction and packing for shipments of artworks framed behind glass. Ideally, pastels and unfixed charcoal and chalk drawings should not travel. When they must, advance planning and special precautions are necessary, every step of the way. *Remember that glass can conduct static electricity also.* Therefore it should always be wiped slowly and with a damp cloth.

Watercolors

The term *watercolor* is used here to mean *thin, transparent washes of finely powdered pigment applied with water.* The binder is a water-soluble gum, such as gum arabic, with an additive such as glycerine to retain moisture. The white paper support reflects light upward and may, used by itself, supply pure white highlights. The pebbled texture of many watercolor papers accentuates their reflectivity. The transparency of watercolors differentiates them from other water-based paints such as gouache, tempera, and children's poster paints.

Although watercolors were used as early as the fifteenth century, they were for a long time reserved for landscapes, genre scenes, and other "light" subjects. In the eighteenth century, watercolor painting matured as artists perfected the use of veils of color, a technique more suited to its natural properties. Powerful and dramatic effects were possible, and soon watercolors involving more heroic subjects competed with oil paintings for gallery space in England and France.

Shortly after the medium had established itself on the art scene, rumors began to circulate about its fading tendencies. The ensuing outcry from artists resulted in one of the first scientific investigations of artistic materials.[9] The reports of these nineteenth-century experiments are of historical significance to conservators. Possibly of more significance were truth-in-advertising policies to which they gave rise. Today, most major manufacturers of paints and pigments acknowledge their responsibility to inform artists of the stability of their products. Many maintain information services that will answer inquiries and will provide color sensitivity charts and other technical data.

The fact that certain pigments used by watercolorists are sensitive to light has thus been recognized for some time. Conservators, chemists, and manufacturers are currently investigating the chemical causes of fading in watercolors. It is thought that because all of the pigment particles in transparent washes are exposed, a pigment used in a watercolor is more sensitive to light than the same pigment used in an oil or gouache painting. It should be noted, however, that some gouache and oil paints will fade.

Fading affects the organic rather then the inorganic colors in an artist's palette, due to their molecular structure.[10] Some examples of organic watercolors are gamboge, sap green, van dyke brown, madder, and alizarin. The rate at which these colors fade is affected by humidity, temperature, and air quality, as well as light. Three lighting variables that influence fading can also be controlled: light intensity, light wave length, and the exposure time of the art to that light.

All light (300 to 700 nanometers) is dangerous to watercolors, so measures should be taken to control the amount of light striking them. Certain kinds of light, however, are more hazardous than others.

All daylight—not just direct sunlight—contains a high percentage of ultraviolet light (below 400 nanometers). It is this range in the spectrum of light that is especially destructive to all organic materials, including the paper on which the watercolor is painted. Fading of colors may be the first visual evidence of such deterioration. Unfortunately, the process is so gradual that it usually passes unnoticed. A shift in the color balance of a composition may occur as some colors fade while others remain intact. The two watercolors by Samuel Palmer shown in color plates 1 and 2, on the jacket for this book depict the same location on the coast of Devon. They were done on the same kind of paper, using the same watercolor paints and painting technique. The painting shown in plate 2, however, apparently faded before it entered a museum collection. The overall tonality has been drastically altered, as we see by comparing plate 2 with plate 1. The color balance has been further modified by the darkening of the paper, also caused by overexposure to light.

Unfortunately, light damage is both irreversible and cumulative. Putting watercolors away for several months will not restore faded colors, nor is there a magic elixir that can rejuvenate pigments. All light is injurious; some organic colors will fade even if protected from ultraviolet light. Incandescent light from ordinary light bulbs contains a high percentage of infrared light, which produces potentially dangerous heat. One protective measure is to retard deterioration by keeping watercolors in total darkness, in a vacuum, or in an inert atmosphere of helium, argon, or nitrogen. More practically speaking, we can also change the way watercolors are displayed and the length of time for which they are displayed. Watercolors should be displayed for times as short as possible in ultraviolet-free illumination of as low an intensity as possible.

Gouache and Tempera

Although gouache and tempera do not have the same composition, the same working properties, or even the same final effect, they do share some conservation problems. They both tend to flake, either because of desiccation of the binder or because the paper moves, below an inflexible layer of paint. Gouache or "body color" is most commonly defined as simply opaque watercolor—opaque because large amounts of white pigment are used in mixing the paint. Like watercolor, gouache is composed of finely ground pigment, water, and a binder, traditionally gum arabic, but often, today, a man-made substance with greater consistency. It is quite possible, therefore, for watercolor and gouache both to occur in the same painting. Gouache rests on the surface of the paper, forming an opaque layer with a matte finish; watercolors, which penetrate the paper, remain transparent.

Like watercolor, gouache did not come into its own as a painting medium until the nineteenth century. In the twentieth century, abstract expressionists enjoyed its painterly qualities.

Egg tempera was used to illuminate medieval manuscripts and may have had much earlier applications. Tempera is generally thought to differ from gouache in that the pigment used for tempera is suspended in an emulsion rather than just being mixed with water. This emulsion, whether egg yolk, gelatin, gum arabic and oil, or a synthetic substance, often makes dry tempera impervious to water, with darker, richer colors than gouache and a tough, satiny finish. The binders or emulsions used in gouaches and temperas can include various sticky substances, including the sap of plants and vegetable and animal glues, some causing more conservation problems than others. It is said that Benjamin West used bear fat. The northwest American Indians developed a form of egg tempera by chewing dried salmon eggs wrapped in cedar bark, which they mixed with pigments.[11] American artists such as Andrew Wyeth, Arthur Dove, and Paul Cadmus have used medieval recipes for egg tempera. Today the traditional distinctions between gouache and tem-

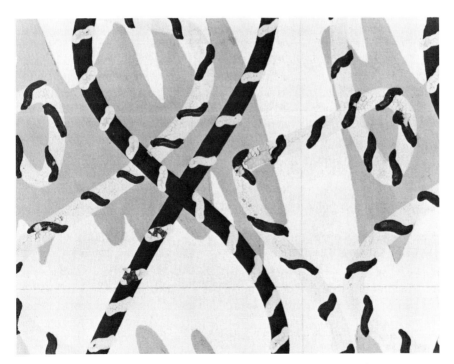

Fig. 2.15. Severe flaking is easily observed on this detail of a gouache painting.—
Stuart Davis, Fabric Design *(detail); the Metropolitan Museum of Art: gift of*
Mrs. Stuart Davis (1981.1002.26); photograph by Sheldan Collins

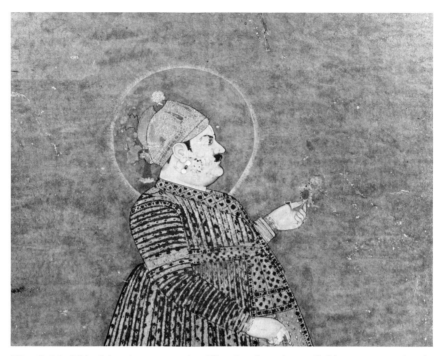

Fig. 2.16. This Islamic manuscript illumination shows flaking tempera in the man's face and the background.—*Rajastan area,* Portrait of a Ruler *(detail); the Madina Collection; photograph by Sheldan Collins*

pera have become blurred, and many commercial formulations are no longer technically one or the other.

Flaking occurs in works of art regardless of age or origin, but it almost always involves a too-thick paint layer containing a desiccated or weak binder on a too-thin, smooth-surfaced paper (or parchment) that flexes or buckles easily. Figure 2.15, a detail of a textile design by Stuart Davis, shows flaking in a gouache. The first warning sign is often a network of small fissures that develops over time. As the paint film ages, its attachment to the paint or the paper support weakens. The thicker and more inflexible the paint layer, the more likely flaking will occur. The danger of flaking also increases in proportion to the flexibility and smoothness of the support. It sometimes appears on medieval manuscripts (see chapter 1 and Figure 1.2). Figure 2.16 shows a nineteenth-century Islamic manuscript with tempera flaking in the background and also in the man's profile, so that the underdrawing is now observable,

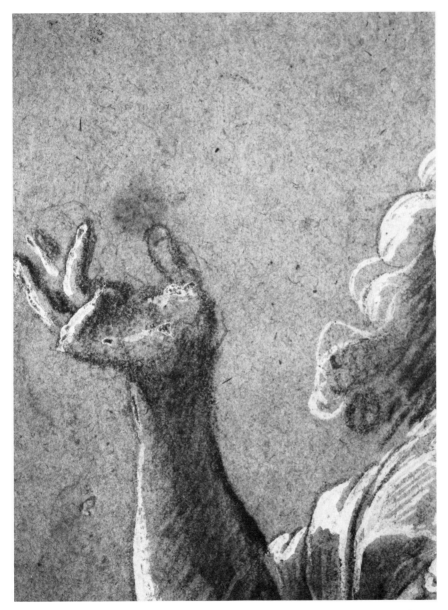

Fig. 2.17. The lead white used to heighten this chalk drawing has darkened from exposure to air pollution. —*Giovanni Mauro della Rovare,* Flying Angel with Upraised Arms *(detail); the Metropolitan Museum of Art: Harry G. Sperling Fund, 1980 (1980.20.2)*

near the eye. Flaking of tempera in manuscripts is exacerbated when the paper flexes—for example, when pages are turned, or as a result of abrasion, perhaps caused by closing the albums.

Handling and storage procedures for gouache and tempera should take into account their tendency to flake, as should the decision to make artworks in these media available for loan. Flaking problems often worsen if the art is jarred or shaken or subjected to fluctuations in relative humidity, both of which are conditions that normally occur in transit. If any evidence of active flaking is present, the object should not travel, nor should it come into proximity with the static acrylic sheeting, rigid (Plexiglas) or flexible (Mylar), that is often used in frames and mats.

A conservator should examine works of art in which flaking is observed or even suspected. It may prove possible to reattach the loose paint to its support through "consolidation." The natural or synthetic substances used for consolidation sometimes darken colors, create a gloss, or otherwise alter the look of the piece, however, so that this procedure may be out of the question. As usual, it is best to prevent the problem altogether through proper care.

One curious phenomenon that sometimes affects older gouaches and tempera is the blackening of a certain white pigment, or colors containing this pigment, when the drawings are exposed to air pollution. White lead carbonate is an ancient pigment and has been used in medieval manuscript illuminations, oil paintings, pastels, and in "heightened" drawings. Hydrogen sulfide, a common ingredient of smog, changes the white lead carbonate into black lead sulfide. Gradually, the white areas of the drawing darken to black, causing an odd shift in tonalities. Figure 2.17, a detail of a chalk drawing heightened with white lead carbonate, shows characteristic darkening from air pollution. The color change can sometimes be reversed by chemically converting the lead sulfide into another lead compound that is white, a process to be undertaken only by a conservator. White lead carbonate has now largely been replaced by zinc white—or, as it is also called, Chinese white.

Metalpoints and Drawings on Prepared Papers

The special conservation problems associated with drawings on prepared papers affect not only rare fifteenth- and sixteenth-century masterpieces in metalpoint, but many twentieth-century drawings, as well—that is, all papers made smooth with a thin coating of an opaque *ground*. In Europe and America, such prepared papers were and still are used for a variety of artistic purposes. Regardless of their age or relative scarcity,

drawings on prepared papers require special handling, to avoid fingerprints, oil and water stains, and scratched and flaking grounds.

Metalpoint—sometimes incorrectly called *silverpoint*, since the exact
metal used cannot be identified without sophisticated testing—is historically one of the earliest of drawing methods, predating graphite pencils
or man-made chalks. Styluses made of various metals were used as early
as the fourteenth century for ruling manuscript pages and other
mechanical purposes before they became artists' tools. Sheets of parchment and, later, paper were prepared by coating them with a liquid
ground, usually white lead pigment, powdered bone, or shell (calcium
white), sometimes mixed with a small amount of colored pigment. A
binder, most often gum arabic or animal glue, was also necessary. Once
the ground dried, it was burnished with a smooth stone or bone. The
purpose of the ground was to provide a surface with enough "tooth" for
the metal stylus.

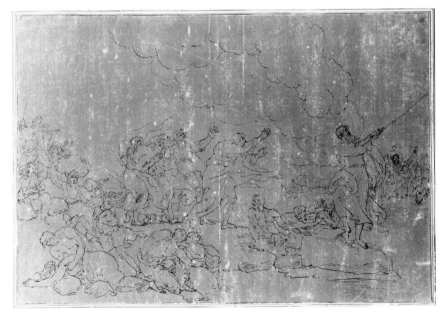

*Fig. 2.18. The ground of this drawing has been damaged by abrasion.—Ben-
jamin West,* Moses Striking the Rock; *the Erving Wolf Collection; photograph
by Sheldan Collins*

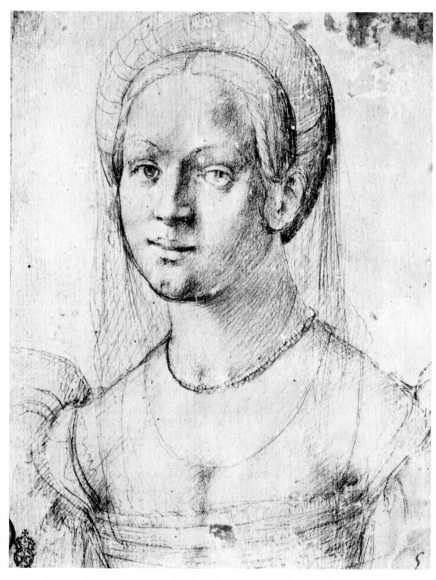

Fig. 2.19. High humidity most likely led to the loss of ground in the upper right corner of this metalpoint drawing.—Attributed to Jacopo Carucci, called Pontormo, Portrait of a Young Lady; *the Metropolitan Museum of Art: the Robert Lehman Collection (1975.1.141); photograph by M. Troiano, from George Szabo,* XV-XVI Century Italian Drawings from the Robert Lehman Collection *(New York: the Metropolitan Museum of Art, 1979), fig. 19.*

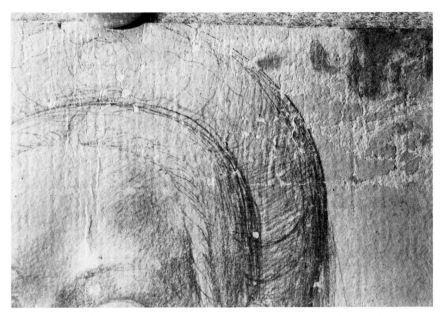

Fig. 2.20. As this detail shows, the paper support of the metalpoint drawing in figure 2.19 is visible in areas where the ground has been lost. —Photograph by M. Troiano

Styluses were manufactured from lead, tin, silver, brass, copper, gold, and their alloys. When the stylus touches prepared papers, tiny bits of the metal are deposited onto the ground by friction. The lines of all metalpoint drawings initially appear light gray, regardless of the metal used in the stylus. Only after oxidation do each metal's characteristic colors appear. Even then, it is difficult to identify the metal used.

The materials and the method of making grounded papers have seen few modifications over time. Commercially prepared papers, available sporadically in response to the medium's cyclical popularity, are generally manufactured according to traditional formulae. Grounded papers do not resist rubbing and scratching as much as untreated papers. Abrasion causes a gradual dulling of the design and eventual loss of the ground. Benjamin West's ink drawing on a grounded paper (figure 2.18) illustrates the effects of years of sliding back and forth against other papers. The artist most likely coated his paper with a ground to create a smooth surface for the drawing. The texture of the original paper is apparent from abrasion. Areas where the ground has abraded appear whitish. Due to their sensitive surfaces, drawings on grounded papers should always be protected from abrasion.

While isolated accidents and long-term abrasion can both cause loss of ground, the problem may also be inherent in the medium. The binder may dry out, and the attachment of the ground to the paper may thus weaken. This problem can be aggravated by wide fluctuations in relative humidity as the paper support expands and contracts. The ground cannot always accommodate such dimensional changes and may eventually separate from the paper. Loss of ground is often seen along creases and fold lines, indicating rough handling. Such damage is disfiguring and may easily worsen. Flaked areas can rapidly expand as the surrounding edges of ground are nicked or scraped.

Drawings on grounded paper should be handled with special care, particularly when they travel. Temperature and humidity should be kept as consistent as possible. If any flaking is visible, the art should not travel. Grounded paper that is flaking should also never be placed near either rigid (Plexiglas) or flexible (Mylar) acrylic sheeting, which is often used in frames and mats.

Paper is naturally absorbent; prepared papers are even more so and are consequently often permanently disfigured by fingerprints and other greasy stains. Because the ground is very easily disturbed by liquids or abrasion, fingerprints cannot be easily removed. While true for prints and drawings in general, direct handling of grounded papers should be kept to a minimum. Water is a particular hazard, because the ground is water-soluble. Softening and dulling of the ground occur as the water and any impurities it contains are wicked up. "Tide lines" form as the water evaporates and dissolved impurities carried to its boundaries are left behind. The action of water or extremely high levels of humidity probably caused the flaking on the metalpoint attributed to Pontormo (shown in figures 2.19 and 2.20), by disrupting the ground's adhesion to the paper.

Ball-Point Pens, Felt-Tipped Markers, and Other Modern Media

Life might be easier for curators and conservators if artists confined their work to the traditional media and techniques with which we are familiar. It seems to me, however, that if artists hadn't turned to new and different media in their search for means of expression, we would be deprived of some of the more important artworks created throughout the history of art. For centuries the invention and development of new materials, usually intended for industrial use, allowed artists to interpret what they saw or felt differently from the way they had, before. Since it seems likely that artists will continue to draw with ball-point pens, felt-tipped markers, waxy crayons, and other materials designed for transitory commercial purposes, we should consider also their conservation problems. Research into the conservation of newly developed artistic materials—or, rather, nonartistic materials used for artistic purposes—has only recently begun. Nonetheless, a few observations and predictions can be put forward with some certainty at this point.[12]

Although Mr. Loud's "rolling pointed pen" was patented in America as early as 1888, ball-point pens were not commercially available until the mid-1940s (the "Biro" pen) in America and shortly thereafter in Europe.[13] The design of the tip—a high-precision steel ball bearing positioned at the end of a metal tube containing ink—has remained virtually unchanged since that time. The composition of the ink has changed over the years, however, in response to various problems.

The earliest inks used in ball-point pens were basically viscous printing inks that tended to remain sticky on the paper. They bled through paper because of their oil and/or solvent content and sometimes

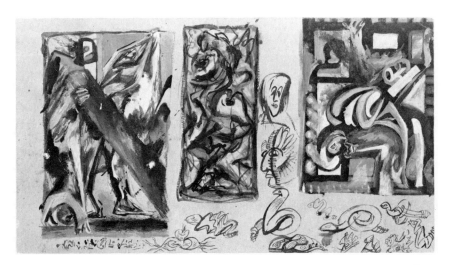

Fig. 2.21. Both the Day Glo paints and the shirt cardboard that Jackson Pollock used in this work challenge those responsible for its preservation.—Jackson Pollock, Three Compositional Studies; *the Metropolitan Museum of Art: gift of Lee Krasner Pollock (1982.147.33)*

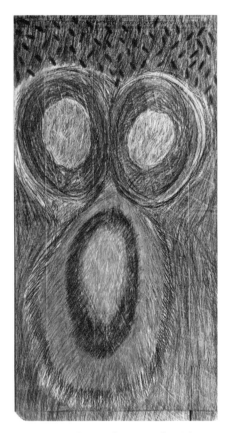

Fig. 2.22. This work was made with wax crayons and a brown paper bag, whose aging characteristics are unknown.— Raphael Ferrar, Untitled; *the Metropolitan Museum of Art: purchase, George L. Aguirre gift (1979.298)*

gummed up the delicate workings of the tip. The proportions of coloring matter, solvents, and other additives were varied in order to improve the quality of the lines produced. As a consequence of this constant experimentation, the inks produced at any given time vary unpredictably in composition. The color of the ink is almost certainly produced by a dye rather than by an inorganic mineral pigment, however, since mineral pigments might clog the ball-bearing tip and would not dissolve in the solvents added to hasten drying. The organic dyes make drawings done in ball-point pen extremely light-sensitive. Black inks, often used for signatures, frequently turn blue. Reds often fade to pink. For that reason, any work of art containing ball-point pen ink must be protected from excessive light.

Felt-tipped markers, whether water-based or solvent-based, also have fugitive colors. Developed after ball-point pens, they too were meant for purely commercial purposes and were not intended to be permanent. They are now available in beautiful, clear colors that span the entire spectrum. Tests have indicated that certain colors, such as yellow, are generally more stable, while others, such as purple, pink, violet, and beige, are more sensitive to light.[14] Even filtering out ultraviolet radiation does not vastly improve the stability of these colors.[15] Consequently, drawings made with felt-tipped pens must be protected from *all* light.

Generally speaking, products designed for commercial purposes have not been subjected to vigorous aging tests, as have some materials that have purely artistic uses and are marketed by established manufacturers. In addition to felt-tipped markers and ball-point pens, our list of impermanent and unpredictable modern media should include wax crayons, colored inks, and many colored pencils (see figures 2.21 and 2.22).

Oil Paints and Acrylics

Instability may also be a problem when artists combine media or papers that respond adversely to each other. As figure 2.8 shows, for example, oil and paper do not always mix. Figure 2.23 shows another case of incompatibility. Brown halos of oxidized oil surround the seated woman painted by Degas. (Degas did perfect a method of painting in oil on paper, *peinture à l'essence;* other artists have been successful, as well.) Acrylic paints, on the other hand, generally combine with paper rather well, because they are alkaline rather than acidic, are more flexible than oil-based paints, and can withstand paper's natural movement. Their long-term aging characteristics are also satisfactory (because they were originally formulated as house paints, acrylics were subjected to a battery of exposure and aging tests). Most conservation problems associated with acrylics on paper arise from too thick an impasto, too weak or thin a paper support, or the mixing together of different brands of commercial acrylic.

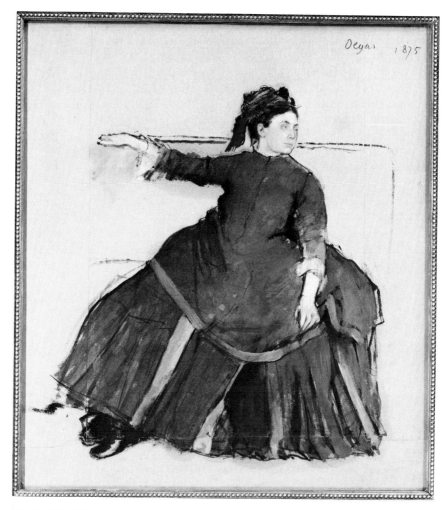

Fig. 2.23. Oil paints and paper are often incompatible.—Edgar Degas, Seated Woman; *the Metropolitan Museum of Art: bequest of Mrs. H. O. Havemeyer, 1929, the H. O. Havemeyer Collection (29.100.185)*

Artists have also used impermanent papers. Franz Kline painted on the Yellow Pages, Jackson Pollock on shirt cardboards (figure 2.21), and Raphael Ferrar on a brown paper bag (figure 2.22). To Paul Klee, the paper support was metaphorical. In *Handbill for Comedians* (figure 2.24).

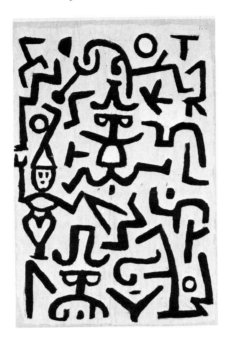

Fig. 2.24. In this work, Paul Klee painted directly on a newspaper advertisement.—Paul Klee, Handbill for Comedians; *the Metropolitan Museum of Art: the Berggruen Klee Collection (1984)*

Klee painted directly on a newspaper advertisement. The printing ink is visible in areas where the gouache has been lost. A 100 percent rag paper, which conservators would no doubt have recommended, would completely have negated the essence of Klee's work; the art might not have some of its present conservation problems, but would it still be an advertisement for actors?

Artists should be aware of the possible consequences when they use unstable materials or create an unstable combination, but we cannot question their selection, assuming, as we must, that the medium and support chosen satisfy an aesthetic intention. Still, as Marcel Duchamp observed in 1933, "posterity will never see a great deal of the work we rave about because of the too frequent use of bad pigments."[16]

Of course, it is impossible to foresee what new media or combinations thereof will come our way in the future, just as it is impossible to list all the unorthodox ones used heretofore. Whenever dealing with contemporary prints and drawings, one must be prepared for some conservation riddles. Because some artists do not consider permanence to be requisite, it is up to us to extend the lifetimes of these works through proper care.

NOTES

1. William M. Ivins, Jr., *Prints and Visual Communication* (1953; reprint, New York: Da Capo Press, 1969), p. 2.

2. Therle Hughes, *Prints for the Collector* (New York: Praeger, 1971), p. 49.

3. I am grateful to Keiko Keyes for bringing these color changes to my attention.

4. I am grateful to Marjorie N. Shelley, conservator of prints and drawings at the Metropolitan Museum of Art, for bringing these contradictions to my attention.

5. Françoise Flieder, "Study of the Conservation of Pastels," *Science and Technology in the Service of Conservation,* ed. N. S. Brommelle and Gary Thomson (London: International Institute for Conservation, 1982), p. 71.

6. Victoria S. Blyth, "Electrostatic Stabilizing Plate (E.S.P.): An Alternative Method for Flaking Tendencies of Works of Art in Pastel," in *The American Institute for Conservation of Historic and Artistic Works Preprints, Sixth Annual Meeting* (Fort Worth: American Institute for Conservation, 1978), p. 29, n. 5.

7. Marjorie B. Cohn, *Wash and Gouache: A Study of the Development of the Materials of Watercolor* (Cambridge, Mass.: Fogg Art Museum, 1977), p. 61, n.2. This 1980s advertising ploy is not as novel as it may seem. As early as the 1890s, the manufacturer of Vibert's Fixatif recommended the product for protecting watercolors from air pollution.

8. Blyth, "Electrostatic Stabilizing Plate (E.S.P.)," p. 29.

9. Marjorie B. Cohn's *Wash and Gouache* is especially recommended for its account of the development of watercolors.

10. For a detailed description of the fading of organic colors, see Thomas B. Brill, *Light: Its Interaction with Art and Antiquities* (New York: Plenum Press, 1980).

11. Anne Wall Thomas, *Colors from the Earth* (New York: Van Nostrand Reinhold, 1980), pp. 48, 20.

12. Highly recommended reading is an article on modern media by Antoinette Owen, "Modern Materials in Drawings: Part 1: Media," *Drawing* 7, no. 3 (September/October 1985): 56–59.

13. Three models (334304 A-C) of Mr. Loud's pen are in the Division of Engineering and Industry, National Museum of American History, the Smithsonian Institution. Hungarian-born William Ladislav Biro introduced his perfected invention from Argentina, where he lived until his death in 1985.

14. Raymond H. Lafontaine, "The Lightfastness of Felt-Tipped Pens," *Journal of the International Institute for Conservation—Canadian Group* 4:1 (Autumn 1978): 11.

15. Lafontaine, "Lightfastness," p. 12.

16. "Fifty and Seventy-five Years Ago in *Art News*," *Art News* 82: 9 (November 1983): 29.

FURTHER READING

Ames, Winslow. *The Mastery of Drawing*. Trans. Josef Meder. New York: Abaris, 1978.

Antreasian, Garo, and Clinton Adams. *The Tamarind Book of Lithography: Art and Techniques*. New York: Harry N. Abrams, 1970.

Brown, Hilton, "The History of Watercolor." *American Artist* 47:487 (February 1983): 46ff.

_____. "Looking at Paintings." *American Artist* 45: 467 (June 1981), p. 40ff; 46: 485 (December 1982), p. 68ff.

Brunner, Felix. *A Handbook of Graphic Reproduction Processes*. 2d ed. New York: Hastings House, Visual Communications Books, 1964.

Cennini, Cennino. *The Craftsman's Handbook*. Trans. Daniel V. Thompson, Jr. New York: Dover, 1954.

Chaet, Bernard. *The Art of Drawing*. New York: Holt, Rinehart and Winston, 1978.

Cohn, Marjorie B. *Wash and Gouache: A Study of the Development of the Materials of Watercolor*. Cambridge, Mass.: Fogg Art Museum, 1977.

Eichenberg, Fritz. *The Art of the Print: Masterpieces, History, Techniques*. New York: Harry N. Abrams, 1976.

Goldman, Paul. *Looking at Drawings: A Guide to Technical Terms*. London: British Museum, 1979.

Goldman, Paul. *Looking at Prints: A Guide to Technical Terms*. London: British Museum, 1981.

Griffiths, Antony. *Prints and Printmaking: An Introduction to the History and Techniques*. London: British Museum, 1980.

Hind, Arthur M. *A History of Engraving and Etching*. 3d ed. rev., 1923. Reprint. New York: Dover, 1963.

Hutter, Heribert. *Drawing: History and Technique*. New York: McGraw-Hill, 1968.

Ivins, William M., Jr. *How Prints Look*. 1943. Reprint. Boston: Beacon Press, 1958.

_____. *Prints and Visual Communication*. 1953. Reprint. New York: Da Capo Press, 1969.

Jirat-Wasiutynski, Voltech, and Thea Jirat-Wasiutynski. "The Uses of Charcoal in Drawing." *Arts Magazine* 55 (October 1980): 128–135.

Jussim, Estelle. *Visual Communication and the Graphic Arts: Photographic Technologies in the Nineteenth Century*. New York: R. R. Bowker, 1983.

Koschatzky, Walter. *Watercolor History and Technique*. Trans. Mary Whittal. New York: McGraw-Hill, 1970.

Lambert, Susan. *Printmaking*. London: Her Majesty's Stationery Office, 1983.

Ludman, Joan, and Lauris Mason. *Fine Print References: A Selected Bibliography of Print-Related Literature*. Millwood, N.Y.: Kraus International Publications, 1982.

Mayer, Ralph. *The Artist's Handbook of Materials and Techniques*. 3d ed. New York: Viking, 1970.

Mayor, A. Hyatt. *Prints and People: A Social History of Printed Pictures*. New York: Metropolitan Museum of Art, 1971.

Mendelowitz, Daniel M. *Drawing*. New York: Holt, Rinehart and Winston, 1967.

Mueller, Earl G. *The Art of the Print*. Dubuque, Ia.: William C. Brown, 1969.

Newman, Richard. "The Microtopography of Pencil Lead in Drawings: A Preliminary Report." In *Papers Presented at the Art Conservation Training Program's Conference, April 28 and 29, 1980*. pp. 31–46. Newark: University of Delaware, 1980.

Pas, Monique de, and Françoise Flieder. "History and Prospects for Analysis of Black Manuscript Inks." In *Conservation and Restoration of Pictorial Art*, ed. Norman Brommelle and Perry Smith, pp. 193–201. London: Butterworth, 1976.

Reynolds, Graham. *A Concise History of Watercolors.* New York: Oxford University Press, 1971.

Sotriffer, Kristian. *Printmaking: History and Technique.* New York: McGraw-Hill, 1968.

Thompson, Daniel V., Jr. *The Practice of Tempera Painting.* New York: Dover, 1962.

Tolnay, Charles de. *History and Technique of Old Master Drawings.* New York: Bittner, 1943.

Watrous, James. *The Craft of Old Master Drawings.* Madison, Wis.: University of Wisconsin Press, 1957.

Weber, Bruce. *The Fine Line: Drawing with Silver in America.* West Palm Beach, Fla.: Norton Gallery and School of Art, 1985.

Wehlte, Kurt. *The Materials and Techniques of Painting.* Trans. Ursus Dix. New York: Van Nostrand Reinhold, 1975.

3

Matting, Hinging, and Framing

ODAY, MATS ARE used almost universally, both to present and to protect prints and drawings. Standard format for them is two pieces of stiff paper board, joined, usually with a length of cloth tape, along either the upper horizontal edges or the left vertical edges. For safety in handling matted works of art, the mats for a collection should open consistently—usually along their longer edges, whether horizontal or vertical. The bottom sheet of the two-board sandwich is left whole, for overall support of the art, while the top sheet has a window opening cut into it so that the art inside is displayed.

Mats play an aesthetic role in the presentation of an artwork by setting it off in a field of neutral color or by surrounding it (in the case of French mats) with decorative bands of pastels, grays, or gold foil. Mats also serve a variety of beneficial protective functions; in addition to providing physical support and an acid-free enclosure, they can prevent the artwork from pressing against the glazing material—glass or Plexiglas—used in a frame. The breathing space between art and glazing lessens the danger of condensation and mold growth by allowing trapped humidity to dissipate more rapidly than it would otherwise. The extra space also reduces the chance that, under some circumstances, some works of art could stick to the glazing: certain substances in some kinds of watercolors may cause the medium to become sticky in elevated humidity, and the breathing space provided by the mat gives the art some protection, in that event.

The British Museum claims to have invented the design for our present-day mat in the mid-nineteenth century, when the curator at the time, Mr. W. M. Scott, noticed that prints kept in portfolios were subjected to rubbing. Called "sunk mounts," mats have become the traditional storage and presentation format for prints and drawings.[1] And for good reason: mats go a long way in protecting paper from the external sources of deterioration listed in Table 1.1 and can reduce the damage from the internal sources of deterioration, as well. As I have stressed throughout this book, conservation matting and hinging are among the most effective ways of protecting artworks on paper.

Mats are cut from stiff paper boards whose composition varies significantly. The ideal materials—rag board, buffered rag board, and conservation board—contain almost pure alpha cellulose. All three are suitable for matting prints and drawings, although they have slight differences. All three have a neutral or alkaline pH (a pH of 7 or more). As the name implies, rag board is made from cotton fibers and usually has a neutral pH. If it has been improperly sized, however, 100 percent rag board can be or can become acidic. Buffered rag board is alkaline because calcium carbonate, usually 2 to 3 percent, has been added. Rag boards have traditionally been available only in cream or white, although several beiges, grays, and pastel shades have recently been introduced. Some colored mat board has been found to fade rapidly. Information pertaining to color permanence should be available from the manufacturer. Any evidence of mat board fading at the very least demands another look into exhibition lighting conditions.

Conservation board, also called archival or acid-free mounting board, is made from wood pulp that has been chemically refined to contain only alpha cellulose (see "pH" below.) This board is also buffered with calcium carbonate. Buffered board lasts longer because its alkaline reserve maintains a higher pH as it neutralizes acid from the environment; boards that contain no alkaline reserve quickly become acidic under poor storage conditions. Conservation board is now available in a wide range of colors.

As mentioned in the introduction, *photographs have different requirements for matting, framing, storage, and exhibition.* In particular, it has been found that mat board with a high pH content is not suitable for certain kinds of photographs. The reader whose work involves photographs is encouraged to consult the specialized literature listed at the end of the introduction. In dealing with suppliers, it is important to specify the kind of collection being cared for, since special types of storage materials have been produced for photographic collections.

Wood pulp mat board—a stiff, bonded sheet of bleached wood pulp compressed between two sheets of paper—should be avoided at all costs. The outer paper is usually decorative in texture and color and may be of good quality. The inner paper is generally smooth and thin. Though it is attractive for matting inexpensive reproductions, board made from unrefined wood pulp should never be used to mat works of sentimental, artistic, or financial value.

Identifying Mat Board

Boards suitable for matting works of art on paper are not always available at framing establishments nor are they automatically used by framers. Always be sure to specify that conservation-quality mat board is to be used. There are several ways of determining whether high-quality board or cheap wood pulp board has been used to mat a print or drawing.

Damage to the artwork. Acidic mat board can cause a gradual weakening and embrittlement of the paper, accompanied by an overall darkening of the artwork where it has come into contact with the mat (figures 1.10 and 1.11). Thin, dark lines of discoloration, or mat burn, quite often appear, following the contours of the window opening. Acid migration from the beveled edge of the window can cause mat burn even when the mat has been lined with acid-free paper. A word of caution is in order, however: fading of papers by light may produce a similar effect by making the protected area surrounding an exposed paper seem darker than it should be.

The presence of plies. Examining the beveled edge of the window— under magnification, if necessary—or by checking the outside edge of the board, you should be able to count two, four, or six plies, if rag board or conservation board was used; both are laminates. In contrast, the edge of wood pulp board will show two thin papers enclosing a compressed mass of what looks like sawdust. The thicker the board, the more "sawdust" is there.

The color of the board's exposed edge. With time, the inner core of a wood pulp board usually discolors, so that an exposed edge shows tan or brown. The interior of rag board and conservation board does not change color. Inner and outer paper layers remain the same color.

General discoloration. Papers containing unrefined wood pulp can sometimes discolor rapidly in strong light, whereas rag and conservation boards are more resistant to such deterioration.

Tear direction and strength. Wood pulp board even a few months old will break easily in a straight line, becoming more brittle as it ages. Rag board and conservation board tear unevenly and peel along the planes of their component layers.

pH. For someone actively involved with matting, the determination of pH (the measurement of relative acidity or alkalinity) of mat board is important. pH is measured on a scale of 14; measurements below 7 are considered acidic, and measurements above 7, alkaline. It should be kept in mind, however, that a pH above 7 does not necessarily indicate that a mat board is of conservation quality, since newly manufactured wood pulp board can be alkaline. pH measurements should be used to monitor incoming or stored supplies of rag board and conservation board. Since the term *acid-free* is loosely applied to all sorts of conservation and framing materials and cannot be defined with precision, it is wise to find out exactly what materials were used to make any board or paper you may consider using. Contents should always be clearly indicated on the wrapper or carton supplied by the manufacturer.

The simplest way to measure pH is with an inexpensive archivists' pen or pencil (Insta-Check-Surface pH Pencil, pHydron Jumbo Pencil), which uses a dye to measure acidity. The paper to be tested is marked with the pencil and is then moistened with distilled water. After fifteen seconds, the sample is compared with a color chart. pH indicator strips carry similar sensitive substances which react when pressed against a damp spot. To use these strips, place the sample paper on a clean piece of glass. Moisten a small area with a few drops of distilled water. Place the colored portion of the strip on the wetted area, cover with a small piece of glass, and add a weight. After five minutes remove the pH strip and compare it with the accompanying color chart. For the sake of accuracy the water must actually penetrate the sample rather than simply sitting on the surface. If the water remains in a bead for several minutes, lightly scratch the surface of the paper to facilitate absorption before you proceed. Measurements of greater accuracy are possible with pH meters.[2]

Chemical tests. Various reagent stains (Tri-Test) are available in kits to test for the presence of groundwood and other damaging substances that signal an inferior board.

Price. Rag board costs most per sheet, followed by conservation board and ordinary wood pulp board. Buffered rag board is the best choice in terms of longevity, strength, looks, and ease of cutting. The more economical conservation board affords nearly identical protection. Four-ply mat board is the usual choice for mats; however, for a large collection, two-ply board is less expensive, and more matted items can be fitted into each storage box. Care should be taken to support larger artworks properly when they are in two-ply mats, as this lighter board can sag and wobble. Besides looking nicer, four-ply mats provide deeper breathing spaces for framed prints and drawings. A particularly heavy or fragile piece would obviously require greater support, perhaps even a six-ply mat.

Preparing a Mat

The first step in making a mat is to measure the artwork. Prints and drawings often have small images and relatively large margins. Failure to take the artwork's overall measurements beforehand has sometimes led people to trim or fold art on paper for insertion into a mat that is too small.[3] Measure the entire sheet of paper before cutting a mat, and record the measurements on a small card. Figure 3.1 shows a sample card that can help eliminate matting mistakes.

After measuring the artwork, determine the outside measurement of the mat. The dimensions of the mat will be influenced by the size of the storage box, the size of a standard frame, the size of any existing frame, and aesthetic considerations. If a "custom mat" (one made to order, not of standard size) is to be made, a three-inch margin around all four sides of the image to be viewed is a good amount to try first. The overall effect will be aesthetically more pleasing if it is made a little wider. Too much margin is better than too little. If standard sizes must be made and if you cannot decide which standard size to use, opt for the larger one; the results are more likely to be visually satisfying, and wider margins offer artworks better protection.

Many institutions save time and expense by using mats that fit standard frame sizes or commercially available storage boxes or both. Standard frame sizes are:

5 x 7 inches
8 x 10 inches
9 x 12 inches
11 x 14 inches
12 x 16 inches
14 x 18 inches
16 x 20 inches
18 x 24 inches
22 x 28 inches

The dimensions of storage boxes vary, but many brands do correspond to standard frame sizes.

Museums housing larger collections with hundreds of storage boxes keep a stock of frames that correspond to the storage box sizes. Their dimensions might be 14¼ x 19¼ inches, 16 x 22 inches, 19 x 24 inches,

Artist and Accession No.	Dove, 78.16.1		Mat and Art Measurements	
			Vertical	Horizontal
Outside dimensions of art work:			8 in.	7 1/4 in.
Outside dimensions of mat (A):		(A)	14 in.	11 in.
Dimensions of window opening (B):		(B)	5 3/4 in.	4 1/2 in.
Width of margins (C) equals A - B, divided by 2:		(C)	4 1/8 in.	3 1/4 in.

Adjustments needed:

Raise lower margin by 1/4 in.: 4 1/8 + 1/4 = 4 3/8 in.
Reduce upper margin by 1/4 in.: 4 1/8 - 1/4 = 3 7/8 in.

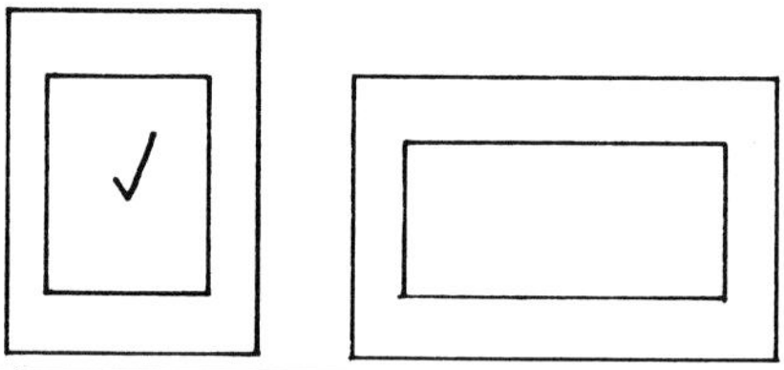

√

Color___Cream_____

2-ply_____

4-ply____√_____

Other_____

Fig. 3.1. An Arthur Dove watercolor is to be measured for a vertical *mat measuring 14 inches vertically by 11 inches horizontally. Dimensions of the mat are predetermined by the standard-sized frame and/or storage box into which it must fit. The paper on which the watercolor is painted measures 8 inches vertically by 7¼ inches horizontally. The design of the painting is vertical. The sheet on which it is painted will be overmatted, so that the image appears in a window measuring 5¾ inches vertically by 4½ inches horizontally. This will create a margin of 3¼ inches on each side, with 4⅛-inch margins at top and bottom. For more pleasing visual effect, the lower margin is raised ¼ inch, which* reduces *the upper margin to 3⅞ inches and* increases *the lower margin to 4⅜ inches. Color and ply of the mat to be used should also be indicated on the card, to avert mistakes.*

22 x 28 inches, 25 x 32 inches, or 30 x 40 inches. Available storage space, the storage environment, and the frequency with which artworks will be exhibited are factors that influence the approach taken to matting a collection. It is also necessary to consider the size of the mat board. Most types come in 32-x-40-inch or 40-x-60-inch sheets. Once standard sizes have been decided upon, the sheets can be cut with the least amount of waste. Many companies will do this work for a "cutting charge," and the service is generally worthwhile, as it saves labor and waste. You can use the leftover strips for other purposes. When you have decided on the outside dimensions of the mat, record them on the card—see figure 3.1.

The next step in mat preparation is to determine the size of the window opening. Dimensions of the window opening (or window) are determined by the dimensions of the image to be displayed. Will the print be "overmatted," with a window smaller than the outside dimensions of the artwork? (This is sometimes called an *overlay mat.*) Or will it be "floated," with the window touching none of the art's borders? Generally speaking, if a drawing or print is to be overmatted, at least ⅛ inch to ¼ inch should be held in place by the mat. Otherwise, the art might escape through the window, as did the lower left edge of the drawing by Modigliani shown in figure 3.2. In such situations tearing or creasing is a danger, especially if the window mat is quickly opened.

Drawings and prints with slight buckling are usually overmatted to prevent them from curling forward and touching the glass or acrylic. When overmatting etchings, engravings, and other intaglio prints, never cover the plate marks; these are important parts of the design. Modern graphics and drawings with designs that extend to the edges of the paper, as well as irregularly sized drawings and Old Master prints that have been cropped are usually floated.

To determine the dimensions of the window opening, first place the object in front of you on a clean blotter or other suitable working surface. Then measure the height and width of the design area that will appear in the window. If the artwork is to be floated, simply add ½ inch to the height and width of the entire piece, which you have already measured. Avoid resting the ruler directly on the art. Record all measurements on the card, perhaps with a small diagram to help you visualize. Never write measurements or indicate placement marks directly on the artwork.

To calculate the width of all four margins, subtract the window's horizontal measurement from the mat's overall horizontal measurement and divide by two. Do the same with the vertical measurements. If the lower margin is to be wider (routinely done for a better visual effect), add

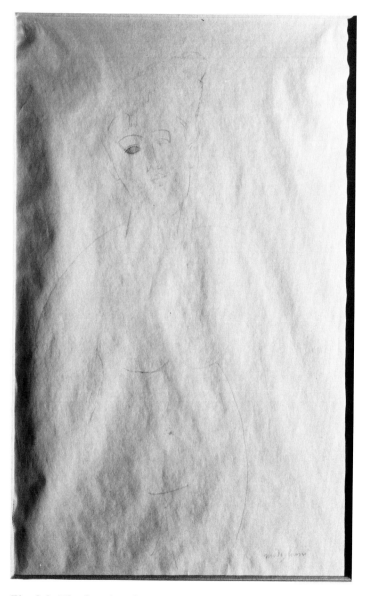

Fig. 3.2. The drawing shown here was not sufficiently overmatted, and the lower left edge has escaped. —Amedeo Modigliani, Torso of Nude Woman; *the Metropolitan Museum of Art: gift of Bella and Sol Fishko (1982.503); photograph by Sheldan Collins*

between ¼ to 1 inch to it and subtract the same amount from the upper margin. It is helpful to record other information, such as color choices and ply, on the card with the measurements in order to guard against inadvertent mistakes.

Unless the mat board has been precut in standard sizes that you intend to use, you will need first to cut two pieces of it to the outside dimensions indicated on the card. To cut the window, lay one piece of the cut board right side down on a clean working surface. Most people prefer to measure on several layers of paper or a thick blotter, to avoid slippage. The actual cutting is always done with the board lying right side down on scrap pieces of board to protect the board and the table surface. To determine which side is the right side, hold the board in raking light that exaggerates the surface texture. One side will usually appear rougher then the other and that side is generally preferred as the "right" side, for its richer effect. The choice, however, is yours. The difference between the two is slight, but will be noticeable if works displayed together are not consistently matted with the same side facing out. Using a pencil with a hard lead and a sharp point, mark out the margins on the back of the board. With increasing proficiency, you will no longer need to mark the lines—only the points that indicate the corners of the window opening.

Mat cutters can be tools as simple as a utility knife, costing less than ten dollars, a hand-held cutter for twelve to twenty-five dollars, or an elaborate table model with tracks and a sliding blade holder, costing several hundred dollars. Many models fall between these two extremes. However the window is cut, the edge should have a bevel of approximately 45 degrees. As you cut, the knife should follow the marked lines, with the blade angling away from the center of the mat board. Because you are holding the knife at an angle, you will need to extend the cut about ⅛ inch beyond each corner of the window opening. Exert even pressure on the knife and make each cut in one continuous movement. If you are using a utility knife or a hand-held cutter, you will need a heavy metal straight-edge to guide your blade. Squares of sandpaper attached to the back of the straight-edge will help prevent slippage. When all four cuts have been made, flip the mat over.

If the center cutout, sometimes called "fallout," does not immediately drop away, carefully extend each incomplete cut with a sharp utility knife, scapel, or razor blade. The tool must be held in the same position as the cutter so that the angle of the bevel remains the same all along the cut. Flip the mat face down again and use a soft white eraser to rub out any pencil marks remaining on the back. (Colored erasers sometimes leave stains.) Using an agate burnisher or bone folder, gently smooth down any sharp edges along the window opening. Extremely fine-grade sandpaper or emery paper can also help smooth rough areas.

Place the window mat face down and align it with the backboard, face up. Secure each piece with weights or sandbags so that they cannot shift during taping. Attach the two along longer butted edges using either wet linen ("Holland") tape or a cloth pressure-sensitive tape designed to sustain folding (Filmoplast SH).

The tape should be at least 1 inch wide. If wet linen tape is used, it must be covered with blotters, glass, and weights while drying. The pressure-sensitive tapes need only to be burnished. Linen tape is strongest and lasts longest, but many people avoid it because of the extra time and effort required for its use.

Our discussion thus far assumes that you have just cut a mat with a single window, such as that shown in figure 3.3. I will also describe the double-window mat, which may be used for storage as well as for display. Instructions for cutting sink mats, double-sided mats, and other sorts of

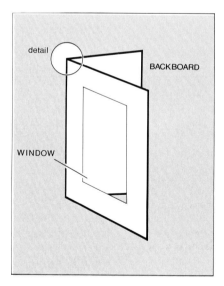

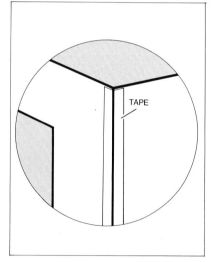

Fig. 3.3. Single-window mat. — Drawing by Lindsey Fisher

Fig. 3.4. Detail of tape needed on single-window mat. — Drawing by Lindsey Fisher

mats appear in Merrily A. Smith's *Matting and Hinging Works of Art on Paper,* listed in "Further Reading" at the end of this chapter.

Double-window mats (figure 3.5) are preferable for items that will be examined and exhibited frequently. During storage or study, the outer window stays in place, but it swings to the back, revealing a second, exhibition window mat, when the artwork is to be framed for display. The double-window mat has many advantages. Unless the artwork uses powdery pigments, clear polyester (Mylar) film can be placed over the outer window so that the image may be examined without opening the mat. When flaking paint is a problem, neutral glassine may be inserted between the two windows to prevent static pull on the surface of the drawing. The double thickness of mat board in front of the art ensures that nothing presses against the image in crowded storage boxes. In addition, the outer window mat keeps the inner mat clean, lengthening its life. Figure 3.6, a detail of figure 3.5, shows the arrangement of tape on a double-window mat.

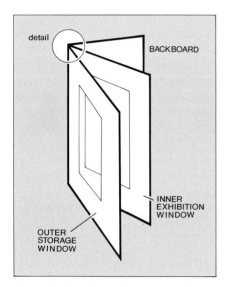

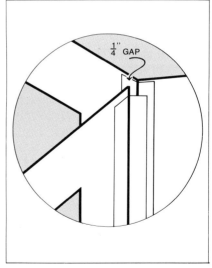

Fig. 3.5. Double-window mat.—Drawing by Lindsey Fisher

Fig. 3.6. Detail of figure 3.5, showing arrangement of tape on a double-window mat.—Drawing by Lindsey Fisher

Hinges and Corners

Matted prints and drawings are normally attached to the backboard of a mat by two folded hinges (also called "V" hinges) or by pendant hinges (also called hanging, bar, or "T" hinges), shown in figure 3.7. Such hinges permit the viewer to examine the back of the artwork and also allow the paper to expand and contract safely with fluctuations in temperature and humidity. Works of art on paper should never be restrained around all four edges; that would prevent their natural expansion and contraction in response to environmental fluctuations (see figure 1.32).

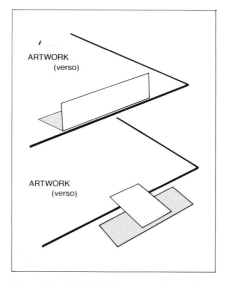

Fig. 3.7. Folded hinge and pendant hinge.—Drawing by Lindsey Fisher

Hinges should be made from Japanese tissue, which offers the advantages of light weight, strength, purity, and flexibility. Various kinds of tissues can be purchased from suppliers of conservation materials or artists' equipment. One should always buy from a reputable dealer, who can guarantee the exact fiber content of imported tissues; due to economic constraints, many Japanese tissues may contain a large proportion of wood pulp, making them archivally unsuitable. A word about the names of these tissues may be helpful. Most often, the name given to a tissue is the name of the area where it was produced. Over the years, that name becomes synonymous with that region's most commonly available paper. Therefore, while *mino-gami* is usually thought of as being a medium-to-light-weight tissue, it is available in heavier grades. The names listed in this book are only meant to be guides for your selection; the ultimate factor in choosing a tissue is the weight and thickness of the object being hinged. Heavy-weight tissues include *okiwara;* among medium-weight tissues, *sekishu* is frequently chosen. For very thin papers, *tengujo* or *chumino* might be appropriate. Hinges should never be so heavy that they emboss the item, nor should they create an opaque area behind it. On the other hand, they should be strong enough to support the weight of the piece. The idea is that if the artwork is subjected to strain or to a sudden jolt, the hinge will tear, rather than the artwork itself. An example of the use of a tissue too strong for mending a work of art on paper is seen in figure 5.1. These considerations explain why linen tape, as well, is usually too strong to be used for hinging art on paper. It is useful to keep an assortment of tissues on hand, an idea that has been packaged by some conservation material suppliers. In no case should art be glued or taped into a mat; results of that treatment are evident in the drawing by William Glackens shown in figures 3.8 and 3.9.

Two hinges at the top of the artwork will be sufficient to hold most art on paper, but larger art—wider than 24 inches—may require three hinges across the top, or even hinges placed around all four sides, to support their greater weight. Artworks should not be hinged along only one vertical side unless there is a special reason—a page from an Islamic manuscript might be so hinged, for example, to preserve its identity as part of a codex.

If a print or drawing on thin paper is not overmatted, and if Plexiglas is used instead of glass in the frame, the art can be easily pulled into contact with the acrylic by static electricity. Antistatic solutions can minimize this, to some extent; sometimes, however, one has no choice but to add a small folded hinge to each lower corner of the artwork, to prevent it from being pulled forward. If hinges are applied to the artwork in any location other than the upper corners, indicate their placement by penciling small arrows on the backboard of the mat. Otherwise, one can easily tear the piece by attempting to lift an attached corner.

Preparing a Folded Hinge

A "V" hinge, as shown in figure 3.7, is simply a strip of Japanese tissue folded lengthwise in not-quite-equal portions. The narrower portion is

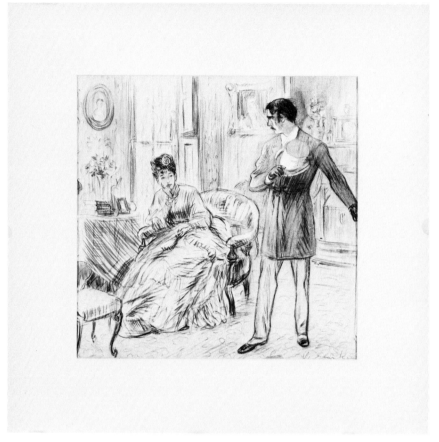

Fig. 3.8. The drawing above has been incorrectly matted.—William Glackens,
The Visit; *the Metropolitan Museum of Art: gift of Mr. and Mrs. Stuart P. Feld*
(1981.446.6); photograph by Sheldan Collins

applied to the reverse side of the artwork; the remaining wider strip is
folded back and applied to the backboard, forming a pivot. Artwork that
floats in its mat (art that is not overmatted) requires folded hinges.

To make the hinge, spread a suitable tissue on a clean blotter. With
a heavy straight-edge and a bone folder (smooth-edged letter-openers
or butter knives can be used), score long strips of tissue between 1 inch
and 1½ inches wide, following the grain of the paper (the direction in
which it tears most easily). Holding the straight-edge in place, fold once

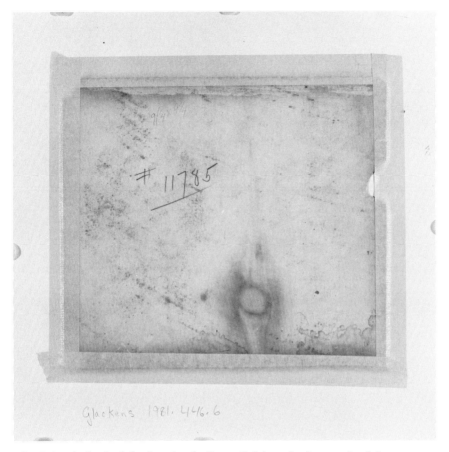

Fig. 3.9. The back of the drawing in figure 3.8 has also been stained from contact with wood.—Photograph by Sheldan Collins

along the score line. Apply a thin line of water to the scored line while it is folded or after it has been opened. Pressing the straight-edge downward with one hand, gently pull the tissue away from it, tearing along the moistened line. Fold the tissue not quite in half lengthwise and tear off the desired number of hinges about 1½ to 2½ inches long, again by scoring. Sometimes water is not needed for tearing, but the moisture helps create a feathered edge, which is softer and bonds more smoothly to paper. Feathered edges are also less noticeable for hinges on smooth or translucent papers. For smaller prints, shorter and narrower hinges are in order, so long as they properly support the weight of the artwork.

The adhesive used in hinging should be a purified rice starch or wheat starch paste. This type of paste is not commercially available, due to its short shelf life. It can easily be made up, as needed, according to the directions given in Appendix 2.

The following procedure for applying folded hinges requires relatively little maneuvering, once the artwork has been positioned, and it reduces the chances of misalignment. Place the item to be hinged face down on a clean blotter, with the top edge of the art closest to you. Insert a small square of waste paper into the folded hinge, and place it on a small piece of glass away from the artwork, holding it in place with forceps. Using a small, flat, stiff brush, apply a thin, even coat of paste to the narrower half of the hinge. Remove and discard the waste paper that has acted as a mask. Then, still holding the folded hinge with forceps, attach the hinge to the artwork so that the folded edge of the hinge exactly follows the top edge of the art. Unfold the hinge. Place a 3 x 6 inch piece of polyester web and a small blotter with the same measurements below the hinge and the artwork and do the same above the hinge. Then cover the ensemble—first, with a 3 x 6 inch piece of glass, and then with a weight (¾ pound to 2 pounds). Repeat this procedure for each hinge.

After five minutes, change both blotters and replace the weights. Allow to dry for thirty minutes (even after the hinge feels dry to the touch). When thin, delicate papers are being bonded, blotters should be changed often, to prevent cockling. Remove the weights, blotters, and polyester, and turn the artwork over. Place it in the mat and position the image in the window opening. Secure the artwork with one or two weights placed on blotter squares. Support extended hinges with another blotter square and apply paste, brushing away from the fold line and away from the artwork. Fold the extended half of the pasted hinge under and attach to the backboard. Cover with a polyester web square, followed by a blotter, glass, and weight. Change the blotter after five minutes and allow the paste to dry for at least thirty minutes. Repeat for the remaining hinge.

Weights used throughout this process can be made by filling small jars with lead buckshot or can be purchased from conservation supply companies or from hardware stores. Some can be improvised; unopened cans of condensed soup are a good weight and work very well, for instance.

Preparing a Pendant Hinge

Pendant hinges are made from rectangles of Japanese tissue measuring approximately 1 inch by 2 inches with feathered edges along the descender of the "T." The size of the hinge can be modified for larger or smaller artworks. They are stronger than folded hinges, because the weight of the object is carried by the entire hinge rather than pulling against the fold. Folded hinges have a tendency to slip.

Place the artwork face down on a clean blotter with the top edge closest to you. Paste out the hinge on a piece of glass by covering one third to one half of the hinge crosswise with a piece of scrap paper that will act as a mask. Apply paste to the exposed portion. Pick up the pasted hinge with forceps and carefully align it along the top edge of the artwork. Place a square of polyester web and a small blotter above and below the hinge and the artwork, followed by a piece of glass and a weight. After five minutes, change both blotters. Wait for at least thirty minutes. Repeat for each hinge. Turn the artwork over, place it in the mat, and position the image in the window opening. Secure the artwork in place with one or two weights on top of blotter squares. Apply paste entirely over another rectangle of Japanese tissue, slightly larger than the first one. Place this piece over the extended hinge, forming a crosspiece. Cover with a polyester web square, followed by a blotter square, glass, and a weight. Change the blotter after five minutes and allow to dry for at least thirty minutes. Repeat for the remaining hinge.

Sometimes the results of hinging a work of art are less than satisfying. Symptoms such as staining through the right side of the artwork, tide lines, curling of the hinge, and puckering of the artwork around the hinge are evidence of too much paste, uneven application of paste, lumpy paste, a too-heavy hinge paper, insufficient drying time, or not enough blotter changes. Hinges easily pulling off or slipping indicate too little paste or paste that is too old. Weak hinges may also be caused by a work of art with a smooth or highly polished surface, or one whose weight is too heavy for the number of hinges provided.

One occasionally encounters a work of art that has been hinged to the window rather than to the backboard of a mat. This is dangerous for the art, because, when the mat is opened, the art is pulled along with it, often resulting in creases or — worse — tears.

Hinging to Bristol

In many collections, prints and drawings are hinged to 100 percent rag bristol (.008 to .012 cal.), a heavy paper, rather than directly to the backboard of a mat. The bristol is attached to the mat with the same kind of tape used to bind the mat together. The separate sheet of paper makes it possible to transfer the artwork from one mat to another without rehinging. In addition, the back of the artwork can easily be examined by manipulating the bristol board, which measures slightly larger than the art, rather than by touching the art itself. Hinging to bristol is highly recommended for study collections. Other papers such as Permalife or two-ply mat board can be used, provided they are smooth-surfaced, flexible, slightly heavier than the artwork to be supported and of archival quality.

Photo Corners

When a print or drawing is sufficiently overmatted, photo corners made from acid-free paper or clear polyester film (Mylar) can be used instead of conventional hinges. These corners are often preferable, because no adhesive is put directly onto the artwork, eliminating possible problems of curling and staining or future hinge removal. Removing an artwork secured with photo corners is an easy operation. One must remember, however, that the photo corners are removed *first* from the mat and then slid from the artwork; the artwork is never curled up and pulled away from the photo corners. Photo corners should not be used on very weak or brittle papers that cannot support their own weight. Furthermore, the size of the photo corner must be appropriate to the size of the artwork. Most commercially available photo corners are too small to support larger items properly.

Photo corners are easy to make from scraps of Mylar, rag bristol, or Permalife paper. To make one average-size photo corner, cut a strip of either material approximately 2 inches long and 1 inch wide (length should measure twice the strip's width). With the strip horizontally in front of you, fold over the upper corners at 45 degrees, so that they meet along the center line of the resulting triangle. See figure 3.10.

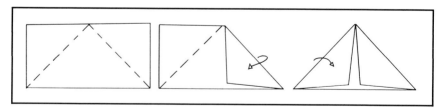

Fig. 3.10. Photo corners.

Framing

Not until the eighteenth century, when the technology for making smooth sheets of glass improved, were prints or drawings framed and hung on walls. Before that time, prints and drawings were normally kept in albums or portfolios, with the exception of devotional or popular allegorical prints, which were usually tacked to the wall. Etched reproductions of popular paintings and drawings by the Venetian artist Piazetta were among the first works of art on paper meant to be glazed, framed, and hung.[4] It has been recorded that the estate of the artist Charles Germain de Saint-Aubin included seventy prints framed behind glass.[5] Writing in 1751, a certain Mrs. Delany, noted for her startlingly realistic paper flower collages and equally accurate social commentary, observed this new trend in interior decoration and noted, "Mr. Vesey has a room filled with prints and they look very well."[6] Folk art—such as decorative frakturs, silhouettes, and scherenschnitte—was intended for display.

Itinerant artists often provided frames, so that satisfied customers could immediately display their purchases (see figure 3.11). Such frames

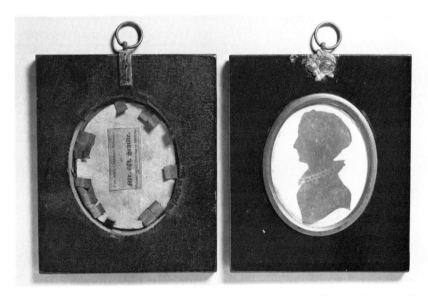

Fig. 3.11. The frames of these silhouettes are original and should be considered part of the artwork itself.—W. Seville, Silhouette of Woman; *private collection; photograph by Sheldan Collins*

are important components of these artworks and should not be thought-lessly disposed of when they are damaged or when they go out of fashion.[7]

Because there was no precedent for framing, prints and drawings were often framed in the manner of paintings—both visually, with heavy gilt molding and deep linen mats, and also structurally. Drawings were lined with canvas, wrapped around stretchers, and left without glass, a procedure also described by the same Mrs. Delany as mentioned above.[8] Figures 3.12 and 3.13 show a drawing by Marie Laurencin that has been treated in this manner. Today, prints and drawings are sometimes still overframed, as if they were simply little paintings, a practice that involves great expense and dangerous mounting techniques.

Conservators consider the primary function of framing to be protective. Their choice of framing materials and techniques is made chiefly with conservation in mind. Both aesthetic and conservation considerations should influence framing decisions, however. When they do, prints and drawings are presented to their best advantage and are still protected from external harm.

When selecting a frame, check to be sure that the molding is sturdy and is securely fastened at each corner. The joints should be tight and properly aligned. If the artwork is large, the frame should be strong enough to carry the weight of the glass or acrylic without bowing, sagging, or spreading at the corners. A slightly deeper molding will usually provide the extra strength necessary for larger graphics. If that does not work, a crosspiece can be attached at the back for reinforcement. The style, color, profile, and overall dimensions of the molding may be decided according to aesthetic preference, but the frame should not overpower the drawing.

Glazing Materials

Glass continues to be the usual choice as a glazing material, because of its availability and lower price. It has disadvantages, however: it breaks easily, is inflexible, is heavy, and provides no protection against ultraviolet rays present in natural and fluorescent light. Some glass has a greenish cast, the result of iron impurities in the sand from which the glass was made.

For these reasons, many people prefer to use rigid acrylic sheets (polymethyl methacrylate), commonly called Plexiglas.[9] Other types of plastics have been recommended (they include polycarbonate), but the acrylics are the most widely available. Acrylic sheeting is lightweight

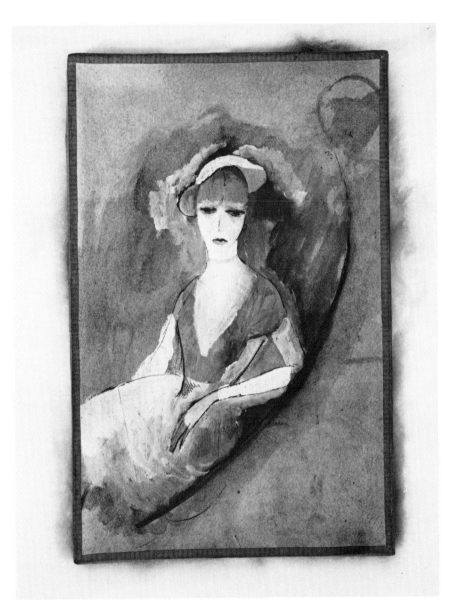

Fig. 3.12. This watercolor and gouache by Marie Laurencin has been lined with canvas and wrapped around a stretcher in the manner of an oil painting.—Marie Laurencin, The Artist's Mother; *the Metropolitan Museum of Art: bequest of Gregoire Tarnapol, 1979, and gift of Alexander Tarnapol, 1980 (1980.21.20)*

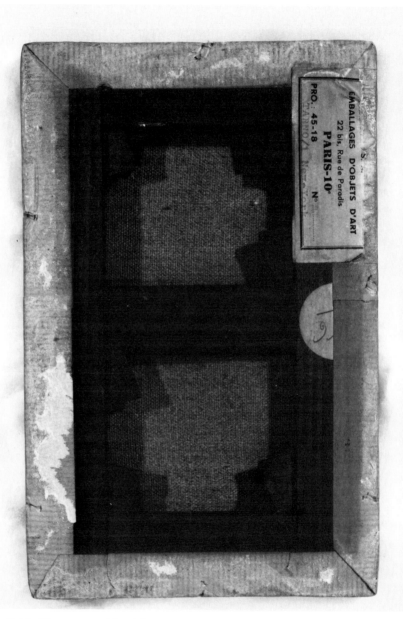

Fig. 3.13. The reverse side of the Marie Laurencin painting in figure 3.12 shows the canvas lining and stretcher.

and has therefore become the natural choice for framing oversized works of art. Because it is somewhat flexible and will not break, acrylic sheeting is also preferred for traveling shows. Rigid acrylic sheets unfortunately scratch more readily than glass and should therefore not be cleaned with rough paper towels and harsh detergents. Acrylic sheets should never be used to frame drawings in pastel, soft graphite, or flaking gouache and tempera. The static charge created by wiping the plastic literally pulls particles of the pigment from the paper. Antistatic solutions can be applied to both sides of the acrylic to reduce its static charge and its natural tendency to attract dust, but their effects are not permanent.

For protecting light-sensitive watercolors or drawings done with felt-tipped markers, or for retarding the darkening of wood pulp papers, special filtering acrylic, available in two types, can be used instead of glass. There are basically two types of ultraviolet filtering acrylic sheets. Their brand names and manufacturers can be found in Appendix 1. The most effective type of acrylic, sold under the name of UF-3 or OP-2, is very slightly tinted and filters out almost 100 percent of harmful ultraviolet light. Also available is a colorless acrylic, known as UF-4, which is slightly less effective. The colorless filter is used when the tinted one interferes with the colors of the print or drawing. Many collectors use ultraviolet-filtering Plexiglas for framing all prints and drawings, regardless of their relative sensitivities to light—a very prudent approach.

Whether ultraviolet filtering acrylic is permanent or not is arguable. Data from one manufacturer, in fact, indicates that the filtering property increases as the acrylic ages. It has traditionally been recommended that filtering acrylics be replaced every ten years. However frequently or infrequently they are replaced, they should certainly be inspected at regular intervals and should be changed as soon as they develop haziness, bubbles, or discoloration. The filtering capacity can be checked with a UV meter. Acrylic sheets, like glass, should of course never rest directly on a work of art.

Nonreflective glass will reduce glare on prints and drawings, but because it is effective only when the glass directly contacts the artwork, it is not recommended.

Another nonreflective product, Denglas, can be used at a distance from the print or drawing, but has a distinctly purplish reflection when viewed from an angle. Denglas is not as effective in filtering out ultraviolet rays as ultraviolet-filtering acrylic sheets. The manufacturers of Denglas also make a laminated nonreflective product, the same type of impact-resistant glass that is used in automobile windshields, with a UV absorber in the middle. Generally, it is too greenish, too heavy, and too expensive for framing purposes.

Glazing material, whether glass or acrylic, should fit properly in the molding. If tension is too great, the glass will snap, while a loose fit will allow dust to penetrate the frame. Taping the glass or acrylic into the rabbet, or lip, upon which the glass rests, creates an effective dust shield.

After the molding and glass or acrylic have been assembled and cleaned, the frame is ready to receive the matted drawing. Old frames being rehabilitated should be thoroughly cleaned. Old tape and adhesive should be removed; corners should be reglued if necessary. "Canned air" (Dust-Off), available in aerosol containers, can help eliminate paint flecks and tiny splinters inside old moldings. Handheld vacuum cleaners also do this job quickly and efficiently. Even better are the tiny, battery-powered vacuum cleaners now available for cleaning computer keyboards and typewriters. Stiff brushes of the type used to paint houses are handy for cleaning debris trapped in old molding.

Mats and Spacers

As previously noted, mats serve the important function of providing a breathing space for the art. This space accommodates the natural movement of the paper with fluctuations in relative humidity. If the print or drawing has been "floated," however, the window mat does not hold down its borders, and care must be taken to keep the artwork's lower edge from curling outward and touching the glass or acrylic. Wherever there is contact between the two, moisture can condense and may result in mold growth.

Contemporary prints and drawings are often framed by simply hinging the artwork onto four- or six-ply rag board and placing it into a frame fitted with a "fillet," or spacer, to prevent the artwork from pressing against the glass or acrylic. A fillet is a strip of wood, rag board, or plastic inserted around the perimeter of the frame and hidden from view by the rabbet of the molding. Framespace, an easy-to-cut clear plastic spacer marketed in strips that are S-shaped in cross-section, snaps around the glass in a frame and rests against the mat. The resulting space protects the art from condensation and can be aesthetically pleasing. Wooden fillets or spacers should never rest directly against the art. If they must—for example, if a work of art must remain in an original antique frame—the fillets or spacers should be faced with strips of rag board firmly attached to the fillet with a purified white glue (polyvinyl acetate, such as Jade 403).

Backing Material

To insert a matted drawing in the frame, hold the frame upright and tip the mat into it, keeping an eye on the artwork. Do not drop the art into the frame face down. After the artwork has been placed in the frame, and you are certain that it remains secure in its mat, turn it face down and fill the remaining space with backing material. If the item is likely to remain framed for a long time, a sheet of buffered paper, (Permalife), placed over the mat's backing, will act as an acidity barrier. Shingles, commonly used in the eighteenth and nineteenth centuries as backing materials, encouraged acid migration, with damage such as that shown in figure 3.14.

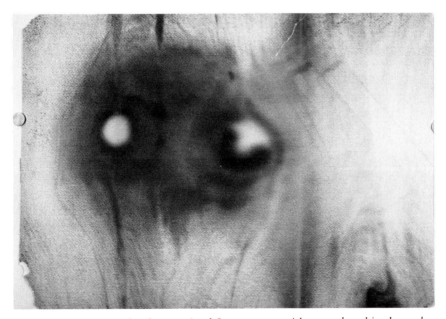

Fig. 3.14. This paper has been stained from contact with a wooden shingle used as backing material in a frame.

A sturdy board such as acid-free corrugated cardboard or a polystyrene-cored board (Fome-Cor) is a better backing material. This board protects the artwork from punctures and damage from the rear. Acid-free corrugated cardboard is preferable, since it is buffered to help it stay neutral longer.

Polystyrene boards cannot generally be considered acid-free, although a new type of Fome-Cor from Monsanto has neutral outer papers. The frame molding should be deep enough to accommodate the glazing material, mat, object, and sufficient protective backing material. This "package" should not protrude beyond the back of the frame.

The backing material is held in place with small nails, called brads, or with diamond-shaped glaziers' points. Brads are inserted with a fitting tool or brad setter, which does not jar the frame as a hammer would. Glaziers' points, shot in with a special gun, are difficult to remove, often requiring much digging. Brass nails, if available, will not rust as will steel brads in moist environments (rusty brads would, however, signal unsafe storage or display conditions). "Turn-buttons," small clamps that rotate around a screw, and similar types of clips secure the contents of a frame without nails and are thus quicker to undo. They also do somewhat less damage to antique frames. Another way of holding in place the contents of the frame calls for a strainer, a rectangle of wooden strips that fits snugly inside the back of the frame and is attached to it by screws. Strainers are helpful for collections that are rotated frequently, because they make framing and unframing faster and easier.

Finally, if the item is to be framed for a long time, a sheet of acid-free wrapping paper is stretched over the back of the frame and adhered to the molding around all four sides with PVA adhesive (Jade 403), or a double-sided tape. This paper acts as a dust shield. On it can be noted the date the artwork was framed, hinging information (if that is out of the ordinary), and any other pertinent information—exhibition dates, exposure times, display restrictions, and so forth. Backing paper is unnecessary if the item is unframed and returned to storage after an exhibition, but the edges of the backing material should nonetheless be sealed with either gummed linen tape or brown paper tape. A cross-section of a typical frame package appears in figure 3.15. Cork circles or rubber "bumpers" attached to the bottom two corners of the back of the frame lift the frame away from the wall and increase air circulation behind it. This ventilation is especially important if items are hung on cool outside walls. Bumpers that come with a small, sharp point, such as tacks have, can be put on the back of the frame as tacks would be; others can be attached with pressure-sensitive adhesive.

Framed prints and drawings may be hung in a variety of ways. Most museums prefer to use flat brass "mirror" plates, which are screwed into the frame, with the whole unit then screwed to the wall. These provide the greatest structural security and at the same time discourage theft. Screw eyes holding a length of braided or twisted galvanized steel wire

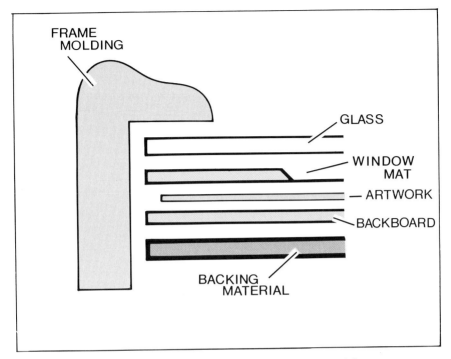

Fig. 3.15. A typical frame package.—Drawing by Lindsey Fisher

are used in most home situations, but are often inadequate for heavy objects. Never put screws back into the old holes of a wooden or plaster frame, as they will easily pull out under the stress of weight. Framed prints and drawings can also be suspended from ceiling molding hooks with nylon or copper wire.

When artwork travels, framing glass should be taped to prevent its shattering and splintering. Figure 3.16 shows the correct way to tape glass. Wide strips of masking tape should be applied side by side to the surface of the glass, with their ends doubled over for pull tabs. To remove the tape, pull it slowly back upon itself (so that the tape forms a U). Pulling it straight up (so that the tape forms an L) exerts a strain that may make old and brittle glass snap. The tape should not extend over the glass onto the frame, because it can damage some types of finishes. The residue left by masking tape can be removed by wiping with glass cleaner, turpentine, naphtha, or benzine. Always dampen the cloth with the solvent before wiping; never pour liquids directly onto the glass. Razor blades can also be used to scrape away adhesive residues.[10] Many mu-

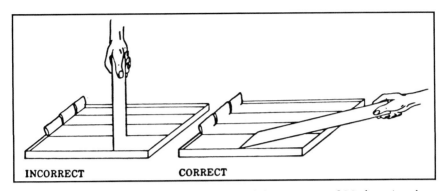

INCORRECT   CORRECT

Fig. 3.16. These drawings by staff members of the Museum of Modern Art show correct and incorrect ways of removing tape placed in strips across the glass of a framed work of art prepared for shipping. Glass on works of art for shipping is taped, as protection against damage to the art: should the glass break in transit, its fragments adhere to the tape, instead of falling and scattering onto the surface of the art. Museum of Modern Art instructions for applying and removing the tape are:

1. Use masking tape or a tape that is similarly pressure-sensitive.

2. Apply the tape in parallel strips that overlap slightly or that are, at most, one-fourth of an inch (0.6 cm.) apart.

3. Do not cover any part of the picture frame *with the tape, as the adhesive from the tape can damage the finish of the molding.*

4. The tape strips can be removed more safely—and easily—if one end of each strip is first grasped firmly and eased back so that it is doubled over itself (see "Correct" drawing, right, above). *Keeping the strip in that alignment,* slowly *pull the tape back along its own length. DO NOT pull the tape at right angles to the surface (see "Incorrect" drawing,* left, above), *as that introduces a strain on the glass that can cause it to break.*

5. TAPE SHOULD NEVER BE APPLIED TO PLEXIGLAS, because it is impossible to remove the marks that tape adhesives leave on Plexiglas.—"Taping Glass on Works of Art," diagram and instructions courtesy of the Department of Registration, the Museum of Modern Art, New York

seums cover glass with clear contact paper instead of using masking tape. Contact paper allows the object to be quickly identified, is easier to remove, and leaves less residue. Acrylic sheeting should never be taped, as the scraping or solvents necessary to remove the residue can damage its surface.

Proponents of so-called airtight framing, which uses sheets of polyester film (Mylar), metal foil, or other impermeable material to seal the backs of frames, argue that the contents are thereby protected from extreme fluctuations in relative humidity. It should be noted, however, that no framing technique commonly used today is really airtight. A frame package such as the one diagrammed in figure 3.15 will be at equilibrium with the environment. A sealed package simply acclimates itself more slowly to surrounding conditions. Since moisture is absorbed by cellulose much faster than it can evaporate, a drawing in a sealed frame may retain moisture for a dangerously long time.

In most instances, standard framing is adequate for protecting prints and drawings. Sealed frames would be appropriate in situations when artworks might encounter short periods of unstable conditions—for example, a traveling exhibition; or when exposure to humidity would be exceedingly dangerous for the supersensitive contents, such as stretched pastels. Sealed frames are no excuse for unsafe exhibition situations.

Depending on the number of items to be framed, the talents of your staff, and the size of your budget, you may decide to have some artworks framed by a commercial establishment. You should not assume that a framer will automatically follow the procedures recommended. The ever-rising costs of quality materials and the labor involved in proper hinging mean that you must demand and be prepared to pay for framing that meets conservation standards. When you have ordered special materials, you will also want to verify that they have been used. Do-it-yourself framing establishments will sometimes provide suitable materials at extra cost.

By the time a conservation problem becomes evident in a framed artwork, the damage may have become extreme. Make a periodic inventory of framed prints and drawings, with close inspection of mat bevels, hinging locations—if visible—and backboards, to help detect problems early. Be on the lookout for hazy glass, areas of contact between the art and the glass, wobbly window mats or backboards, brown mat bevels, rust on hanging wires, screw eyes, or brads, and musty odors.

Unframing

From time to time, art must be unframed. The most important principle to keep in mind is to *take nothing for granted*. Many prints and drawings seem to have been framed in ways that seem designed to try the wits and patience of those who must unframe them. First, cover a table with a soft material, such as felt, bubble wrap, foam rubber, carpet remnants, or several blotters, to protect the finish of the frame from being chipped, scratched, or crumbled. When moving a framed object, hold it firmly by its edges, with both hands, rather than trusting the strength of the hanging wire, screw eyes, or molding, which may have weakened with age.

Place the framed item on the table and examine it carefully from the front, to see whether any conditions might make unframing risky. Has the item slipped out of the mat along one edge? Does a buckling pattern indicate where the hinges are? Is the artwork so flat that it might be dry mounted to a board that has become brittle? Do you see flaking paint? Is the artwork in contact with the glass and, if so, has the art adhered to it? Is the glazing material glass or acrylic?

After learning as much as possible about how the picture has been inserted into the frame, turn the frame face down on the padded table. First, remove any screw eyes and hanging wire. Resist the temptation to slide the artwork out from beneath the wire. Cut the hanging wire completely away so that loose ends cannot cause scratches. With a soft brush, gently clean the back of the frame, taking care not to tear any peeling labels.

Next, cut away the backing paper, being sure to save any writing or labels that you find on it. As you do so, look for water stains, dirt, insects—any clues regarding the probable condition of the frame's contents. List them on a separate sheet of paper, so that they can be considered when the artwork is later examined. Do not discard anything until you know with certainty that it has no archival value. If the back of the frame has not been covered with paper, cut away any tape over the nails or glaziers' points and carefully pull them out with pliers. You may need to dig with a sharp knife before you can grip the head of each nail with the pliers. Glaziers' points must often be bent upward with a blunt knife to pull them out. Be sure to remove all the nails, so that the backboard will not catch when it is lifted out.

When the backboard has been fully exposed, lift the frame upright with one hand and tilt it backward slightly to see whether the contents will fall out gently into your other hand. Push gently on the glass. If the contents remain firmly packed into the frame, coax the backboard, gently, lightly, with a thin metal spatula inserted along the upper edge. Avoid prying the boards; if they are brittle, they may suddenly crack in half when pulled out under pressure, and you may inadvertently damage the art itself. Prints and drawings are sometimes dropped into frames with no backboard at all. Check for this possibility beforehand, and avoid peeling away or otherwise damaging backboards while they are still in the frame.

If your observations suggest that the item was dry mounted to a brittle board or that some other risks are involved, turn the entire frame face up, holding its contents in place with your hand. Lift away first the molding and then the glass. Two people may be needed for this operation. Remember, old glass can spontaneously shatter, so lift from at least two sides, never by a corner.

If possible, separate the backing materials from the artwork and from anything to which it is directly adhered. The artwork, its mat or backboard, labels, and any other information taken from the frame should be stored in an acid-free folder pending examination, treatment, and rematting. Discard old framing materials. Wrap and label the frame, after placing cardboard against the glass and cushioning its corners. Store the ensemble until it is needed again. If works of art have adhered to brittle backboards or mats, provide them with rigid horizontal support—acid-free corrugated cardboard, for instance—after they are unframed.

Oversized Artworks: Framing and Handling

Any item whose dimensions exceed your framing and storage accommodations can be considered oversized. Works of art whose size makes them difficult to handle include posters, maps, architectural drawings, contemporary graphics, and wallpapers. Not only are these objects cumbersome; the costs of framing them are higher, as well.

Oversized works of art also require more storage space, often at a premium in many institutions. The need for special allowances that must be made in storing large, cumbersome works of art—a formidable problem, sometimes—is discussed in chapter 4, under "*Storing Oversized Artworks,*" which suggests types of storage, containers, shelving, and organization for these special items. Such works are usually in deplorable condition when acquired, because they often served a practical function prior to becoming part of a museum collection. Many deteriorated from neglect, simply because of their large, unwieldy size. As an example of that, today only one map survives of the 868 Mercator wall maps engraved in 1554 on six joined sheets of paper.[11]

Speaking generally, historic posters were never intended to be works of art. Consequently, they were often printed on newsprint of the poorest quality, as were those by Toulouse Lautrec. More often than not, posters and broadsides were actually used as advertisements, sometimes outdoors. They are likely to be found rolled, crushed, and tattered; or, worse, they may have been patched with scotch tape, dry mounted, or lined with heavy canvas.

Maps likewise lead a hard life before they come to rest in a collection. Old ones that were usually rolled up for use and transport were often lined with fabric for strength and were bound with a separate strip of ribbon or fabric at the edge. Wooden sticks were attached to each end for ease of rolling. To create a map of the desired size, several sheets of paper were frequently joined. Sheets that were varnished to protect them from the elements have in many cases darkened. Maps may also have cracked and stiffened from their linings, and may be soiled and torn from long and heavy use.

Architectural drawings and prints can come in many sizes and shapes, the most common being preliminary sketches, more complete studies, presentation drawings for clients, and detailed construction drawings called "working documents."[12] Architectural drawings were done on many types of supports, including commercial illustration boards for display and linen-lined tracing paper for rolling. Copied documents, such as blueprints, have special conservation requirements that relate to the copying technique used. Like maps, architectural drawings were made to scale and were used specifically to illustrate details. Consequently, they can reach massive proportions.

Wallpaper is often the largest artwork on paper to be found in a collection. Historic wallpapers are now being preserved *in situ* and also as separate sheets in museum collections. Preservation *in situ* has many limitations, since the wall behind the wallpaper is often the source of its deterioration. A more complete procedure—and one considerably more expensive—is to remove the wallpaper from the wall, carry out the conservation treatment, and reinstall the paper on panels that are archivally sound and easily removable. Many historical societies have chosen to replace their wallpapers with reproductions while saving the originals in their collections. These various options are discussed in the reading matter listed at the end of this chapter. Extensive planning is necessary before any action is taken in treating wallpaper.

Wallpaper samples that enter collections are very often in need of conservation treatment. They are dirty or torn, and bits of plaster often still adhere to their backs, which may have been lined with layers of cloth or paper. Flaking paint, frequently a problem, is aggravated by the paper's having been rolled. Odd sizes are especially difficult to handle and store (see figure 3.17).

Oversized objects often require conservation treatments, such as flattening, tear repair, washing, deacidification, or lining before they can be framed or placed in storage. You can undertake the first two procedures, described in chapter 5, providing that you have large enough flattening

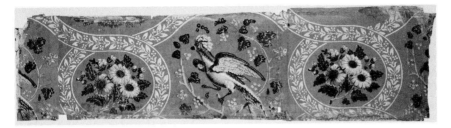

Fig. 3.17. The thickly painted or printed surface of historic wallpaper is often flaking, and the odd sizes of wallpapers present storage problems, as well.— Anonymous, Wallpaper, American (?), Early XIX Century (?); the Metropolitan Museum of Art (62.651); photograph by Ken Taronto

glass and space in which to maneuver it. Because treatment of oversized items does require great space, many private conservators simply cannot accept them. Generally speaking, regional conservation centers are better equipped to handle oversized works of art. Some, like the New England Document Conservation Center, have become known for their treatment of maps and posters.

Lining with canvas is often recommended for oversized items, but in my experience it is often badly done and is not worthwhile. Linen should never be used to line items whose paper has deteriorated to the point where it cannot withstand the tension that heavy cloth will exert on it. Most conservators prefer to use Japanese tissue for lining because of its lighter weight and better compatibility with the paper of the object. For very large graphics, such as billboard advertisements, linen or other cloth may be the only practical lining material. In these instances, the item should still be lined with Japanese tissue first, followed by fabric. This will facilitate removal of the cloth if that becomes necessary in the future.

Large works of art on paper should be framed and stored with the same care as smaller prints and drawings. Whenever possible, lighter-weight materials should be chosen for ease of handling and safety. Traditional framing is ideal, budget and storage space permitting. The framing guidelines described above should be followed. Unless flaking paint or other friable media are present, rigid acrylic sheeting is preferable to glass because of its lighter weight. Since the possibility that a work of art will touch its glazing increases with its dimensions, use of a deeper breathing space or additional hinges is prudent for larger works.

Framers often suggest dry mounting large items to keep them flat, but I do not recommend doing so, for reasons already discussed. If necessary, place several hinges around the sides and bottom of the piece to keep it flatter. Several hinges may also be necessary to support the greater weight of large objects. Framers also often suggest clips, which sandwich the work between the glazing and backboard, thus eliminating the need for expensive moldings. Although these clips are easy to use and attractive for contemporary posters, they are recommended for use only with disposable items and not with works of art. Dust and other contaminants can easily enter all sides of the package, accelerating deterioration. Furthermore, the clips leave no breathing space, encouraging condensation and mold growth.

Less costly alternatives are possible by eliminating the need for glass and molding. Encapsulation—sandwiching the artwork between two layers of Mylar, a clear polyester film—is a practical solution for oversized problems. The objects can be easily handled and readily identified. Neatly encapsulated objects can be displayed as they are. Encapsulation should not be confused with lamination, which is permanent sealing between plastic sheets. Lamination is not recommended for works of art. Obviously, encapsulation is not appropriate for artworks having powdery media or insecure paint layers. Directions for encapsulation are found in chapter 4.

Partial encapsulation is another inexpensive method for displaying large graphics and is preferable if they are acidic. In this method, the art object is sandwiched between Mylar and rigid acid-free corrugated cardboard or heavy ragboard to which it has been hinged. Again, if partial encapsulation is done neatly, the object can be displayed as it is.

"Shrinkwrapping," often done to protect posters for sale, stretches a thin sheet of plastic around the object and a backboard, sealing the enclosure with heat. Shrinkwrapping is not recommended for works of art because it uses materials that are not inert.

Posters, maps, architectural drawings, and other oversized objects should be stored and displayed under the same environmental conditions as other works of art on paper (see chapter 4).

NOTES

1. Alfred Whitman, *Print-Collector's Handbook* (London: George Bell and Sons, 1903), p. 106.

2. These directions are not intended for measuring the pH of prints and drawings. For more information regarding pH, see M. Holben Ellis, "The pH of Drawings and Its Implications," *Drawing* 3:4 (November –December 1981): 84–87; A. King, A. Pelikan, and W. E. Falconer, "The Use of the Archivist's Pen and Universal pH Solution for Estimating the Surface pH of Paper," *Studies in Conservation* 15:1 (February 1970): 63–64; and Anne

Moncrieff and Graham Weaver, *Science for Conservators*, Vol. 2: *Cleaning* (London: Crafts Council, 1983), pp. 86–103.

3. The issue of trimming down artworks deserves serious attention. I address it here in a footnote only to avoid diverting the reader's attention from the matting instructions. Too often, it is not recognized that the placement of an image on the page reflects the decision of the artist and is not accidental. In modern graphics, especially, the entire sheet is often intended for display, and its proportions in relation to the design are aesthetically meaningful. The sheet that carries the image may also indicate the item's provenance and method of manufacture. Stone or plate marks, deckle edges, and tacking edges are often removed when edges are trimmed. If an item has been cut from a book (*not* recommended) intact edges will provide that evidence. Artworks whose edges have been trimmed decrease in value, as well. This same prohibition against trimming applies to secondary supports when they are intimately related either historically or aesthetically to the print or drawing.

4. A. Hyatt Mayor, *Prints and People: A Social History of Printed Pictures* (New York: Metropolitan Museum of Art, 1971), No. 579.

5. Mayor, *Prints and People*, No. 91.

6. Merle Hughes, *Prints for the Collector* (New York: Praeger, 1971), p. 29.

7. Folk art suffers from many conservation problems having to do with the way in which it has been framed. See Marjorie Shelley, "Preserving American Folk Art on Paper," *Art and Antiques* 5:1 (February 1982); 16ff; William Adair, *The Frame in America, 1700-1900: A Survey of Fabrication, Techniques, and Styles* (Washington, D.C.: The American Institute of Architects Foundation, 1983).

8. Hughes, *Prints for the Collector*, p. 29.

9. Plexiglas brand acrylic sheet is manufactured by Rohm and Haas. Other brands are also available. See also Appendix 1.

10. This information is available free of charge on a sheet that can conveniently be posted in the framing area. Write to the Office of the Registrar, the Museum of Modern Art, New York, New York.

11. Mayor, *Prints and People*, no. 180.

12. For an overview of the materials used in architectural drawings, see Thea Jirat-Wasiutynski, "Architectural Drawings and Prints: Materials and Storage," *Association of Canadian Archivists Bulletin* 8:3 (May 1983): 9–10.

FURTHER READING

American Institute for Conservation. "Wallpaper Conservation." Special issue. *Journal of the American Institute for Conservation of Historic and Artistic Works* 20:2 (Spring 1981).

Bartlett, James, and Douglas Marshall. *Maps in the Small Historical Society*. Technical Leaflet 111. Nashville: American Association for State and Local History, 1979.

Capps, Marie T. "Preservation and Maintenance of Maps." *Special Libraries* 63:10 (October 1972): 457–462.

Ehrenberg, Ralph E. *Archives and Manuscripts: Maps and Architectural Drawings*. Chicago: Society of American Archivists, 1982.

Frangiamore, Catherine Lynn. *Rescuing Historic Wallpaper: Identification, Preservation, Restoration*. Technical Leaflet 76. Nashville: American Association for State and Local History, 1974.

_____. *Wall Papers in Historic Preservation*. Publication 185. Washington, D.C.: National Park Service, Office of Archeology and Historic Preservation, n.d.

Hinging and Mounting of Paper Objects. HMS–6. Washington, D.C.: Smithsonian Institution, Office of Museum Programs Audiovisual Program Coordinator, n.d. [158 slides, script, bibliography, sources of supply, glossary, paste recipe, instructions for watercutting paper].

Jirat-Wasiutynski, Thea. "Architectural Drawings and Prints: Materials and Storage." *Association of Canadian Archivists Bulletin* 8:3 (May 1983): 9–10.

Jones, William K. *The Exhibit of Documents: Preparation, Matting, and Display Techniques.* Technical Leaflet 75. Nashville: American Association for State and Local History, 1974.

Kidd, Betty. "Preventative Conservation for Map Collections." *Special Libraries* 71:12 (December 1980): 529–538.

Smith, Merrily A. *Matting and Hinging Works of Art on Paper.* Washington, D.C.: Library of Congress, Preservation Office, 1981.

Thompson, Enid Thornton. *Collecting and Preserving Architectural Records.* Technical Leaflet 132. Nashville: American Association for State and Local History, 1980.

4

Storage and Environment

Storage

*T*HE CHOICE OF a storage space for works of art on paper should be influenced by several factors: the location of the space; its suitability, in general; and the size of the collection to be stored.

Because roofs leak and underground areas flood, attics and basements are unsuitable for storing prints and drawings unless elaborate precautions are taken. If there is any possibility of a leak, even from pipes in the next room or several floors above a proposed storage area, water detectors should be installed.

Attics and basements are also difficult places in which to maintain proper environmental conditions; more sophisticated technology is required to keep them safe for collections than is needed for space with a more consistent climate. Rooms adjacent to parking garages are not suitable for storage because of the danger of air pollution entering through vents or other passageways.

Security considerations should also influence the choice of location for a storeroom for prints and drawings. Then, too, the storeroom should be near curatorial staff offices or study rooms for the convenience of those who will be using it most. Since damage to museum objects most often occurs as they are handled in transit the need to move them from room to room, up and down stairs, or from building to building should be minimized.

Any room in which prints and drawings are stored should be clean, well ventilated, and equipped with good lighting. Lighting should not come from windows unprotected by drapes and ultraviolet-filtering shades or from unfiltered fluorescent tubing. There should be a small table or cart just inside the storage area, on which objects being moved to or from assigned storage locations can temporarily rest. Everything must be well-organized and clearly labeled. Cement, plaster, and paints used to renovate a storage area should have completely cured and dried before works of art are placed in the room. All storeroom shelves, floors, and walls should be cleanable. Light-colored walls, ceilings, and floors will make detection and elimination of rodents and insects easier. Objects stored should be clearly visible; unnecessary clutter should be kept to a minimum.

Security equipment and fire detection devices are beyond the scope of this book, but they should be present, in more or less sophisticated form, in any storeroom. Museums choosing fire prevention systems specifically for storage areas that will house prints and drawings have traditionally avoided sprinkler systems, because of the threat of water damage. Halon gas is usually preferred, but is expensive for smaller institutions. Carbon dioxide fire extinguishers are recommended instead of extinguishers using fluid or foam. Place the fire extinguisher next to the door, where it is readily visible. For more specific information on security and fire-prevention equipment, get in touch with specialists in those areas and consult the literature cited at the end of this chapter.

The room or area chosen for storing prints and drawings should be large enough to accommodate the storage system selected and to hold future acquisitions, as well.

For more specific advice on design and construction of the ideal museum storeroom, see Hilberry and Weinberg's "Museum Collections Storage," listed in "Further Reading."

Storing Framed Artworks

By far the best method of storing prints and drawings is to store them framed, provided that they have been properly hinged and matted with materials of conservation quality. The frame protects the picture itself from careless handling. The glazing material—acrylic or glass— allows the work to be quickly examined, protects it from soot, and, to some extent, helps to prevent damage from air pollution. Pastel, chalk, and charcoal drawings, which have a natural tendency to smudge, are always best stored in their frames, as are other especially fragile drawings. Particularly fragile artworks should be stored framed and kept horizontal on a shelf.

Because storage space is often limited, few institutions are able to store a collection of prints and drawings in their frames. When such space *is* available, framed artworks can be slid into open-ended bins.

Within each bin, they should be separated from each other with sturdy pieces of cardboard or foam board. Framed items should not be stored in bins that are too small, where the frame moldings could be damaged or the glass broken during moving or rearranging. Identification labels affixed to the sides of the moldings will provide ready identification for the artworks and eliminate the need for haphazard rummaging to find a specific picture. The bottom of each bin should be padded with protective strips of carpet or cardboard. Vertical bins should not contain more than three to four items and should stand with their bottoms several inches above floor level, for cleanliness as well as protection from water, in case of flood. Framed objects should never be stacked on the floor. If possible, it is preferable to construct open-ended storage bins from metal rather than wood.

An alternative storage method—less satisfactory than the use of bins—is to hang framed drawings on wire screens, either the stationary kind or those that slide on tracks affixed to the floor and ceiling. Such screens are frequently used in painting storerooms. Pastel, chalk, and charcoal drawings should not be hung on movable screens, because the vibration caused by rearranging them may damage the artworks. The front of each frame should be covered with heavy paper or cloth to protect the enclosed artwork from light. Generally, hanging a collection of prints and drawings on screens is not an efficient use of space.

Storage Containers

Flat files of wood or steel. When lack of space must be considered, flat print files can accommodate many more drawings in a given amount of space than framed storage would safely allow. Flat print files, available from art supply and office furniture stores, are commonly constructed of either wood or steel.

Traditional wisdom has long held that wooden storage furniture could be used for prints and drawings if the wood were sealed beforehand with polyurethane varnish. The theory was that the varnish coating would serve as a vapor barrier, preventing the wood's acidic vapors from coming into contact with the stored artworks. This theorizing has now changed. Recent investigations into the action of vapors exuded by various types of wood and wood products, in particular formaldehyde emissions from plywood and particleboard, indicate that even varnished wood is not a suitable material for storage furniture intended for art on paper. Especially dangerous is oak and particleboard, the very combination frequently found in expensive oak-veneered flat files.

Opinions on the best sealants for wood vary. If wooden cabinets are the only storage option available for one's prints and drawings, those cabinets should be painted with several coats of epoxy paint and allowed to air-dry for several months to a year before they are put into use. Even epoxy paint cannot effectively seal out harmful vapors exuded by wood. Ventilation to the cabinet should be provided; the cabinet's wooden back might be replaced with screening, for instance. Each wooden shelf should be lined with heavy, acid-free paper or blotters. Artworks stored within wooden cabinets must be surrounded by acid-free materials and, preferably, placed in solander boxes.

While there is little agreement about which sealant is best for wooden surfaces—acrylic, epoxy, or polyurethane paint—one conclusion is unanimous: *wood is not a suitable material for constructing storage or display furniture to be used for art on paper.* For more on this, the reader is directed to the articles by Miles, Carpenter, and Hatchfield listed at the end of this chapter.

Flat steel files should be of sturdy construction and should open and close smoothly. Steel with an electrostatically secured or "baked on" finish is the safest and most durable material for cabinets intended as storage for art on paper.

Care should be taken to avoid overloading flat file drawers; cramming in more pieces of art than a drawer has room for can result in crumpled artwork lodged in the back of the cabinet. Each drawer should be arranged to prevent its contents from sliding back and forth when the drawer is opened and closed, which could result in abrasion of the designs or other damage.

Steel cabinets. Storage arrangements now commercially available include a system of steel boxes that can be stacked in a locked steel cabinet. These steel boxes—the ultimate in durability—are more expensive and much heavier than their cardboard counterparts, which seem sturdy enough and are equally available. It should also be noted here that condensation can be a problem in closed metal containers and cabinets when relative humidity fluctuates. Relative humidity may actually be lower on muggy summer days than it is when a sudden drop in temperature has just occurred. In climates with greatly fluctuating relative humidity, storage boxes or cabinets must be checked frequently for condensation, most often detectable by rust along joints and edges or by mold growth. Although their accuracy varies, dial hygrometers and small humidity indicators made of paper scales carrying patches of sensitive salts that change color as humidity levels change can be useful in checking for high humidity levels within each box. Unless adequate ventilation is provided or unless the environment can be strictly maintained and the interior of storage boxes monitored, I do not recommend the closed steel storage system. For the reasons just mentioned, valuable prints and drawings are not always better off stored in locked vaults.

Storage boxes. One of the most common and most adaptable methods of storing prints and drawings involves print storage boxes arranged along steel shelves or wooden shelving. Again, it should be noted that wood is not the best material for constructing storage furniture for prints and drawings. The bottom-most shelf must be several inches above the floor, both for cleanliness and also for protection from damage by water in case of flood. Store the largest and heaviest boxes on the lower shelves and the smaller ones higher up. If boxes are placed beyond easy reach, use a sturdy step-stool to get to them, for the safety of both the art and the keeper. Storage by shelving should be set up only in well-ventilated rooms, and steel shelving should be regularly checked for signs of rust. Do not place steel shelving directly against exterior walls, which can be cold and damp. If boxes are stored in cabinets or closets, adequate ventilation should be provided.

Print storage boxes—called *solander boxes,* after their inventor, Daniel Charles Solander (1736–1782), a pupil of Linnaeus—are made from sturdy pressboard, binders' board, or other paper laminates. Solander boxes are available in several sizes and vary in price according to their components and degree of craftsmanship. Over the years, with growing interest in their use for archival storage, there have been many improvements in the materials used to make them. Major manufacturers of these boxes are now using a buffered acid-free paper or other neutral material almost exclusively as linings for the boxes. Traditional starch-filled cloth outer coverings (attractive to vermin and not very durable) are still made, but they have largely been superseded by pyroxylin-coated or pyroxylin-impregnated cloth. Fabrics coated with acrylics have recently replaced the pyroxylin-coated cloths. Chemically unstable and weak adhesives used in applying linings and coverings to storage boxes have largely been improved. The rigid board of boxes still varies in composition from nonneutral cardboards to buffered binders' board. Any woods used in the box framework may also vary.

When choosing a storage box for art on paper, it is important to consider these points:

• Is the box rigid and durable? A box that cannot properly support its contents or one that falls apart after a few years of handling is useless.

- Is the box lining acid-free and will it act as a barrier to acid migration from the exterior boards if they are not neutral? Manufacturers usually emphasize that their lining materials are of archival quality. When in doubt, better inquire.
- Does the box lining cover the interior entirely, or just the top and bottom? An overall acid-free lining covering all sides is preferable.
- Does the box open and close easily? Does it close snugly? Too loose a top allows dust to penetrate; too tight a top makes the box difficult to open.

When costs must be curbed, there is no simpler, more practical solution than boxes made of acid-free corrugated cardboard or heavy-duty buffered fiberboard. The container manufactured from acid-free corrugated cardboard is precut and ready to be assembled. Extra containers can be stored flat in little space. These boxes weigh less than solander boxes, are less durable, and are therefore less suited to heavy use in print study rooms or libraries. Their corners, lacking rigid supports, adhesives, or metal fasteners, tend to fold inward; and cardboard boxes do not always open or close smoothly.

No adhesives are used in the boxes made of buffered fiberboard; heavy metal clips provide strong corner supports. Because of their lighter weight and lack of overall framework, fiberboard boxes lack the rigidity of solander boxes, and the larger sizes in fiberboard tend to wobble. They also may be hard to open and close; and because their parts sometimes do not fit snugly, they are not as dustproof as solander boxes. By and large, however, pure materials and low cost make these fiberboard boxes, as well as those made from acid-free corrugated cardboard, an economical solution for safely storing large collections.

In general, the more neutral and more chemically stable its adhesives, boards, coverings, and linings, and the more it can withstand years of use, the better a box is for conservation purposes. Price increases in proportion to quality. Several less expensive boxes that can easily accommodate a collection are of course preferable to one premium-priced model crammed to overflowing. Money is well spent, however, if it provides better protection for the valuable contents of the box. Apart from matting, these boxes are one of the best conservation buys available, in terms of the protection they afford.

However, one fact is as true of storing in solander boxes as it is of framing artworks for safer storage or storing them in flat file drawers: none of those precautionary measures will work unless the artworks are protected by materials of archival quality before they are put into storage.

Storage mats. Ideally, prints and drawings should be matted (see chapter 3) before being placed in containers of any sort. Matted items should be consistently inserted into boxes with the hinged side or the spine of the mat along the spine of the box, for easier, safer retrieval. When prints and drawings are stored in mats, the surface of each work should be protected by a slip sheet placed between the artwork and the window mat. Many kinds of papers are suitable for use as slip sheets. Silk tissue, a Japanese tissue containing a high percentage of gampi, is silky, translucent, and neutral. Neutral glassine has a smoother surface and a neutral pH. Interleaving tissues are offered by many companies and are generally lightweight tissues of either Japanese or Western manufacture, suitable for use as slip sheets. Permalife paper (bond weight, .003 to .004 cal.), paper manufactured specifically for longevity, is stiffer than tissues or glassine and can be used, but is not translucent, preventing rapid "see-through" identification of the matted object. Reflex Matte paper, likewise a bond-weight paper, is treated to be smooth and translucent. It is also neutral. Buffered tissue, an opaque tissue containing a filler of calcium carbonate, is not as smooth as these other papers, but can be used. Clear polyester (Mylar) film (.003 to .005) can also be used as slip sheets. *Polyester film should never be used near soft graphite, charcoal, chalk, or pastel drawings.* Many people prefer to use polyester film as a slip sheet, because its transparency makes the matted items immediately identifiable, so that they are—theoretically, at least—subject to less handling. Unless one works very carefully, however, the film's sharp edges can scratch both the artwork and the person handling it.

Neutral glassine and nonbuffered tissues do not retain their neutrality over long periods of time and must periodically be replaced. Ways of buffering glassine are now being explored, but none is yet commercially available. Buffered tissues contain an adequate reserve of calcium carbonate, and tests indicate that polyesters remain stable.

How frequently neutral glassine and nonbuffered tissues should be rotated is difficult to state categorically. Obviously, if such a slip sheet is covering a print with a pH of 4, the slip sheet will become acidic faster than its neighbor covering a print with a pH of 7. A good rule of thumb is always to keep a supply of slip sheets on hand and to change them whenever a work of art with a slip sheet of glassine or nonbuffered tissue is examined. This practice, however, does little for the protection of the unpopular print that never sees the light of day. Any signs of brittleness or darkening of a slip sheet is proof that that slip sheet is doing little to protect the artwork within the mat. Such a slip sheet should be replaced immediately. A pH indicator pencil can be kept nearby, to test papers used as slip sheets—a corner snipped off can serve as a sample.

It can be expensive to mat an entire collection, especially if double-window storage mats are used. Although such mats are preferable, less expensive alternatives still provide adequate protection for prints and drawings.

Folders. Folders made from heavy acid-free bristol, or acid-free folder stock (.020 cal.) can be used instead of mats. You can make these easily yourself, or you can purchase standard sizes. Such folders can be used in drawers and in solander boxes or can simply be stacked on shelves (a useful option for oversized items). Slip sheets should still be used to protect the surface of each work of art within the folders. Folders can have many different designs. The simplest has three sections. The middle section is made either slightly larger than the object it is to hold or the size of the drawer of solander box in which it will be stored. On either side of the middle section are two flaps of the same height as the middle, but not as wide. These two outer sections, when folded, overlap each other to cover the item inside.

Folders with flaps on four sides that fold up and over the art to be stored provide additional protection for the object inside. For folders made of heavy card stock, each fold line should be scored with a bone folder for greater overall flexibility. A piece of mat board or acid-free corrugated board placed below the artwork gives these folders rigidity and makes them easier to handle.

Encapsulation. Prints and drawings in drawers or solander boxes may also be protected by encapsulation. In this procedure, the artwork is sandwiched between two sheets of flexible polyester film (such as .003 or .005 Mylar). The edges of the polyester package either are sealed with double-sided tape or are joined ultrasonically. The static electricity of the two sheets of polyester hold the artwork in place, and both sides are protected by a neutral, chemically stable material. Encapsulation must not be confused with lamination, which heat-seals an item more or less permanently in cellulose acetate. Lamination is not recommended for works of art under any circumstances.

Encapsulation is not always desirable for prints and drawings because the glossy surface of the encapsulating film can interfere with a viewer's appreciation of the enclosed art. Documents and other archival materials are usual candidates. If funds are lacking for matting, however, encapsulation provides maximum protection with the least equipment and technical experience required. Drawings done in soft graphite, charcoal, chalk, or pastel should not be encapsulated, because of the static electricity polyester film generates under friction. Encapsulated items are best stored in acid-free folders, so that their surfaces cannot scratch and dull one another.

To encapsulate an artwork, first place a grid of graph paper (available from drafting supply stores) on a clean working surface. Cut two pieces of polyester film about 1 inch larger all around than the item to be encapsulated. Cutting the film is easiest with a paper-cutter, but scissors or a utility knife will work as well. Polyester film can be purchased in standard sizes or special-ordered in custom sizes. Place one piece of polyster film on the grid and clean it with a lint-free cloth. The resulting static charge will attract any dust in the immediate area, so the work space should be kept scrupulously clean. Next, place the print or drawing on the film and align it along the grid lines so that it is centered on the plastic. Add a small weight, protecting the artwork's surface with a blotter square. Using only 3M Double-Sided Tape No. 415, tape around the item, leaving at least ⅛ inch between the tape and the edge of the item. Leave small gaps for air exchange where the tape meets at each corner. Use the tape only for encapsulation; never permit it to touch the print or drawing. Ultrasonic edge sealers are available; but, due to their cost, they are practical buys only for those with large collections of archival materials. Remove the weight and the blotter square and place another cleaned sheet of polyester film on top of the artwork. Once again, weight the center so that nothing shifts. Working in a clockwise manner (or counterclockwise, if you are left-handed), pull the paper covering from the tape at the top and side. Using the lint-free cloth or a squeegee, smooth the layers of polyester film, stroking away from the two attached sides. Remove the paper covering the final two strips of tape and smooth out the entire package with the cloth or squeegee. With a paper-cutter, scissors, or a knife, trim the excess polyester film to within ¹⁄₁₆-inch of the tape. Round the corners, using scissors or a special device available from archival supply stores, so that these corners cannot cut other papers—or the handler's fingers.

Instructions for encapsulating problematic items and for making a polyester "book" appear in the Library of Congress's *Polyester Film Encapsulation* (see "Further Reading").

Continuing research indicates that very acidic items do not benefit from encapsulation—that is, in a closed system, acid deterioration is accelerated. Items that have become acidic either through internally generated sources or from external causes should be matted for optimum protection. Partial encapsulation, in which the item is hinged to a piece of buffered mat board and then faced with Mylar is another alternative to full encapsulation. If a highly acidic item must be encapsulated, it should be deacidified beforehand—a decision to be made and a procedure to be carried out only by a conservator.

Archival supply houses now offer a variety of envelopes and folders in standard sizes made with polyester film. These are useful for large collections of similarly sized items, such as postcards. *Only pure polyester film is acceptable for storing prints and drawings, so avoid any unidentified plastics.*

Whether they are in mats, folders, or envelopes, encapsulated or not, prints and drawings should be the appropriate size for the drawer or box they are put into. A small item in an oversized container can be damaged by sliding.

Storing Oversized Artworks

As mentioned in the discussion of framing, in chapter 3, special allowances must also be made for size and weight when the storage of oversized objects is being planned. Flat storage for oversized works of art is preferable.[1] Horizontal all-steel cabinets with shallow drawers are best for storing large items and are available from library and drafting supply companies. All works going into storage should first be encapsulated or wrapped in sturdy folders made from acid-free folder stock or acid-free wrapping paper. It is advisable to put encapsulated items into acid-free folders, also, to prevent surface scratches caused by the artwork's sliding. Placing the folders in the drawers with their folded spines facing out will encourage anyone handling the art to remove the entire folder from the drawer before extracting the drawing.[2] Encapsulated objects and objects in acid-free folders can also be stored in flat map-storage boxes, although these boxes are cumbersome to handle and usually require two people to lift and carry them safely. Map-storage boxes can be stacked on sturdy metal shelving.

Oversized items can also simply be stored on wide metal shelving. This option is the least satisfactory one, but it can be safe if the objects are held securely in folders and are not stacked too high. The more items in a pile, the more rummaging is necessary to find a specific one. Clear labeling and a filing system are crucial for trouble-free storage of oversized items.

Artwork should be rolled only temporarily or in situations of extreme necessity. If rolling is unavoidable, the art object should be wrapped, *face out*, around the exterior of a tube that is large in diameter and is acid-free or wrapped with Mylar. The art itself should then be wrapped with acid-free paper and clearly labeled. Triangular storage tubes made from acid-free corrugated cardboard are now available and are easier to stack, but with triangular tubes, the rolled artwork is placed *inside* the tube, not wrapped around the outside. Heavily painted historic wallpapers should never be rolled nor should any artwork on brittle, deteriorated paper.

Careful organization and clear labeling are the best ways of preventing accidental damage to oversized works of art. Storerooms should be arranged so that handling of very large items is kept to a minimum. They should be readily accessible, however, when necessary.

Routine Handling of Matted Prints and Drawings in Storage

Because objects are frequently removed from storage at the request of individuals other than in-house staff people, printed copies of proper study room procedures should be posted in the study room area, with additional copies available to give to outside students or viewers. Awareness of the need for observing such procedures can significantly lengthen the life of many prints and drawings. The following rules establish basic precautions. Your institution should compile and enforce additional rules appropriate to its particular situation.

Visitors should never touch a print or drawing with their fingers or point toward art with pencils. Pens should not be allowed in the vicinity of artworks being studied. Beverages and food should not be allowed in the study room.

Visitors should be instructed in the safe and correct way to view matted prints and drawings. The matted artwork, removed from its box or folder, should be placed on a clean, uncluttered table. The mat should be opened from the lower right corner, not by reaching into its window. The slip sheet may then be pulled out by its corners and the mat closed. For viewing, the mat should be held with both hands and tilted upward. Visitors should look *across toward,* not directly *down,* on an unprotected print or drawing, to minimize the chances of damage in the event of coughs or sneezes or eyeglasses falling. Neckties and dangling jewelry should be removed, tucked in, or otherwise firmly secured to the viewer's person. Small tabletop easels and bookstands are useful supports for matted prints and drawings. After viewing the artwork, the visitor should replace the slip sheet, making sure it is centered and smooth before closing the mat.

As a safety measure for the handling of matted artworks in storage, the mats for all works in a collection should be fitted so that they all open in the same direction. Most often, for vertical prints and drawings, this is from right to left, as the pages open in an ordinary occidental book. For horizontal artworks, opening a mat by lifting the bottom edge is standard. Similarly, all prints and drawings should be consistently hinged in the same manner. If hinges are placed in a location where they may not be expected, small arrows penciled inside the mat should so indicate.

Environment

While small museums and historical societies may be unable to afford storerooms and exhibition galleries as technically sophisticated as those found in major museums, you will want to give your collection the best protection possible within the limits of your budget. Artworks intended to last need to be well kept. As noted in the preceding chapters, the deterioration of art on paper can be slowed by matting, storing, and exhibiting it in accordance with good conservation practice. Without being an air conditioning specialist, a heating engineer, a lighting designer, or a professional exterminator, the individual concerned about protecting these fragile works of art can determine the proper environmental conditions for prints and drawings and learn how to measure and monitor these conditions. The term *proper environmental conditions* is used here to mean the conditions under which we can reasonably expect artworks to survive the longest. The term denotes suitability, rightness, and appropriateness: it represents a compromise between *what we know to be optimum* and *what we recognize as realistic*.

Equipped with that knowledge, one can work with specialists to design and install appropriate systems. There is always the economic question of whether one can afford specialists. In most instances, however, their expertise will save money; a piecemeal approach to climate control for works of art on paper may actually make the environment worse than it already is.

A simple, relatively uncomplicated system is preferable to a more sophisticated arrangement that one does not have the necessary staff to maintain and monitor. If you cannot afford total climate control, evolve a long-range plan and start on a small scale, working within your financial and technical limitations. You might start with just one storage area and gallery (an approach called *zoning*) or even with one vitrine or cabinet (called a *microclimate*). Or you might start by simply closing curtains, dusting regularly, and slipping UV shields over fluorescent lights. The list of references at the end of this chapter includes two particularly useful works: *The Museum Environment* and *Museum Climatology*, both by Garry Thomson.

The first step in improving environmental conditions is to understand how the interaction of air pollution, temperature, humidity, and light causes prints and drawings to deteriorate. Next, one must learn how to measure these conditions in one's own collection environment. Finally, methods successfully used by other institutions to maintain satisfactory environments should be studied. This study should consider climate control systems that have failed, whether due to the design of the system itself or to the fact that the building simply could not accommodate the levels of temperature and relative humidity it needed to maintain. Some historic structures, especially those in northern areas of America, cannot withstand elevated humidity levels during winter months. The impact of perfect environmental conditions on the building is often overlooked in our haste to improve the building's interior.

Air Pollution

The deleterious effect of air pollution on prints and drawings has long been recognized. Vibert's Fixatif was marketed in the 1880s as a product that would theoretically protect watercolors from pollution produced by gas lamps.[3] The darkening of lead white from exposure to air pollution has also been seen (figure 2.17).

Far more insidious than color changes, however, is the physical breakdown of paper from gases such as sulfur dioxide, hydrogen sulfide, nitrogen oxides, and ozone. Probably the most dangerous single pollutant is sulfur dioxide, produced when fossil fuels are burned. With elevated temperature and humidity levels, sulfur dioxide readily combines with water to form sulfuric acid. Ozone, a powerful oxidant, is prevalent in photochemical smog, produced by the action of sunlight on car exhaust fumes.

Sulfur dioxide and hydrogen sulfide can be detected and measured by sensitive salts on indicator cards or contained in tubes connected to air pumps. Ozone and other gases require more sensitive instruments operated by an engineer. Your local Environmental Protection Agency can assist you in analyzing the air quality within your building.[4] Until our air becomes cleaner, you should assume that air pollution is attacking your collection. Its effects can be lessened, however, by study and careful use of your present system, with workable controls added as the budget permits.

Air pollution exists in solid forms as well as gaseous ones. Particles of smoke, dust, pollen, lint, and salt all find their way into art collections and settle on any unprotected work. Tobacco smoke is a prime particulate pollutant. Particulate pollution can spoil the appearance of art on paper by causing abrasion, introducing acidic gases, increasing humidity levels through retention of moisture, providing food for the growth of fungi, and in various other ways. One recommended standard for air quality is no dust particles greater than two microns and no more than fifty micrograms per cubic meter of sulfur dioxide.[5]

Many museums have successfully filtered out gaseous air pollution by installing water washes or sprays in their air conditioning system. Alkaline washes (pH 8.5–9) are sometimes used, but they can cause corrosion and may not be effective, in the long run.[6] Water sprays are not easily installed in existing systems, nor are they effective in removing ozone. An activated charcoal filter will remove ozone and is cheaper to fit into existing systems. More recently activated alumina filters have been used to remove sulfur dioxide and ozone from incoming air by absorption. Such filters must be periodically replaced.

Filters for removing dust and soot from the air can be fitted into existing systems; but the more effective the filter, the more energy is necessary to force the air through it, and the more frequently it must be changed.[7] Such filters can vary from simple to sophisticated.

Some collectors use electrostatic air cleaners, which are widely advertised as removing dust, pollen, and soot from the air in homes. These devices have strongly charged negative plates that draw positively charged particles into an electronic field and trap them there. While such air cleaners are more effective than filters for particulate matter, *they can endanger prints and drawings:* the ozone produced by the electronically catalyzed reaction of air molecules around the machine is especially destructive of cellulose. Since ozone can be destroyed by activated charcoal filters, *electrostatic air cleaners should be used only in conjunction with these filters;* an unaided household unit alone should not be placed in a storeroom. Photocopying machines and germicidal lamps also produce ozone and should therefore be kept away from prints and drawings.

Some simple and practical methods of controlling particulate pollution are these: seal collections area windows and doors tightly; allow people to enter storerooms and galleries only through vestibules (dirt clings to shoes and clothes); regularly clean radiators, fireplace openings, heating ducts, and chimneys, as well as storage furniture and floors. Treated cloths, such as One-Wipe (Guardsman), Stretch 'n' Dust (Chicopee), and Endust spray are efficient dusting products for furniture only, never to be used on works of art.[8] Avoid waxes or polishes for cleaning purposes in collections areas; while they appear to pick up dust readily, they leave behind a sticky film that will only trap more.

Some methods of reducing gaseous and particulate pollution are possible only within a system for total climate control. Others can be undertaken by any museum. All require surveillance and maintenance. Specialists can help you establish a schedule for regular maintenance and monitoring.

Heat

All facets of a museum's environment—pollution, heat, humidity, and light—are interrelated. For example, the damaging effects of air pollution are multiplied many times over as temperature and humidity increase. Acids are formed as the pollutants combine with available water vapor, a reaction that is speeded up by heat, as are yellowing and embrittlement—visible evidence of the aging of prints and drawings. Heat, a form of energy that speeds up chemical reactions when absorbed by paper, is sometimes used specifically to age paper artificially for analysis. Art stored in attics where temperatures soar to 120 degrees Fahrenheit undergoes a great deal of unnecessary artificial aging. Besides being a catalyst, heat also encourages the establishment of insect colonies and nests of other parasites.

In museum storerooms and galleries, temperatures must be maintained in a range that is comfortable for people, as well as safe for the art objects. Works on paper should ideally be kept in cool storage, but a temperature of 60 to 70 degrees Fahrenheit is likely to prove more practical to maintain. Much more important than the actual temperature within this range is the prevention of fluctuations in temperature. Heat is intimately related to relative humidity, so that a sudden drop in temperature can cause relative humidity to reach dangerous levels in a short time, resulting in condensation—as, for example, when a room air conditioner is turned up to super-cool on a muggy summer day. The temperature in museum storerooms and galleries should be kept as constant as possible, drifting only two to three degrees in either direction. If temperature must fluctuate, it should do so as slowly as possible, to give the art in the area a longer period of adjustment. Double-glazed windows and extra insulation will help minimize temperature fluctuations and will save energy as well.

It is important to realize that heat within buildings does not come from furnaces alone. Spotlights can substantially increase temperatures in galleries. A table lamp can heat a picture that hangs nearby. For this reason, avoid using small lights designed to be clipped onto picture frames. Sunlight striking dark curtains and furniture produces heat. Electrical equipment generates heat. In most buildings, localized "hot spots" are common. Try to avoid hanging prints and drawings over radiators, heating ducts, or working fireplaces. Artworks should be stored as far as possible from steam risers or other heating equipment.

Place accurate thermometers throughout your building. Several days of readings will give a profile of fluctuations in temperature. Thermostats in each area can activate heating or cooling equipment as needed. If heat distribution is uneven, fans or some other built-in circulation system may be in order. Fans can also help keep humidity levels down.

Humidity

Regulating humidity is the most difficult technical challenge met in climate control. High levels of humidity are particularly troublesome for paper artifacts. Since paper is hygroscopic, its being placed in a humid environment will cause it to absorb water vapor rapidly, only slowly giving it up again. Figures 1.24 through 1.31 illustrate the effects of high humidity. Drastic dimensional changes brought about by fluctuations in relative humidity can disrupt paint layers and permanently deform paper. Mold growth sustained by prolonged periods of high humidity can stain and weaken paper. Because humidity is closely involved with temperature, both must be carefully monitored, to prevent fluctuations.

To make that possible, it is necessary to know how to operate the various devices used to measure humidity in a meaningful way—that is, *relative* humidity. Air can hold water vapor in varying degrees—hot air can contain more than cold air, which is why condensation takes place when the temperature drops suddenly and water in the air passes from the gaseous to the liquid stage. Simply measuring the amount of water by weight contained in a certain volume of air provides the *absolute* humidity, but since air can hold varying amounts of water at different temperatures, this is not a meaningful measurement for our purposes. Relative humidity is the percentage obtained by comparing the amount of water vapor in a given volume of air to the maximum amount that volume of air could hold at that temperature. Most humidity levels are expressed in terms of RH. In addition to knowing how to operate the instruments needed, you must be aware of their limitations.

One convenient device for measuring relative humidity is a sling psychrometer, but it takes practice to use it correctly. It consists of a conventional dry-bulb thermometer and wet-bulb thermometer with a gauze-covered tip, which is thoroughly wetted with distilled water before use. The wick must be kept clean and in close contact with the bulb. The sling psychrometer is twirled, or slung in a circle, for one full minute, or until the wet-bulb thermometer registers its lowest point. The wet and dry temperature readings are then compared, the difference between the two calculated, and the RH interpreted from a chart.

An aspiring psychrometer incorporates a small battery-run fan that draws air across the bulbs of the thermometers, eliminating the need for twirling. In using either model, always read the wet-bulb thermometer first. Keep both psychrometers away from your body during use and take care not to breathe on the bulbs when reading them. Buy the best model of psychrometer you can afford. Accuracy is crucial; temperature readings that are inaccurate by a degree or two can mean a 5-to-10 percent error in relative humidity. Aspirating psychrometers are more accurate, because of their more consistent air flow. Again, buy the best model your budget will allow, and—most important—maintain and use it correctly.

Dial hygrometers, small circular gauges, are the most practical way to monitor relative humidity in small spaces such as drawers, display cases, and closets. The sensor in these instruments is either hair or paper. As it expands and contracts with changes in humidity, it causes a pointer to move along a scale on the face of the dial. Dial hygrometers need to be maintained according to the manufacturer's instructions. One should keep in mind that they incorporate delicate sensors; a rap on their glass faces does nothing beneficial. They are slow in reacting to humidity changes; but if properly calibrated and maintained, they can be quite accurate. As always, the most expensive instrument means nothing if it is not properly maintained, calibrated frequently, and used correctly.

Another useful instrument—but one that still requires calibration—is the hygrothermograph. This device simultaneously records temperature and humidity levels on a revolving paper graph. These graphs can span a day or several weeks, thus giving an accurate profile of the changing climate in gallery or storeroom. Some time and practice are needed to master the operation and interpretation of the hygrothermograph, which may explain why many hygrometers conspicuously displayed in galleries and museums are, in fact, not running at all.

The Office of Museum Programs of the Smithsonian Institution offers a slide presentation on use of the hygrothermograph.[9] Gael de Guichen's book *Climate in Museums* (see bibliography at the end of this chapter) has exercises to help one learn to interpret the graphs.

Handy smaller humidity gauges are paper indicator cards with patches of sensitive cobalt salts that change from a pink to a blue color with varying moisture levels. These cards can be placed in boxes, cases, and drawers, and on the backs of picture frames. While they can indicate in which direction RH is moving, they are largely inaccurate and should be used only to warn of dangerous situations or to serve in back-up situations when *nothing* else is available.

The liquid crystal hygrometer, recently introduced, is relatively easy to interpret, never requires calibration, and is more accurate than the indicator cards. In the liquid crystal hygrometer, a piece of polarizing glass is placed over a series of compounds arranged in order of reactivity. As each compound changes its crystal structure in response to a shift in relative humidity, it becomes brighter and more visible. The brightest number on the scale is the relative humidity. While this sounds quite simple, in actuality, it is difficult to determine exactly which number is the brightest; consequently, the determination of RH is dependent upon the viewer. Liquid crystal hygrometers can give only general ranges; they must never be used instead of more precise instruments. Because they never require calibration, however, they may be more accurate than more sophisticated but poorly maintained instruments.

Temperature and humidity sensors have been recently introduced that can be used alone or hooked up to a central microcomputer for continuous monitoring of the environment for as long as four weeks. These sophisticated instruments are not yet widely available, but will presumably find many applications in the museum world soon.

As with the control of temperature, the objective in controlling humidity is to avoid subjecting art on paper to continual, irregularly changing levels of humidity. Turning on a humidifier occasionally in the winter may worsen the climate for prints and drawings. Again, the easiest way to control humidity is with a total climate-control system. Since this is not feasible in many situations, free-standing humidifiers or dehumidifiers are often used to eliminate extremes. A humidistat in each area, properly calibrated, can control the cycle.

Even with all the options available for measuring humidity, it is still prudent to have several different instruments on hand.

The ideal range of relative humidity for prints and drawings is 45 to 55 percent, with fluctuations between the two not to exceed five percentage points. This sounds deceptively simple; and checking the references to relative humidity given throughout this book, readers will find a wide range, from 40 percent to 65 percent, of recommended relative humidity levels for the preservation of paper, with lower ranges gaining in popularity. In truth, to make this kind of statement at all is misleading, if it is not immediately followed by the exhortation that it is not the *exact level* of relative humidity, so much as its *constancy*, that is critical. If, in attempting to maintain one exact level of relative humidity, one is constantly turning on air conditioners or humidifiers, or resorting to makeshift solutions, such as simmering tea kettles, it is better to accept gradual shifts in either direction, even if the 45-to-55-percent limits are exceeded. This is my rationale behind the recommended range given above; better to exceed the limitations, if drastic fluctuations can be leveled out.

There are many types of humidifiers on the market. Many are designed for centrally heated homes, whose interiors in winter are often as dry as the Sahara. Trays of water on stoves and radiators do little to alleviate the problems of dry air.

Avoid atomizers that spray a fine mist of water into the air. The penetration of the water vapor into the surrounding atmosphere is uneven. Objects close to the atomizer will be soaked. The better humidifiers work on the principle of evaporation, either with or without heat. Of course, all humidifiers require water and therefore need daily maintenance.

Dehumidifiers are available in several designs. Those using desiccating agents are recommended for colder climates; refrigerant dehumidifiers are recommended for warmer climates. Dehumidifiers must be checked periodically and their collecting trays emptied, unless the water they remove from the atmosphere is discharged directly into a drain. Climate can be controlled within display cases by creating microclimates. Conditioned granular silica gel is usually the choice for lowering humidity. A new type of silica gel, Art Sorb, is more effective than the earlier product and is available in sheets or beads. Nathan Stolow's articles on microclimates and case design (see bibliography at chapter's end) are recommended reading if you are contemplating climate control on a small scale.

Windows are trouble spots for temperature and humidity control. As they allow heat from sunlight into the room, relative humidity decreases around them. In cold weather, moisture condenses in their vicinity. Double or triple glazing can ease these seasonal—and daily—fluctuations. Within the same room, uneven pockets of humidity occur and shift locations, in response to temperature changes caused by the presence of windows, radiators, or lighting fixtures.[10]

Localized high humidity can result when collections area floors are washed, or even when a crowd gathers in any enclosed space, as people release minute particles of moisture in breathing. Figure 4.1 shows a print that was hung on a freshly plastered and painted wall by a well-intentioned borrower. In a short time, buckling in the print signaled a dangerous situation. At the first hint of high humidity, action must be taken. For this reason, it is crucial to have accurate measuring devices. Relative humidity of 60 to 65 percent is dangerous for prints and

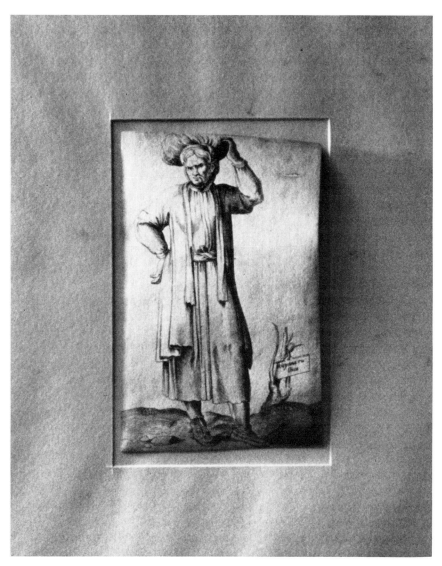

Fig. 4.1. This print quickly buckled after it was hung on a recently plastered wall.—Enea Vico, Hispana Rustica; *the Metropolitan Museum of Art: purchase, Whitney Fund (49.97.446)*

drawings. When RH at those levels is detected, turn on an electric fan to circulate and help to dry the air. At 68 to 70 percent relative humidity, the danger of mold growth is great. At that point, if there is no centrally operated equipment for lowering the moisture content in the immediate area, a portable dehumidifier should be obtained and put into operation. Inspect all framed prints and drawings and make sure air is circulating around them. Check for condensation along shelving. Move all artworks away from the source of the dampness, whether it is outside walls, leaky pipes, or anything else. Open any containers, closets, or vitrines in which moist air might be trapped or lingering. Place moisture-absorbing blotting paper on shelving or between stacked items. A blotting paper containing 67 percent silica gel by weight (Natrasorb SG145 desiccant paper) is also available, as are reusable desiccating canisters (Dri–Can). These in addition to silica gel and Art Sorb products are useful for dehumidifying small enclosed spaces. Current thinking suggests that, since mold cannot grow in RH of 45 to 55 percent, simply placing artworks in proper RH is the best way to prevent damage to them from mold growth.

If you observe mold growth or smell a musty odor, and it is impossible to remove the artworks to a drier environment, it may be appropriate to use thymol or some other fungicide to kill any active mold spores. Such chemicals must be handled with extreme caution and used only in emergencies; they are more toxic than was once supposed.[11] A design for a thymol cabinet recommended by the Center for Occupational Hazards is given in Appendix 3, with precautions and operating instructions.

Certain items should not be exposed to thymol fumes. These include works of art done in oil paints, synthetic resins, or varnishes, which thymol fumes soften. It has been suggested that thymol fumes cause parchment or vellum to become embrittled.[12] Photographs should not be placed in thymol cabinets except under the direction of a conservator specializing in the care of photographs. It is important to realize that fumigation with thymol or other fungicides will not remove mold growth, make it disappear, or prevent it from growing again if the art affected is returned to a humid environment. I have found that artworks may sometimes be exposed to thymol more for the psychological benefit of owners unwilling to grapple with the tedious problem of humidity control than for any real threat of mold growth to the art itself.

The vapors of naphthalene (moth balls) will also disinfect papers placed in an airtight container with some crystals of the chemical. The naphthalene crystals should never actually touch the art, as they can

cause oily stains. A three-week exposure period has been suggested.[13]
Like thymol, naphthalene has harmful vapors; it should not be inhaled,
and it should be handled as little as possible.[14] Naphthalene can recrys-
talize on nearby surfaces, in high concentrations.

Cabinets, closets, solander boxes, and framed pictures are sometimes
mistakenly provided with strips of thymol-impregnated papers (blotting
paper soaked in a 10 percent thymol/ethyl alcohol solution and allowed
to dry), to discourage mold growth. The preparation of these disinfec-
tant blotters presents hazards. It cannot be overstressed that thymol is a
chemical requiring special handling. Do not handle the crystals without
adequate protection in the form of a gas mask, solvent-resistant gloves,
and a fume hood. Because people should not breathe the fumes released
by the solution or the dried blotter strips, these strips cannot simply be
scattered indiscriminately throughout storage areas. Instead of using
such strips, ways of controlling the humidity should be explored.

In very high concentrations, thymol can even soften plastics. Thymol-
impregnated papers put into frames fitted with Plexiglas have caused
artworks to adhere to the softened and sticky plastic.

Thymol strips are recommended only in emergency situations when
damage to artworks from high humidity is imminent. Under such conditions as these, it is preferable to make fungicidal strips from a 10 percent
solution of o-phenyl phenol (Dowicide 1) in ethyl alcohol or sodium
o-phenyl phenate (Dowicide A) in water. Although these compounds are
less toxic than thymol they still must be handled with care. For guidelines, consult the literature listed at the end of Appendix 3.

Light

Light is another destructive force that must be reckoned with in
controlling the collection's environment. At this point, I should like to
suggest that the reader consult Thomas B. Brill's *Light: Its Interaction with
Art and Antiquities,* for a discussion of what light is. As Brill says, "efforts
made to explain light have produced the stormiest debates in . . . phys-
ics." The actions of light are intimately related to those of temperature
and humidity. Figures 1.21, 1.22, and 1.23 (see chapter 1) show papers
that have been damaged by light. Light-sensitive media include the
watercolors used in hand-colored prints, the inks in Japanese prints, iron
gall inks, modern colored inks made with aniline dyes, pastels, watercolors, gouache and the inks of felt-tipped pens and ball-point pens. The
effect of light on prints and drawings is twofold: it causes papers to
deteriorate, and it makes colors fade or otherwise change.

Serious deterioration of paper will occur in just two to four weeks of exposure to full sunlight. This breakdown is further aggravated by unstable fillers, sizings, and other noncellulosic components of paper. Papers containing lignin, such as newsprint, are especially light-sensitive and will very quickly darken.

Light, and especially certain wavelengths, attacks the long cellulose molecules, causing chain-breaking and the production of "chromophores," the color bodies that cause paper to appear yellow. Chain-breakage is responsible for brittleness in paper.

Air pollution, temperature, and humidity interact with light in complex ways. Oxygen and humidity promote the deterioration of cellulose and are also involved in the fading of colors. The interaction of water, air, and light has been extensively researched in the fading of dyes, which are used to make the media that are particularly light-sensitive. Thanks to research involving the textile industry, and especially the segment concerned with denim, we now have a tentative theory of fading as a self-generating cycle of decay.

Heat, often a product of light, acts as a catalyst. In the case of a newspaper left in the sun, heat is generated when light is absorbed by the paper. This speeds the breakdown of cellulose and hastens other chemical reactions within the paper. A fair rule of thumb is: for every rise in temperature of 10 degrees Centigrade, the rate of a chemical reaction doubles.

Damage to prints and drawings correlates positively with certain wavelengths of light, increases in the intensity of light, and increases in the duration of exposure to light. While all light is dangerous to art on paper, certain wavelengths are more harmful to paper and pigments than others. Ultraviolet light, 300 to 400 nanometers on the spectrum, is invisible to humans, but is especially destructive to prints and drawings. Because of ultraviolet light's invisibility to the human eye and its destructiveness to art on paper, we must learn how to measure it and how to remove it from our galleries and storerooms. Because it cannot be seen, the motivation for removing it is not always strong. Many people are under the impression that removing ultraviolet light means using colored lights or changing the color of the light emitted from existing fixtures. UV-free light is no different in color from light that is seen normally by the human eye; the appearance of displays under it does not change.

Ultraviolet light is found in high proportions in daylight and in slightly smaller proportions in fluorescent lighting. Most commonly encountered incandescent (tungsten) light bulbs do not produce appreciable amounts of ultraviolet light. The proportion of UV light contained in light sources is measured with a UV meter. A typical one will indicate whether the amount of UV light present is safe or whether filtration is necessary. (The standard against which this safe level is measured is the amount of UV light produced by a tungsten light bulb or 75 microwatts per lumen). If you do not own a UV meter, it is wise to assume that UV light is present in any gallery or storeroom illuminated by natural or fluorescent light.

Methods of removing UV light from galleries and storerooms include physically blocking out all daylight, removing fluorescent tubes, and substituting incandescent (tungsten) lights. If it is not possible to block out daylight or replace fluorescent lights, UV filters should be installed. Exterior windows and skylights can also be treated with a UV-filtering film adhered directly to the glass, a job for a professional. Films can also be applied to the glass of display cases. Flexible blinds made of UV-filtering film can be hung in windows. These are quite inconspicuous, especially if they are placed behind translucent curtains. Panels of rigid UV-filtering acrylic can be positioned in front of windows or suspended below skylights. Cylinders of similar filtering material can be slipped around fluorescent tubing.

Prints and drawings can be framed behind ultraviolet-filtering acrylic except in instances where static may interfere with fragile paint layers or powdery media. The tinted acrylic (UF–3, OP–2) removes almost 100 percent of harmful ultraviolet rays, but because of its color, which most often remains unnoticed, tinted ultraviolet filtering acrylic sheeting may not be suitable for framing very pale drawings on very white paper. Instead, the colorless ultraviolet-filtering acrylic (UF–4, formerly called UF–1), slightly less effective in stopping the transmission of ultraviolet light, can be substituted. These types of rigid acrylic sheeting are available through framers and distributors of plastics. Plastics containing ultraviolet filtering compounds should be inspected periodically for haziness or bubbles and also for filtering efficiency.

The intensity of the light to which art on paper is exposed in general is another important factor that contributes to light damage. Again, we must use instruments to measure it, because the human eye is not reliable. The eye very quickly adjusts to available illumination. For example, when one comes into a dimly lit room from outdoors, the room appears darker than it really is.

Light intensity is usually measured in footcandles, lumens, or in lux (lux and lumen units prevail in Europe). Light meters that translate readings directly into footcandles are highly recommended for measuring illuminance. The Gossen Panlux Electronic Footcandle Meter is one. Photographic meters can also be used, but it must be kept in mind that these are not as accurate as meters designed especially for measuring footcandles. When photographic meters are used, footcandles can usually be calculated according to formula supplied by the manufacturer, or by the following: Set ASA scale to 100. Set the f-stop scale to f5.6. Take a reading from a white card held in front of the artwork. The indicated shutter speed will be equal to the footcandles. To measure incident light, hold the sensor in the same location and at the same angle as the artwork. Do not tilt the sensor toward the lights. Make sure that your body is not casting a shadow over the sensor. Slowly move the sensor from the center of the sheet toward the edges. This will detect "hot spots" from uneven illumination.

The proper level of illumination for prints and drawings has been much debated. It has been generally agreed that 5 to 8 footcandles are acceptable for displaying artworks on paper for *limited amounts of time.* This figure represents an uneasy compromise between the need to exhibit an object and the desire to protect it. Most museums in America and Europe now have lighting restrictions of 5 to 10 footcandles (50 to 100 lux or lumens) for prints and drawings. Light intensity can be minimized by placing shutters, blinds, or curtains over windows, draping display cases, lowering the wattage of the light bulbs used, using fewer lighting fixtures, placing gauze draperies under skylights, manipulating movable screens, and so forth. Used creatively, these protective measures can enhance an exhibition area and provide some measure of greater safety from light damage to art on paper.

To monitor lighting conditions, many museums use simple and inexpensive "fadometers" made of several strips of blue wool attached to a card. The wool strips quickly react to light. Each strip of wool is calibrated to fade at a certain rate and can thus be used to measure the amount of light that has fallen on an art object. It must be remembered, however, that these fading cards are only useful if they are regularly examined. More important, if a fading card registers a change, a permanent change has likewise occurred in the work of art, even if the change is not readily apparent. Therefore, fading blue wool strips on cards may be more appropriate for evaluating the safety of lighting conditions in display areas *before* the artworks are actually installed.[15]

Regardless of the type of light selected, works of art on paper should never be permanently displayed. A prudent policy might provide for a maximum of three months of exposure per year under the lighting restrictions described above. Accurate records of exposure times may be kept, if not on catalog cards, then on backs of frames or penciled inside mats. When artworks are requested for loan, the duration of the loan and the past exposure records of the objects will be important considerations, as are the lighting conditions of the borrowing institutions (not to mention the extent of their control over temperature and humidity). Exposure times can be kept down by installing automatic timers in little-used rooms, by turning on gallery lights only during exhibition hours, or by covering display cases with cloths that can be pushed to one side.

To many people, the lighting restrictions enforced by museums and galleries seem unnecessarily conservative. It has been claimed that restrictions have been adopted arbitrarily. Inasmuch as the behavior of pigments and their paper supports cannot accurately be predicted in all instances, this complaint may to some extent be true. It must be remembered, however, that fading is irreversible.

There is a popular—and persuasive—argument that works of art can be truly appreciated only when they are bathed in all the delicate nuances of natural daylight. I can agree with that, in theory; however, the sight of a magnificent Winslow Homer watercolor faded to a shadow of its former self by having been displayed in natural daylight is more than enough repudiation for that point of view.

The importance of controlling the type, intensity, and duration of light that strikes prints and drawings cannot be stressed enough. It is wise to issue periodic reminders to lighting engineers, consultants, maintenance people, and other museum staff members, emphasizing that light can shorten the life of prints and drawings and that they can be irreparably damaged by what might be considered no more than a normal amount of light over extended periods of time.

Insects and Rodents

An improperly maintained environment may also prove inviting to insects and rodents. Figures 1.36 and 1.37 (chapter 1) illustrate the damage that insects can cause. The most common insect enemies of paper are termites, cockroaches, silverfish, book lice, and bookworms. They are attracted not only to the paper, but also to glues, sizes, and certain media. Insects can cause damage very quickly, and infestations should be dealt with promptly. Once that is done, regular, thorough good housekeeping procedures can help to keep collections areas free of such pests by eliminating the damp, dark places they love as habitats and by keeping the area clear of any stray bits of organic matter on which they might feed. Humidity control and regular cleaning of storerooms, closets, and cabinets are essential. Obviously, no food should be permitted in these areas. Only if the problem persists are more serious measures warranted.

Insecticides are not new. Pliny wrote that books of papyrus entombed for 535 years with citrus leaves had been found to be in excellent condition. During the Ming and Ching dynasties in China, sheets of paper coated with lead compounds were bound into books to protect them from moths. A traditional Japanese yellow dye made from the bark of the kihada tree has also been proven effective in warding off insects. In the past, arsenic has been used to disinfect paper pulp and textiles— with deadly effects for everyone involved. Exposure of artifacts to sub-freezing temperatures is one modern approach to insect control.

Any insecticide or rodent poison selected for museum use must be safe for people as well as for art on paper.

Even insecticides considered safe for use by museum personnel must never come into contact with prints and drawings. Always follow the manufacturer's instructions. Avoid touching or breathing the chemical, and keep it away from food. As a result of government restrictions, insecticides sold over the counter in spray cans kill insects only on contact and therefore do not prevent future infestations. Sources of information include the local office of the Occupational Safety and Health Administration, the Center for Occupational Hazards in New York City, and Harvard University's Office of Environmental Health and Safety.[16] In addition, several highly worthwhile seminars and short courses have been sponsored—and continue to be held—by state agencies, universities, and conservation associations. Announcements of these seminars usually appear in museum-and-conservation-related periodicals.

Naphthalene has traditionally been used as an insect repellent in museums. Naphthalene crystals can be put into closets, cases, or other closed spaces, but they should not be sprinkled at random in open storage areas where people work. The concentration of vapors may become dangerously high when crystals are used in small, enclosed spaces and it should be kept in mind that naphthalene can also recrystal-lize on nearby surfaces in high concentrations. For this reason, it is advisable to wear a respirator fitted with organic vapor cartridges when the chemical is present in such areas, to prevent nasal irritation and headaches. Guidelines for selecting a respirator may be found in Michael McCann's article listed in "Further Reading."

Paradichlorobenzene has been used in the same way as naphthalene for many years. Questions have recently been raised concerning its generation of chlorine gas in high concentrations. Very little information is available on the subject at this point. Better to banish all insecticides containing chlorine from proximity to prints and drawings.

Pyrethrum is an insecticide that has been recommended for use in public buildings because of its low toxicity. Like naphthalene, pyrethrum can be used in storage cases and in small enclosed areas not frequented by people.

In storerooms, offices, and public spaces, roach traps and other sticky tapes containing insecticides can be used. They are not generally toxic, but they should not be handled carelessly.

Items entering collections often look suspect. Old moldy scrapbooks, worm-eaten frames and bindings, piles of papers, and so forth, can be carriers for insects. Many institutions have fumigation boxes located in the vicinity of entering material. These boxes can be constructed in-house. They should be airtight and large enough to accommodate a variety of items. Respirators should be used by people opening and closing the box. The insecticide used within can be naphthalene or pyrethrum.[17]

Two other alternatives to solving insect problems are vacuum fumigation chambers and fogging. Both involve the services of a professional exterminator. To select a reliable firm, talk to other museums or institutions similar to yours. Ask about their arrangements and find out whether the program has been effective. Consult with the conservators if they supervised the project. The exterminator of your choice should be a member of a national or local pest control association. Each state requires exterminators to be registered and certified. Information on exterminating services can be obtained by writing to the National Pest Control Association.

Vacuum fumigation chambers using ethylene oxide, methyl bromide, or sulfuryl fluoride are not routinely necessary for works of art on paper. In most instances, insects and their eggs can easily be detected and can be brushed away from prints and drawings. Occasionally, frames containing burrowed-in larvae or beetles enter a collection. These insects can be dealt with using over-the-counter preparations placed with the frame in an air-tight container. If the frame has no archival value, simply dispose of it entirely. Obviously, vacuum fumigation chambers are in order for institutions processing large numbers of items, such as the Library of Congress.

Fumigation chambers must be operated by trained personnel, according to strict governmental regulations. Such chambers are also very expensive and require a location away from personnel work areas. Ethylene oxide is lethal, and precautions must therefore be taken to ensure that objects fumigated with it do not continue to exude gases when they are returned to storage and that they do not form poisons by secondary reactions. These dangerous aftereffects of fumigation are being investigated. If your institution routinely fumigates with ethylene oxide, purchase small ETO monitors or alarms that can be placed near the objects treated or that can be worn by workers.[18] Because of the potential health hazards associated with ethylene oxide, some museums have ceased using it completely and are exploring nonchemical methods of insect control. A publication on the safe use of ethylene oxide is available from the Health Industries Manufacturers Association in Washington, D.C.[19] The Occupational Safety and Health Administration (OSHA) has published its final standard on *Occupational Exposure to Ethylene Oxide* in the Federal Register, June 22, 1984.

Methyl bromide or sulfuryl fluoride can also be used in vacuum fumigation chambers. Methyl bromide should not be used for parchment or photographs.[20] Both are toxic and must be used according to strict regulations.

An entire gallery or storeroom can be fogged by professionals or by a trained staff member. Pyrethrum is the usual chemical used for this because of its relatively low toxicity. Nonetheless, even with pyrethrum, the room must be emptied and sealed, with adequate precautions taken to protect other workers in the building. Works of art should not be left unprotected during this procedure.

Fumigation should never be approached lightly. It is essential to know which fumigation methods have been found safe and effective for museum collections and their personnel.

Environmental control is much easier if everyone participates. All staff members should be routinely on the lookout for unsafe conditions in galleries and storerooms: automobile exhaust fumes entering through a back window or ventilating duct, a curtain left open, a leaky pipe, an overflowing dehumidifier, and insects or their debris. Everyone must be aware that environmental control is an essential part of caring for art on paper, both in storage and on exhibition.

NOTES

1. One system of vertical map storage has been suggested by Joanne M. Perry, "Vertical Map Storage," *Special Libraries* 73:3 (July 1982): 207–212. The system she proposes does not, however, supply support for the items in each file, and it uses acidic materials to make the folders. With modifications, it might nonetheless be acceptable for oversized works of art.

2. Thea Jirat-Wasiutynski, "Architectural Drawings and Prints: Materials and Storage," *Association of Canadian Archivists Bulletin* 8:3 (May 1983): 10.

3. Marjorie B. Cohn, *Wash and Gouache: A Study of the Development of the Materials of Watercolor* (Cambridge, Mass.: Fogg Art Museum, 1977), p. 61, n. 2.

4. This practical suggestion was made by Anne F. Clapp, whose book, listed in the general bibliography, contains an excellent section on environmental problems and solutions.

5. P. Michael Bottomley, "Conservation and Storage: Archival Paper," in *Manual of Curatorship,* edited by John M. A. Thompson (London: Butterworth, 1984), p. 240.

6. See Garry Thomson, *The Museum Environment* (London: Butterworth, 1978), p. 149; Carl Wessel, "Environmental Factors Affecting the Permanence of Library Materials," in *Deterioration of Library Materials,* ed. Howard W. Winger and Richard Daniel Smith (Chicago: University of Chicago Press, 1970), p. 78. There are no hard-and-fast rules in the science of climate control. Many practical suggestions are available from the American Society of Heating, Refrigeration, and Air Conditioning Engineers.

7. Thomson, *The Museum Environment* contains a more sophisticated description of particulate filters.

8. Michele V. Cloonan, "An Analysis of Dust Cloths for Library Materials," *Abbey Newsletter* 7:3 (July 1983): 35.

9. *The Hygrothermograph,* HTS-8 (Washington, D.C.: Smithsonian Institution, Office of Museum Programs Audiovisual Program Co-ordinator, n.d.), contains eighty slides and script.

10. Bottomley, "Conservation and Storage: Archival Paper," p. 240.

11. In preparation for work with thymol, read Deborah Nagin and Michael McCann, *Thymol and o-phenyl Phenol: Safe Work Practices"* (New York: Center for Occupational Hazards, 1982). The publisher will answer written and telephone inquiries about health hazards in fumigation.

12. See Anne F. Clapp, *The Curatorial Care of Works of Art on Paper,* 3d rev. ed. (Oberlin: Intermuseum Conservation Association, 1978), p. 38.

13. Clapp, *Curatorial Care of Works of Art on Paper,* p. 58.

14. A fact sheet on naphthalene is available from Harvard University, Environmental Health and Safety, Industrial Hygiene Department.

15. Robert L. Feller and Ruth Johnston-Feller, "Use of the International Standards Organization's blue-wool standards for exposure to Light. I. Use as an integrating light monitor for illumination under museum conditions" (Preprints of papers presented at the Sixth Annual Meeting of the American Institute for Conservation of Historic and Artistic Works, Washington, D.C., 1978), pp. 73–80.

16. *Safe Pest Control Procedures for Museum Collections* and *Pest Control in Museums* are both useful sources of information. Appendix F in the latter work lists the personnel in each state who are in charge of pest control. It also lists the regional office of the Environmental Protection Agency and the Occupational Safety and Health Administration. For information regarding a specific pesticide, consult the manufacturer or the *Pesticide Handbook (Entoma),* ed. Robert Caswell, Kathleen DeBold, and Lorraine Gilbert, 29th ed. (College Park, Md.: Entomological Society of America, 1981–1982). Also see "Pest Control Roundup: Guide to Manufacturers and Suppliers of Products and Systems for Treating and Eliminating Insects and Bugs in Cultural Facilities," *Technology and Conservation of Art, Architecture, and Antiquities* 8:1 (Spring 1983): 25–26.

17. Ward gives a design for a simple fumigation box in *Getting the Bugs Out,* Museum Methods Manual 4 (Vancouver: British Columbia Provincial Museum, 1976), p. 13.

18. 3M manufactures the Ethylene Oxide Monitor 3550, Occupational Health and Safety Division. Audiovisual alarms are made by American Sterilizer Company, Erie, Pennsylvania.

19. James F. Jorasky, ed., *The Safe Use of Ethylene Oxide* (Washington, D.C.: Health Industries Manufacturers Association, December 1980).

20. A brochure on the safe use of methyl bromide is available from Dow Chemical U.S.A., Midland, Michigan.

FURTHER READING

Amdur, Elias J. "Humidity Control: Isolated Area Plan." *Museum News* 43:4 (December 1964): 58–50.

Bachmann, Konstanze. *Basic Principles of Storage*. Bulletin 1. New York: New York State Conservation Consultancy, 1982.

Bottomley, P. Michael. "Conservation and Storage: Archival Paper." In *Manual of Curatorship*, edited by John M. A. Thompson, pp. 239–244. London: Butterworth, 1984.

Brawne, Michael. *The Museum Interior: Temporary and Permanent Display Techniques*. New York: Architectural Book Publishing Co., 1982.

Brill, Thomas. *Light: Its Interaction with Art and Antiquities*. New York: Plenum Press, 1980.

Brommelle, Norman S. "Museum Lighting, III: Aspects of the Effects of Light on Deterioration." *Museums Journal* 62:1 (June 1962): 337–346.

———. "Technical Services: Air Conditioning and Lighting from the Point of View of Conservation." *Museums Journal* 63:1, 2 (June–September 1963): 32–36.

Buck, Richard D. "A Specification for Museum Airconditioning," *Museum News* 43:4 (December 1964): 53–57.

Cameron, Duncan. "Environmental Control: A Theoretical Solution." *Museum News* 46:9 (May 1968): 17–22.

Carpenter, Jane M., and Pamela B. Hatchfield. *Formaldehyde: How Great Is the Danger to Museum Collections?* Cambridge: Center for Conservation and Technical Studies, Harvard University Art Museums, 1985.

Chapman, Joseph. "Fire." *Museum News* 50:5 (January 1972): 32–35.

Douglas, R. Alan. "A Commonsense Approach to Environmental Control." *Curator* 15:2 (June 1972): 139–144.

Edwards, Stephen R., Bruce M. Bell, and Mary Elizabeth King, eds. *Pest Control in Museums*." Lawrence, Kans.: Association of Systematics Collections, 1981.

Feller, Robert L. "Control of Deteriorating Effects of Light on Museum Objects." *Museum* 17:2 (1964): 57–98.

———. "Control of Deteriorating Effects of Light on Museum Objects: Heating Effects of Illumination by Incandescent Lamps." *Museum News* 46:9 (May 1968): 39–47.

———. "The Deteriorating Effect of Light on Museum Objects: Principles of Photochemistry, The Effect on Varnishes and Paint Vehicles and on Paper." *Museum News* 42:10 (June 1964): i–viii.

Fennelly, Lawrence. *Museum, Archive and Library Security*. London: Butterworth, 1982.

Fisher, Walter R. "Fire Safety Systems: Protecting Our Treasures from Threat of Fire." *Technology and Conservation of Art, Architecture, and Antiquities* 1:2 (Fall 1976): 14–17.

Guichen, Gael de. *Climate in Museums: Measurement*. Rome: International Centre for the Study of the Preservation and the Restoration of Cultural Property (ICCROM), 1980.

Hilberry, John D., and Susan Kalb Weinberg. "Museum Collections Storage." *Museum News* 59:5 (March–April 1981): 7–21; 59:6 (May–June 1981): 5–23; 59:7 (July–August 1981): 49–60 [Reprinted as a pamphlet by the American Association of Museums]

Johnson, E. Verner, and Joanne Horgan. *Museum Collection Storage.* Technical Handbook 2. Paris: UNESCO, 1979.

Keck, Caroline K. "Conservation's Cloudy Future." *Museum News* 58:5 (May–June 1980): 35–39.

_____. "On Conservation: Relative Humidity Controls." *Museum News* 50:8 (April 1972): 13–14.

Keck, Caroline K., Huntington T. Block, Joseph Chapman, John B. Lawton, and Nathan Stolow. *A Primer on Museum Security.* New York: New York State Historical Association, 1966.

Lafontaine, R.H. *Recommended Environmental Monitors for Museums, Archives, and Art Galleries.* Ottawa: Canadian Conservation Institute, 1975.

Library of Congress. *Environmental Protection of Books and Related Materials.* Preservation leaflet 2. Washington D.C., 1975.

_____. *Polyester Film Encapsulation.* Wshington, D.C., 1980.

Lull, William P., and Linda E. Merk. "Lighting for Storage of Museum Collections: Developing a System for Safekeeping of Light-sensitive Materials." *Technology and Conservation* 7:2 (Summer 1982): 20–25.

Lusk, Carroll B. "Museum Lighting: Parts I–III." *Museum News* 49:3 (November 1970): 20–23; 49:4 (December 1970): 25–29; 49:6 (February 1971): 18–22.

McAusland, Jane. "Conservation and Storage: Prints, Drawings, and Water-Colours." in *Manual of Curatorship,* edited by John M. A. Thompson, pp. 245–262. London: Butterworth, 1984.

McCann, Michael. *Respirator Use in Conservation Laboratories.* New York: Center for Occupational Hazards, 1986.

McGiffin, Robert F., Jr. "A Current Status Report on Fumigation in Museums and Historical Societies." AASLH Technical Report no. 4. Nashville: The American Association for State and Local History, 1985.

Miles, Catherine E. "Wood Coatings for Display and Storage Cases." *Studies in Conservation* 31 (1986): 114–124.

Musgrove, Stephen W. "A New Look at Fire Protection." *Museum News* 62:6 (August 1984): 11–16.

National Fire Protection Association. *Fire Protection by Halons.* SPP–26. Quincy, Mass., 1975.

_____. *Fire Protection Handbook.* FPH1581. Quincy, Mass., 1981.

_____. *Fire Safety Self-Inspection Form for Museums.* Quincy, Mass., 1976.

_____. *Portable Fire Extinguishers: Installation, Maintenance, and Use.* NFPA 10. Quincy, Mass., 1974.

_____. *Protection of Museum Collections.* NFPA 911. Quincy, Mass., 1974.

Paine, Shelley Reisman. "Basic Principles for Controlling Environmental Conditions in Historic Agencies and Museums." AASLH Technical Report No. 3. Nashville: The American Association for State and Local History, 1985.

Peltz, Perri, and Monona Rossol. *Safe Pest Control Procedures for Museum Collections.* New York: Center for Occupational Hazards, 1983.

Perkinson, Roy. "On Conservation: Lighting Works of Art on Paper." *Museum News* 53:3 (November 1974): 5–7.

Plenderleith, H. J., and P. Philipott. "Climatology and Conservation in Museums." *Museum* 13:4 (1960): 243–289.

Shelley, Marjorie. *Storage of Archival Documents and Works of Art on Paper.* Bulletin 2. New York: New York State Conservation Consultancy, 1983.

Stolow, Nathan. "Action of Environment on Museum Objects, Part I: Humidity, Temperature, Atmospheric Pollution." *Curator* 9:3 (September 1966): 175–185.

————. "The Action of Environment on Museum Objects, Part II: Light." *Curator* 9:4 (December 1966): 298–306.

————. "Fundamental Case Design for Humidity Sensitive Museum Collections." *Museum News* 44:6 (February 1966): 45:52.

————. "The Microclimate: A Localized Solution." *Museum News* 56:2 (November–December 1977): 52–63.

Thomson, Garry. "Air Pollution—A Review for Conservation Chemists." *Studies in Conservation* 10:4 (November 1965): 147–167.

————. *Museum Climatology.* London: International Institute for Conservation, 1967.

————. *The Museum Environment.* London: Butterworth, 1978.

————. "Some Hints on Measurement and Control of Climate in Historic Houses." In *Conservation within Historic Buildings,* pp. 6–8. London: International Institute for Conservation of Historic and Artistic Works, 1980.

Tillotson, Robert G. *Museum Security.* Trans. Marthe de Moltke. Paris: International Council of Museums, 1977.

Tiszkus, Alphonse T., and E. G. Dressler. "Fire Protection Planning for Cultural Institutions: Blending Risk Management, Loss Prevention, and Physical Safeguards." *Technology and Conservation of Art, Architecture, and Antiquities* 5:2 (Summer 1980): 18–23.

Trinkhaus-Randall, Gregor. *Effects of the Environment on Paper: A Review of Recent Literature.* Technical Leaflet 128. Nashville: The American Association for State and Local History, July 1980.

Ward, Philip R. *Getting the Bugs Out.* Museum Methods Manual 4. British Columbia Provincial Museum, 1976.

Weiss, Susan E. "Proper Exhibition Lighting: Protecting Collections from Damage." *Technology and Conservation* 2:1 (Spring 1977): 20–25.

Wessel, Carl J. "Environmental Factors Affecting the Permanence of Library Materials." *Deterioration and Preservation of Library Materials,* ed. Howard W. Winger and Richard Daniel Smith, pp. 39–84. Chicago: University of Chicago Press, 1970.

Williamson, Samuel J., and Herman Z. Cummins. *Light and Color in Nature and Art.* New York: John Wiley, 1983.

Note: A Museum Environment Test Kit is available from the Arizona Commission on the Arts for one-week rentals. It contains an instruction manual by Barbara Moore and Robert Herskovitz and a copy of *The Museum Environment,* by Garry Thompson, plus a meter for measuring ultraviolet light, a footcandle meter for incident light, a psychrometer, and blue-scale fading cards. Write to the Arizona Commission on the Arts, 2024 North 7th Street, Suite 201, Phoenix, Arizona 85006.

5

Basic Conservation Procedures

Examination of Prints and Drawings

ALL INCOMING ART should be examined to determine the nature and causes of any existing problems, to propose a method of handling such problems and eliminating the causes, if possible, and to repair any existing damage. Even if no conservation treatment is immediately required, routine examination reports will provide points of reference in the future, should the condition of the objects change. On a day-to-day basis, examination reports are useful for quick reference. For instance, if an item is requested for loan, a look at its examination report will show whether the item can be lent, to begin with, and if so, whether it has special requirements that would affect its travel or exhibition arrangements.

Every object in a collection should be examined periodically, with continuing records kept of its condition. Ideally, conservation inventories of collections should be conducted every few years. Unfortunately, few institutions have the staff and the time for regular collections surveys. If that is true of your collection, initial and "special-event" examination reports at least can be compiled when objects enter the collection, when they are requested for loan, or when they go into an in-house exhibition.

Routine observance on the part of vigilant guards, technicians, installers, volunteers, and curatorial staff can help keep all staff people alert to evidence of damage to prints and drawings, which should be promptly examined on being reported. Everyone on the staff should be familiar with the common conservation problems of prints and drawings. Information on routine points to check in examining a work of art appears in chapter 1 and could be useful as a checklist for conducting a conservation inventory. The examination of each work of art can be

done more quickly—and the entire collection examined more uniformly—if such a checklist is followed. A comprehensive list of symptoms should help the examiner note and identify most problems, and a
quick look at the index of this book will provide the numbers of pages
that carry information on suitable ways of dealing with such problems
and their causes.

Suppose, for example, that a pen-and-ink study for a painting in your
collection has been donated to your institution. Using the checklist
compiled from the information in chapter 1, you examine the study and
note that dark rectangles appear in one area of the design. On closer
examination, you observe that the back of the drawing has been repaired
with pressure-sensitive tape, which has caused staining in the same area.
A dark line of discoloration surrounds the design—mat burn, indicating
that poor-quality wood pulp board was used in framing the piece. Small
dark spots, or foxing, extend over most of the paper support, and a
water stain appears along the lower edge. These symptoms suggest that
the drawing was stored or displayed in a humid environment and may
have suffered from actual water damage. Indeed, as you consult your
unframing notes, you recall that the framing materials, now discarded,
were somewhat damp and moldy. Since the drawing is done in pen and
ink, you turn to the index for help in finding information on pen-and-
ink drawings. There you learn that the drawing was very likely repaired
with tape, in the first place, because what you have determined to be the
iron gall ink used by the artist had eaten through the paper support; the
tape was added for reinforcement.

By using the book in this way, you can identify most common problems of works of art on paper and find information that will be helpful in
dealing with them.

A work of art *must* be thoroughly examined *before* any conservation
procedures are carried out. Finally, and perhaps most important, the
thorough and periodic examination of prints and drawings serves many
useful purposes.

Data to be Recorded

Examination reports vary a great deal in format and can be more or
less detailed. Some have been published and can be adapted according to
individual needs.[1] Remember, as you assess changes in the condition of
works in your collection, that more detailed information will be of
greater help in the future than terse and general comment.

An examination report should include the following information:

1. Identification of the object (artist, title, accession number, collectors' marks, signature, labels, stamps, seals, inscriptions, other distinguishing marks).

2. Description of the artwork and its components (outside dimensions, plate mark dimensions, paper type, medium and technique used, frame, framing materials, unframing notations, mat, hinges).

3. Description of condition (paper losses, flaking, skinning, tears, breaks, buckling, creases, discoloration, fading, accretions, scratches, brittleness).

4. Evidence of past treatment (repairs, lining, dry mounting, use of fixatives, cosmetic restorations).

5. Date of examination and name of examiner.

6. Proposed treatment if it is to be done in-house, by examiner: problems to be treated, materials to be used. If artwork is to be examined by a conservator, for more involved treatment, that should be indicated on initial examination report.

7. Signature of official custodian acknowledging proposed treatment.

8. Record of treatment: date, name of individual doing the treatment, materials used.

9. Photographic documentation.

The above description of information to be included in an examination report is based on that outlined in Section IV, Part II, *Standards of Practice*, of the AIC *Code of Ethics*. First drawn up in 1963 and revised in 1979, the *Code of Ethics and Standards of Practice* presents the accepted criteria for the practice of conservation by its professional members. A similar examination report including the same information in more detail should be provided by conservators to whom works of art are taken for treatment.

Examination Area and Procedure

The area in which works of art are examined should be well lit, uncluttered, and scrupulously clean. A large working surface is essential. That surface should be covered with clean blotters, with ready replacements kept at hand. In addition to a pencil (and pencil notations are preferred to those made with a pen, for these examinations) and the examination form, you should work with a ruler (either a twenty-inch or a forty-inch one, whichever is appropriate), calibrated in centimeters and in inches; a magnifying glass or a headband magnifying loupe (Optivisor); and a small stainless steel microspatula. If a tape measure is used, it should lock, to prevent unexpected retractions.

Remove the unframed print or drawing from its acid-free folder, together with any labels from the frame and your unframing notations. If you have been unable to separate the artwork from its mount or mat, include that information in your report. Complete the examination form, keeping the actual manipulation of the artwork to a minimum. Measure the piece's greatest dimensions—and *do not rest the ruler on the art.* If the shape of the piece is irregular, note that fact and illustrate the note by drawing in on the report a small diagram for clarity. Also note the dimensions of any plate marks evident. Transcribe all information from any labels and unframing notes. Set labels aside to be encapsulated. When you have finished with the front of the piece, carefully turn it over. The microspatula can lift a corner of the sheet so that you do not need to pull it up with your fingers. Always turn the paper support sheet over while holding it by at least two corners. If the artwork is brittle or weak, it should be examined in its acid-free folder. To turn it face down, close the folder and turn the entire package over. The folder will provide the piece with overall support.

The surface of pastel, charcoal, and chalk drawings should be protected by glassine or silk tissue during examination of the reverse side. Pastels with exceptionally powdery surfaces and works with flaking paint should obviously not be turned over at all.

Describe the artwork and its condition as accurately as possible, so that future examiners will be able to focus better on what you have observed and make a clear assessment of any changes. You may find the word *discoloration* clear enough, but other observers may not know exactly where the discoloration is, how severe it is, what may have caused it, and so on. A magnifying glass may be useful for examining defects, as well as for determining the medium used and the technique of the artist.

When you are handling a work of art, avoid touching it with your fingers as much as possible, especially within the design area, and—as mentioned earlier—wash your hands frequently.

Photographs as Part of Record

A photograph of each work of art examined should be part of the examination record. Even if you are not particularly adept as a photographer, you can take adequate record photographs. Ideally, a small photography area should be permanently set up in your offices or storeroom. Before you invest in expensive photographic equipment, however, discuss your needs with a professional photographer. The equipment does not have to be elaborate, but it should include a 4-by-5 view camera or a 35mm camera with a lens of good quality, a light meter, a tripod, lights (tungsten lamps are most practical), light stands, and a copy stand or an easel for the art to rest on while being photographed.[2]

A safe and convenient method of securing prints and drawings so that they can be photographed is to attach them to a board covered with Velcro cloth and held steady by an easel. Soft Velcro woven nylon "loop cloth" in a neutral color may be wrapped around a homosote or other lightweight board and stapled to the back. The print is positioned as the board lies flat on a table. Velcro "hook tape," available in either small strips or half-inch circles, is used to hold each corner or edge of the art in place. The board, with the art attached, is then slowly lifted into a vertical position. Confirm *first* that the art is secure; *then* place board and art on the easel. A gray scale or color scale photographed alongside the object is useful in assessing exposure times and color accuracy, as well as dimensional scale of the artwork.

Photograph the work of art itself; then, if its medium permits, photograph the reverse side of it, as well. Take close-ups of conservation problems, which can be recorded with greater precision by rearranging lights. Because photographic lamps produce heat, leave them on as briefly as possible and turn them off between shots. Be particularly cautious when photographing parchment, which reacts quickly to both temperature and humidity changes.

Photography should be considered a kind of conservation procedure. During picture-taking, the artwork should receive the same careful handling required at any time it is moved. Throughout the time it is being photographed, the artwork should be manipulated as little as possible. Always support the artwork with its acid-free folder, its mat, or a sheet of acid-free cardboard; *never dangle it by one corner.* If the surface of the work is powdery or otherwise sensitive, protect it with a piece of glassine or smooth silk tissue whole photographing the back of it. Wash your hands frequently.

A work so fragile that it cannot be lifted vertically can be positioned and photographed horizontally on a copy stand—or even on the floor. The photographer may have trouble positioning the camera, however, for a horizontal shot, and increased precautions against accident should be taken when this is done.

Because photographs serve as valuable records for a number of years, they should be archivally processed and stored properly. Archival processing may be difficult to obtain consistently, especially if developing and printing are done by a commercial establishment. If you are fortunate enough to have a darkroom in-house, you can follow published guidelines for archival processing.[3] Black-and-white prints archivally processed and properly stored are the most permanent type of photographic record. Color slides are generally considered to be impermanent. Their color accuracy can be preserved longer if they are stored away from heat and light in pure polyester sleeves or acid-free paper envelopes and are projected as little as possible.

Photographs and slides should be promptly identified, as soon as they are received after processing. Artist, title, accession number, and other pertinent information, such as date and purpose of the photo, may be obvious to the individual who photographed the art or ordered it photographed, but for someone seeing it for the first time, with no information about it, a photograph of the back of an unidentified drawing can be not only frustrating, but totally pointless. It is especially important to note when the photograph was taken and whether any type of treatment is to follow. Any special lighting arrangements used should also be noted. *When writing on the backs of photographic prints, use a lead pencil with a very soft lead; place the print face down on a hard surface—glass, for instance—to avoid embossing it, and never use a ball-point pen.*

If photographs and slides are stored separately from examination reports, indicating their location or negative numbers on the report will be a very worthwhile time-saver in finding them for future reference.

Dry-Cleaning Prints and Drawings

After examining the artwork thoroughly, you will usually have a good idea of the conservation treatment it requires. One of the most common procedures performed on prints and drawings is *surface cleaning*, otherwise known as *dry-cleaning*.

Prints and drawings are often covered with a thin all-over layer of grime, or they may be soiled from handling. Dust, soot, salts, silica crystals, textile fibers, accidental marks, and other foreign matter are inevitably deposited on artworks by air pollution and human contact.

Such surface dirt should be removed, not only for aesthetic reasons, but also to eliminate it as a source of damage to the art itself. Dirt is abrasive. It may also be acidic and hygroscopic, helping to nurture mold spores, which it also carries.

Procedure

To begin this delicate surface cleaning, place the art on a spotlessly clean surface and assemble the tools you will need: a very soft-bristled brush; an air bulb, available from photographic supply stores; a drafting brush; a good supply of 3-x-6-inch blotter squares, the same as used for hinging; weights; a stainless steel spatula; and crumbled erasers. For crumbled erasers, *drafting powder* (Opaline, Skum-X) can be used, or you yourself can make an eraser powder by finely grating white vinyl erasers (Magic Rub). It should be noted that drafting powders can contain pumice, which is too abrasive for softer papers. Also, if drafting powder is used, it should be fresh—because, as it ages, its soft particles become dry and gritty. A powder made with grated white vinyl eraser particles provides more gentle cleaning.

Before you begin, you must ascertain whether the artwork can tolerate the mechanical action of dry-cleaning. Brittle papers that cannot easily be handled should not be dry-cleaned. Heavy-handed cleaning can make slight tears and fold lines worse. Design areas are generally to be avoided in this procedure. Powdery media and heavily printed areas must plainly also not be subjected to overall dry-cleaning.

It is also important, *before* you begin this kind of cleaning, to determine whether the surface character of the paper supporting the art will be altered by dry-cleaning. With unsized paper and other extremely soft papers—most tissues, for example—even slight rubbing will pull up fibers and roughen the surface. Highly polished "parchment" papers can be dulled by rubbing, and colors sometimes offset easily. Always test the effects of any erasing technique in an inconspicuous corner of the artwork before proceeding. *Permanent damage in the form of mottling and haloing can result from a too-vigorous dry-cleaning.*

Begin the dry-cleaning procedure by gently blowing away any loose surface dirt on the face of the art with the photographer's bulb blower. Follow that by going over the surface with the soft brush—a soft Japanese brush about three inches wide is ideal. Brush from the center of the item out toward the edges. Use *very* light pressure and be especially cautious near powdery design areas. Brushing should be so light that the paper does not move. Very thin papers can be held in place under a blotter square secured with one's fingers. As dust accumulates around the working surface, whisk it away with the drafting brush. Do not use the drafting brush on the art; its bristles are too stiff.

If the artwork remains dirty, after the surface has been carefully blown and lightly brushed, try the next step in the dry-cleaning process: use a powdered eraser, such as Opaline or Skum-X, available from art supply stores. Opaline comes in a small, open-weave bag, in which it is ordinarily used. To clean prints and drawings, however, it is better to cut the bag open and use the eraser crumbs directly on the paper. Sprinkle a small amount of eraser crumbs onto the area to be cleaned. Working around sensitive design areas, lightly roll the eraser crumbs in a circular motion with your clean fingertips. As the eraser powder turns gray, blow or gently brush it away and apply more fresh crumbs from the bag. So that your hands remain free, secure the art in place with a weight placed over a blotter square. Work systematically from the center of the art outward, replacing the eraser powder as it picks up foreign matter and becomes grayed and soiled. As you approach the edges or corners of the artwork, use less pressure, to avoid making crimps and creases. Work around colored areas of powdery pigment, graphite, or heavily printed areas. To keep the artwork from shifting as you work around a particularly delicate area, place a small blotter square atop the art, near where you are working; place the fingers of one hand on the blotter, to hold the work still, as you continue cleaning with the other hand. Tears and creases in the paper support for prints and drawings can be made worse by dry-cleaning. If they are present, work very slowly, *in the direction they take—never against it.*

What NOT to Clean Away

As you clean, keep in mind that any penciled marks that are potentially meaningful in any way should be left alone—such marks may represent signatures, dates, or artists' inscriptions. And be especially sure that any numbers you may feel tempted to erase do not indicate some sort of inventory or artists' code. Many artists—Paul Klee and Lyonel Feininger are two whose names come to mind—used a complex numbering system to identify their prints and drawings. Artists also use as signatures monograms and letters that, at first glance, may not seem relevant.

If you appear to be picking up anything other than surface dirt—anything such as pigment or paper fibers—stop at once and reassess your cleaning procedure. Your powdered eraser may be too abrasive, your motions too vigorous, or the pressure exerted by your fingertips on the art too heavy. What you want to do is not to remove *all* the dirt on the surface of the art, leaving it spick-and-span but clearly the worse for the cleaning; rather, dry-cleaning is done to remove only the surface dirt that is *loosely adhered.*

Finishing Touches

As you work, carefully brush away accumulated eraser particles with the soft-bristled brush. Eraser crumbs inadvertently left on the surface of a print or drawing could eventually harm it and other surfaces with which they might come into contact. Clean the working surface, as well, and—again it bears saying—wash your hands frequently. Clean both the front and the back of the artwork with the eraser crumbs, being careful never to put the art face down onto eraser powder that may be left on the working surface. Use the spatula to lift a corner of the artwork— gently—before grasping the entire sheet to turn it over.

When you have completed the above procedure, record your work in full on the examination report. Also record any changes in the item's appearance.

Repairing Tears

Old tears, new tears, weak plate marks, cracked lines of iron gall ink, and skinned patches of paper require repairing and sometimes reinforcement, work that can often be done simply by following or extending the processes described below.

Tools and Materials

Assemble the necessary tools and materials: an assortment of Japanese tissues, paste, a flat, firm-bristled brush one-fourth to a half-inch wide, brushes with pointed tips in several sizes, distilled water, blotter squares, polyester web squares, bone knife or folder, forceps, cotton swabs, a sharp scalpel with Number 10 or Number 15 blades, small glass or Plexiglas plates, and small weights. Useful sizes for the blotter, polyester, and glass squares are 3 x 3 inches or 3 x 6 inches.

First, examine the tear carefully. Are the edges worn and dirty, or are they fresh? Do they join neatly, or is there a gap , showing that the edges have been worn down? Are the edges of the tear beveled? Proceed only after having determined the configuration of the tear.

Procedure

The next step is to clean and align the edges of the tear. To some extent, the tear will already have been cleaned, during the dry-cleaning of the art's surface. Place a polyester web square below the tear. With the artwork remaining face up, on a clean blotter, very gently clean the edges of the tear with a *white* vinyl eraser (Magic Rub is a good one), taking care not to disturb the exposed fibers. Do not use colored erasers, as their color might permanently stain the paper. Then turn the artwork face down and clean the other side of the tear. Always remember that torn prints and drawings should be given extra overall support when turning them over.

Align the edges of the tear, overlapping the fibers as much as possible. The better an edge of a tear meshes with the opposite edge, the better the repair, both structurally and aesthetically. Gently rolling a dampened swab in the direction of the fibers will help to both clean and align them. If the tear spreads apart easily, hold the edges in place by weighting the artwork on either side of the torn area. Do not remove the weights until the repair has fully dried, or the tear will pull apart.

Place a small amount of strained paste in a dish and stir it briskly with the flat brush, to eliminate any lumps in the paste. If the paste has been stored in a refrigerator, it may be too stiff for use, just at first; and you may find that, even at room temperature, it may need thinning. If so, mix it thoroughly with a few drops of distilled water until it has the consistency of yogurt or heavy cream. Paste that is too thick will constrict as it dries, while paste containing too much water may penetrate through to the front of the paper and may be too weak to hold. Starch pastes do tend to retain their strength when diluted.

Next, choose the tissue needed for the repair. The actual type of the tissue is not so important as is its compatibility with the paper of the artwork. If the mending tissue is too thin, the tear will not be sufficiently reinforced, so that, when the artwork is curled or flexed, the tear is likely to reopen or spread. If the mending tissue is too thick, it will produce an opaque, stiff area behind the tear. Generally speaking, the mending tissue should be slightly lighter in weight than the paper of the print or drawing. For light-weight papers, *tengujo* or *chumino* can be used; for paper of medium weight, *sekishu*; and for heavy papers, *okiwara*. When reinforcing skinned areas or weakened plate marks, use a lighter tissue, since only slight reinforcement is necessary. Tear off narrow strips—one-eighth to one-fourth of an inch wide—of the tissue. The repair should be made with several short strips of tissue, rather than with one continuous piece.

Figure 5.1 shows a work of art with several tears that were mended with a tissue too heavy for the job: it is so thick and so strong that it is causing deformation of the entire sheet. In addition to that, the mends are clearly visible as opaque, raised welts when the art is viewed from the front. Aesthetic issues aside, however, a new tear formed directly to the right of the old one, when the print was carelessly handled, because the earlier tear was so strongly repaired.

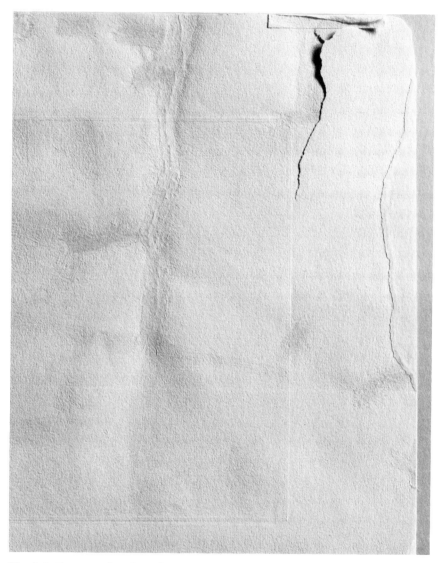

Fig. 5.1. One occasional result of mending a tear in a print or drawing is pictured on the back of such a work here: the mended tear, at left, continues in fine condition; but a new tear has formed and is spreading, directly to its right. The new tear might have been prevented by using a thinner, weaker mending tissue for the old torn place.—Photograph by Sheldan Collins

After the edges of the tear have been cleaned and aligned, use a small brush with a pointed tip to apply paste just along the tear line. With the brush tip, carefully stroke out the fibers of both torn edges, working to place the paste between areas that overlap. *Do not let any paste seep through the tear to the front of the artwork.* The polyester web square will prevent the artwork from sticking to the blotter if paste does reach the front surface—but it should be prevented from doing so if at all possible. Rub the joined parts of the tear lightly with a bone folder through a polyester web square placed on top of the new mend. If you wish, the tear can be dried at this point by using a polyester web square, a blotter square, glass, and a weight. Or you can continue with the next step in the mending.

Brush paste along a strip—a half-inch to an inch long—of mending tissue, using the flat, firm-bristled brush. Hold the strip against a piece of glass and brush outward, making sure the fibers of the mending tissue are fully extended for better holding power. Grasp one end of the tissue with the forceps and quickly apply it, paste side down, to the tear. Work from the innermost end of the tear out toward the edge of the paper. Using a brush or a bone folder, tamp the repair in place. Cover with polyester web square and rub lightly with the bone folder, to ensure complete, overall contact. Working quickly, apply more sections of tissue strips, until the tear has been completely mended. A long tear may require mending in separate stages, one section being allowed to dry before the next is tackled. To ensure that the mend is properly aligned as it dries, cover it with polyester web squares, blotter squares, glass, and small weights. Change blotters after five minutes and allow it to dry thoroughly, under pressure, even after it is apparently dry to the touch. Mending tissue extending beyond the edges of the artwork should be trimmed off with a sharp scalpel. Record what you have done on the examination report.

Varied Uses for Mending Technique

By modifying the mending technique slightly, you can repair a variety of tears and cracks or reinforce skinned patches in art on paper. If you misalign a tear or use the wrong tissue, remove it immediately by lightly rolling over it a swab that has been dampened—*not soaked*—with distilled water. Work in only one small area at a time, an area approximately a half-inch to an inch long. As soon as the repair and its adhesive are sufficiently softened, start to push or roll the tissue back upon itself, working outward from the end closest to the center of the artwork, using a blunt knife or scalpel or the tips of the forceps. *Do not simply pull the repair off*; to do that would exert too much stress on the back of the artwork, which is already somewhat softened from moisture. As you push back the repair, also gently scrape up the adhesive. Clean your knife often, with a tissue, to prevent the sticky adhesive from accumulating on it. Work along the entire area that has been moistened. If the going is slow, the artwork may become saturated by the time you reach the end of the repair, or it may even have dried out. For these reasons, work on only small portions at a time and be especially cautious when ending the work in each area, since that is where the paper will have been exposed to moisture for the longest time.

When you have removed the tissue used for the repair and as much of its adhesive as possible, you will notice that some of the adhesive remains embedded in the paper. This residue should be removed, because, if left, it will shrink as it dries and that will cause the paper to curl. To remove the rest of the adhesive, lightly roll a dampened swab over it once or twice. Blot quickly and often with blotter squares, to pick up the dissolved adhesive and prevent it from penetrating further into the artwork. Use a fresh swab as often as necessary. When you feel that all the paste has been removed, cover the area worked on, front and back, with polyester web squares, followed with blotter squares, and dry the area under a weighted glass square. Change blotters after five minutes, and allow a total drying time of at least thirty minutes. More time will be needed if the paper of the artwork was penetrated by water in the process.

As you remove incorrectly applied repairs, keep in mind that you are working above an area that has already been damaged, and be aware that its earlier problems can easily be aggravated by your activity nearby.

Please note that the above procedure is intended only for removing tissue repairs recently applied with starch paste. *Do not attempt to remove old repairs applied with aged, unknown adhesives, or severe, irreversible damage to the artwork could easily occur.*

With experience, you will soon instinctively choose the right tissues, the proper consistency of paste, and so on. Tears in pastels or flaking gouaches or tears that interfere with the design of a print or drawing should be repaired by a conservator. Sometimes a sheet is so extensively torn or weakened by thinned areas that overall lining with thin Japanese tissue is advisable for additional support. This, also, is a job for a conservator.

Flattening Creases and Wrinkles

Whenever moisture is applied to paper, whether in the form of water or in paste, the dampened area must be dried promptly under weight. Every effort must be made to blot up excess moisture and to prevent it from remaining within the paper, where it increases the chances of buckling and staining. Drying the area under weight gently encourages the paper support to return to its original configuration as it dries.

Localized flattening—that is, pressing only specific areas of the artwork that have been moistened—is discussed above, in connection with repairing tears. The same principle can be applied to flattening creases or wrinkles occurring in one area. The material and tools needed are distilled water, cotton swabs, brushes with pointed tips in several sizes, polyester web squares, blotter squares, glass or Plexiglas squares, small weights, and a magnifying glass or head loupe (Optivisor).

First, examine the deformation, to determine its origins. Wrinkles occasionally result from the way in which the artwork was made. Sometimes the paper support of etchings or engravings has been creased by the printing press, and because such wrinkles are evidence of artistic technique, they *should not be removed.*

Most creases, however, are simply the result of careless handling. Try to determine the severity of the crease. If the paper fibers have actually ruptured along the fold line or if the piece has been folded for several years, so that dirt has entered the fold line, the creases will not be made invisible by any flattening effort. Finally, note any risks involved in reducing the crease. Tracing papers and translucent drafting "parchment" papers react erratically to water and require special flattening techniques. Obviously, if powdery pigments are involved, if the support is parchment instead of paper, if the paper is coated or "grounded" ("grounded" paper has a smooth, chalky look, and its original surface texture is not apparent), or if an embossed area or plate mark is affected by the crease, more elaborate procedures will be needed to remedy the problem, and the job would be best left to a conservator.

Spot-Testing for Water Sensitivity

Water should never be applied to a work of art until all the components of the work of art have been tested for sensitivity to water—a procedure called *spot-testing.*

To spot-test for water sensitivity, use distilled water, which is free of impurities. Place a tiny droplet of the water—no more than one-sixteenth of an inch in diameter—on the surface of the paper in an inconspicuous area. Observe the droplet carefully, through a magnifying glass or a head loupe, noting saturation time. Allow the droplet to saturate the paper, then blot the area dry. If a brown ring forms around the perimeter of the wetted area, the paper contains substances that can cause staining when water is applied. If this is so, do not proceed. Cover the test area with a blotter square, a small glass square, weight them, and allow the work to dry thoroughly.

Next, apply a tiny droplet of distilled water to one color used in the design of the work of art. Again, observe the testing area carefully, noting saturation time, color changes, softening or "feathering" of pigment edges. Before the droplet dries, press it firmly with a blotter square. Check the blotter to see if any trace of color has been picked up. Examine the area of the artwork tested for any changes in appearance— textural differences, color shifts, shininess or dullness. If the artwork is affected by application of water, even if the color tested did not transfer to the blotter, do not proceed.

Repeat the water sensitivity test on every color in the design. Record the results on your examination form. Keep in mind that no moisture should be used on or even near any color that is water-soluble or any paper that contains substances that cause staining.

The Flattening Process

Soiled creases in paper can be gently cleaned with powdered eraser. The artwork should be face-up on a clean blotter. Take care not to disturb roughened fibers that may be evident along the fold line and carefully brush away all eraser crumbs. Start the flattening process by applying the very slightest amount of moisture to the crease. You may or may not have an idea of the paper's sensitivity to water, depending on your work with it up to this point. The small amount of moisture needed can be applied by lightly rolling a *damp* swab—not a *wet* one—over the deformed area on both the front and the back of the paper.

Quickly cover the dampened area with blotter squares on both sides and add a small weighted glass square. Change blotters after five minutes. At this point, you will be able to see whether the paper is flattening. If there is little change, apply a very small amount of moisture once more, and press. You should eventually observe the crease beginning to relax. If the paper is highly sized, it may be nonabsorbent and may require several applications of moisture.

If the fold line is particularly sharp, lightly brush a small amount of distilled water along it. Relax the area on either side, using a swab. Slowly work along the crease, never actually wetting out the paper, merely relaxing it. The procedure cannot be rushed. Remember always to apply moisture to both sides of the paper and to weight the dampened area after each application. Routinely examine used swabs and blotters frequently, to ensure that no pigment is adhering to them.

Plate marks are valued parts of the artwork and must never be flattened. Never apply moisture directly to their embossed lines; work carefully around them. If necessary, make a template of blotters that follows the contours of the plate mark. The moisture and weight involved in any flattening technique should never be so great as to lessen the depth of a plate mark.

Overall Flattening

Localized flattening of creases and overall flattening are often undertaken together. Sometimes this procedure simply involves applying more moisture to a troublesome area before overall flattening. Overall flattening is sometimes undertaken to counteract paper deformation caused by localized flattening; as one spot flattens, the paper may buckle on either side. The technique involved is the same in both instances: relaxation of the paper fibers and drying under even pressure, which helps the paper return to its original configuration. In both instances, the process is slow and requires sensitivity to the surface characteristics of paper. Such extreme measures as smoothing the paper out with an iron can easily— and permanently—destroy the subtle, fragile topography of prints and drawings. In working with art on paper, one must always keep in mind the three-dimensional quality of seemingly "flat" prints and drawings.

Materials and tools needed for overall flattening include a device that produces a fine, even mist of water, such as an air brush, a spray gun and compressor, a sprayer connected to canned pressurized air, or a plant mister (dahlia misters are ideal); distilled water; blotters; plate glass with beveled edges, a quarter-inch to a half-inch thick; lens tissue; printers' felts, a quarter-inch to a half-inch thick; and weights, such as felt-covered bricks, the unabridged *Oxford English Dictionary*, and small lithographic stones or other found objects. It is useful to have one or two "flattening stations" permanently set up, with two sets of plate glass, blotter, and felt squares cut to match. One set, for smaller items, should measure 20 by 26 inches; the other set, for such things as posters, architectural drawings, and other large pieces, should measure 30 by 40 inches. Since no two artworks are identical, the thickness of blotters and felts to be used should vary accordingly.

Each "flattening station"—or "press," as they are also called—consists of printers' felt, six to eight blotters, and a piece of plate glass. Printers' felt is different from ordinary felt, being as much as a quarter-inch to a half-inch thicker than the ordinary kind. Weights and a few sheets of lens tissue or other smooth-surfaced tissue should be readily available, nearby, to protect sensitive surfaces during flattening.

Place the item to be flattened face down on a clean blotter. It should already have undergone dry-cleaning and any mending needed. Also, the paper and colors should have been tested for water sensitivity beforehand. If the piece is nonetheless still quite soiled, do not proceed—excessive surface dirt can cause tide lines from the movement of moisture through the paper. If the work is reasonably clean, however, begin the flattening by holding the water sprayer at least two feet away from the object and spraying the back of the work lightly with a fine mist of distilled water. The paper may darken as it absorbs water. If it is nonabsorbent, droplets may form on its surface. If they do not penetrate the paper in a few seconds, but settle and grow larger, instead, use a blotter square to blot them up and get them off the paper. Continue spraying—the objective is to relax the paper, but not to saturate it with water. The paper will probably begin to move, as the cellulose molecules expand with their intake of water. Short-fibered wood pulp papers like newsprint will move quite a bit and may even begin to roll up. If they do, quickly place another blotter on top of the artwork, turn the entire sandwich over, remove the top blotter, and lightly spray the front of the artwork. This will counteract the expansion on the other side and the paper will soon relax.

Works in Water-Sensitive Media

Prints and drawings made with water-sensitive media can usually be sprayed in this way because only a small amount of moisture is involved. Certain dyes, however—most notably the red ones used in felt-tipped pens and in some stamping inks—will feather or bleed with even the slightest moisture. Therefore, before attempting to flatten any artwork, it is essential to test carefully, under magnification, not just the design media, but the inks used in signatures or collectors' marks, as well, to see whether their edges appear to soften with moisture or whether they seem to sink into the paper. If the work does contain water-sensitive areas, and if they are small, simply mask them with Mylar or paper scraps during spraying, so that they will be protected from moisture. *If the color in question is used extensively throughout the design, do not proceed.*

With small water-sensitive areas safely masked, dampen both sides of the object and carry it to the press between the two blotters on which it was sprayed. Open the press, leaving the felt and three or four blotters on the bottom. The design side should be covered with a sheet of lens tissue. This step is especially important if any adhesives remain on the face of the artwork, or if certain colors have been "glazed" with gum arabic. Commonly used in nineteenth-century prints, gum arabic saturates colors and causes them to appear shiny in a raking light, and they may also be sticky when moist. If glazed areas are thick, or if a crackle pattern appears in them, leave the flattening to a conservator. Lens tissue over these areas will prevent the art from adhering to the blotters as it dries under weight. Place one of the blotters from the press over the face of the artwork. Holding the art and the two blotters on either side of it together, turn the work over, face down, and into the press. If the artwork is large, you will need two people for this task. Dampened prints and drawings are weak and can tear or abrade very easily. For that reason, they should always be supported by a blotter when they are being moved from place to place. Remove the blotter from the back of the artwork, which is now face down in the press. If the work has on it, from old repairs, any adhesive that may have become sticky during spraying, place a sheet of lens tissue over that area. Add three to four blotters to the top, followed by the plate glass.

There are no hard-and-fast rules governing weights to be used during flattening. Often the weight of the glass alone is sufficient.

Keys to Successful Flattening

The success or failure of the flattening operation depends on the sensitivity of the paper to water, the degree of dampness applied, the drying speed, the cause of the deformation, and the ambient temperature and relative humidity of the room. A good general rule to follow is: do not overdo any step of the procedure, proceed cautiously, and *never rush.*

Make sure the object is evenly weighted. Place one or two medium weights, such as the felt-covered bricks, on top of the glass. After half an hour, change the blotters above and below the artwork, leaving the lens tissue in place, and continue drying under the same weight. If the artwork became almost saturated during spraying and still feels damp, change the blotter again in an hour or so. The item should remain in the press for several days. Afterward, you should remove the object, place it on a flat blotter in the open, and observe it. During the next few hours, its deformations may return.

Stubborn paper deformations that defy initial attempts to flatten them may require several tries. More weight is not necessarily the answer; more blotter changes may be needed, or more time spent in the press—up to a week, in some instances; greater dampening to begin with may help; or the work may simply need repeated attempts to eliminate the buckling gradually.

One method to ensure that the item is fully relaxed before it is weighted is to place it between impermeable sheets of Mylar, after spraying—*keeping in mind that this cannot be done if any water-sensitive media are present in the art.* If the artwork remains between these Mylar sheets for a few minutes, all of the moisture will be absorbed by the paper, rather than by the blotters. This method is very effective when flattening large, heavy sheets of paper, but it increases the danger of water-spotting.

Flattening Rolled Items

Rolled-up objects, such as posters, frequently pose special problems in collections. Often the materials used to make these kinds of objects were of poor quality, to begin with, or the objects may have been generally mistreated during their periods of use. It is not unusual to find such works crushed and torn at either end of the roll. To make matters worse, such items are often quite large, making handling difficult in general. Attempts to unroll or open the item out often produce more damage. Prints and drawings that have been rolled up for many years must be unrolled very slowly. The procedure is similar to that of overall flattening, but the process must be more gradual.

Examine the rolled-up item as thoroughly as it may be possible to do without unrolling it, in order to identify the medium and to note any colors that may be water-soluble. Remove any insect droppings or heavy dirt on the exterior of the roll.

The Humidity Chamber

Place the item in a "humidity chamber." Such a device can be very simply constructed from a large plastic garbage can with a tight fitting lid. For unusually long rolls, another plastic garbage can be inverted on top of the first one. In the bottom of the chamber, place a tray filled with water and a small dish or sachet of thymol or *o*-phenyl phenol crystals (*o*-phenyl phenol is less toxic than thymol). Over the tray of water, invert a plastic crate, dish drainer, or stretched plastic mesh, to prevent the artwork from falling into the water in the tray. Place the rolled-up item in the chamber and close the lid tightly. After five to six hours, check on its progress. The humidity level inside the container should have risen by this time; a small paper gauge or dial hygrometer placed inside the chamber will indicate the level of humidity present. The paper of the rolled work should feel softer and the "curl" should seem less tight. If the humidity has not risen significantly, increase the amount of water in proportion to the cubic footage of the container, add some hot water to the tray, or lightly mist the interior with a fine dahlia sprayer or the vapor emitted from an ultrasonic humidifier before closing the chamber again. It may be necessary to keep the item in the container overnight.

Unrolling the Artwork

When the artwork feels most relaxed, remove it and place it first on polyester webbing and then on an impermeable surface, such as Mylar or Formica. This will slow down the evaporation of water. Using long strips of rag board—scraps left over from precutting can be used—or blotters, weight down the outermost edge of the item. Glass plates may be placed on top of these to provide a better anchor. Slowly start to unroll the artwork, inserting long strips of rag board parallel to the roll as you go. These will help hold the paper flat and will help keep the item from rolling up again. If the paper is sufficiently relaxed, no more weight than this should be necessary at this time. If the artwork begins to resist your efforts to unroll it, lightly mist it with water—or, better, with the vapor emitted from an ultrasonic humidifier—so that it again relaxes. It is important that water droplets do not actually form on the paper—they could easily cause staining if they should penetrate the paper and dry. When the work has been completely unrolled, proceed as you would in routine flattening, but remember that more relaxation in the paper will be needed before the artwork is placed under weight. Premature weighting will cause the paper to crack along its undulations.

Record both successes and failures in flattening procedures. Such notes will help you and others working with this problem in the future, when similar papers must be flattened.

Deacidification

Deacidification, also called acid neutralization, or buffering, has received a great deal of public attention. The procedure for it involves depositing an alkali mixed with water or a solvent on or within the paper being deacidified, to protect the paper from either internal or external acidity. Most people apparently assume that this process is routine treatment for prints and drawings. Current advertisements reinforce this belief. Under no circumstances, however, should deacidification of works of art on paper be attempted by any lay person using any commercial product—not only for the sake of the art, but because some solutions used in this process are toxic.

The value of deacidification in libraries and archives cannot be overemphasized: it is a necessary procedure, if the millions of books and records made on poor-quality papers are to be preserved.

A Cautionary Word

The deacidification of works of art, however, is an entirely different matter. The uniqueness of prints and drawings is emphasized, throughout this book. Deacidification procedures for such works can alter the colors of both paper and pigments.[4] Wood pulp papers containing lignin, which probably could benefit most from deacidification (see figure 1.8, chapter 1), will darken from the process. Uneven penetration of the solution into paper can alter the paper's subtle surface characteristics. Deacidification treatments of works of art on paper must take into account the subtle, subjective qualities that differentiate them from archival materials. This distinction is not always easy to make, since many archival materials are valued for aesthetic reasons, also. Deacidification may seem desirable for prints and drawings, even when its effects have been taken into account, but—all possibilities considered—*prevention* of those effects remains preferable to cure. Proper matting, framing, storage, and environment can go a long way toward protecting prints and drawings from acid and can slow down its effects. Internal sources of acid can be gently reduced by other conservation procedures that do not subject the artwork to drastic shifts in pH and to changes in its appearance.

Finding a Good Conservator

The time to select a conservator is *before* events catastrophic to prints and drawings occur. Conservators cannot prevent disaster *after* a state of emergency has developed; but delays in implementing repairs and proper conservation procedures to prevent *further* disasters can be minimized if every institution establishes a conservation strategy plan before emergencies arise. Such a plan should include commitment to provide the best possible care for the collection, regular examination reports and conservation surveys, a disaster plan in case of fire or flood, and a good working relationship firmed by a formal agreement with a professional conservator or conservation center. Obviously, the degree to which this strategy is set forth on paper will depend upon the type of collection involved and upon the financial resources available. Proper conservation for any collection of art on paper requires continuing, steadfast commitment to providing proper care for the collection, expressed not only by the maintaining of proper matting, framing, storing, and exhibiting procedures for them, but also by consideration of environmental issues. Everyone involved with conservation—and everyone who comes into contact with a collection *is* involved—should share this philosophy.

Examination reports and conservation surveys are one valuable means of monitoring the continuing condition of works of art on paper. Such reports and surveys are a part of the commitment to preserving a collection, as well as an important aspect of the overall conservation strategy. They can play a critical role in answering the insurance company's questions when damages occur in transit or while an artwork is on loan. Condition reports put the current facts about an artifact's condition at your fingertips; and, properly noted, they provide a better understanding of suggested remedies at the time that you speak with a conservator on that point. They are tremendously helpful to conservators, who find it helpful to know about past damages, treatments, and repairs to an artwork.[5] Conservation surveys are now required by government agencies to ensure that grants awarded best serve the needs of the collection as a whole.

Disaster plans in the event of fire or flood are a must for every institution housing a collection of works of art. Published examples of such plans—and there are many; see "Further Reading"—can help to formulate one appropriate for individual circumstances.

Each aspect of a conservation strategy will, sooner or later, require the help of a professional conservator, perhaps to set up a conservation survey or advise treatment when a preliminary examination of a print or drawing indicates that an expert's help is needed. The experience of conservators may be helpful in planning storage or exhibition areas. Quick response when disaster strikes is another service that most conservators and conservation centers can give, provided they have some acquaintance with the institution and its holdings beforehand.

Where, Why, and How to Begin

Most paper conservators will be found in and around metropolitan centers, and the properly qualified professional usually has affiliations with several institutions or organizations.

But—you may ask—why bother spending a lot of time looking for a conservator, when there are several restorers conveniently listed in the Yellow Pages, and the local frame shop advertises restoration services?

There are several reasons for finding—and getting to know—a qualified professional conservator. To begin with, the field of paper conservation has changed drastically, within a very short time—many earlier amateur "bathtub" treatments are now recognized as being destructive to paper. Of equal importance is the recent change in the philosophy of conservation versus that of restoration. Treatments are no longer carried out if they harm the art in the long run or if the treatment alters the original character of the piece. Secret elixirs and instant cures have gone the way of the smocks and berets of the "artist" stereotype of earlier years. Superficial cosmetic alterations have been replaced by carefully documented, pretested procedures carried out with extreme sensitivity to aesthetics. Today's conservators respect the integrity of the artwork at the expense of satisfying prevailing tastes or the desire for the financial appreciation of the artwork.

The Qualified Professional

A conservator working in the United States today should be a member of the American Institute for Conservation of Historic and Artistic Works, familiarly called the AIC. Members of the AIC have agreed to comply with the institute's Code of Ethics and Standards of Practice. The first Standards of Practice were adopted by the AIC in 1963; the first Code of Ethics came into use in 1967. Both were revised in 1979. Copies of each are available from the AIC. (The address: Klingle Mansion, 3545 Williamsburg Lane, N.W., Washington, D.C. 20008.)

The Code of Ethics and Standards of Practice of the AIC gives all conservators something in common. Their agreement to adhere to its tenets is the only form of licensing that presently exists for conservators. This can be misleading. Anyone can become an Associate Member of the AIC by simply paying annual dues; the organization is open to all, even those with only a passing interest in conservation. The title of *Associate*, therefore, cannot be construed as an endorsement of competence or even as any assurance that the member is a practicing conservator. The rules of the organization forbid its use on business cards or stationery.

The next level of membership in the AIC is the *Professional Associate*. To attain this level, a conservator must have a number of years of training and experience and must have submitted reports and photographs of various treatments, which are reviewed by a special committee. *Professional Associates and Fellows*, the highest membership category, includes members who have experience that has been recognized by their peers, and they have demonstrated that they comply with the Code of Ethics and Standards of Practice. Again, the titles are not an endorsement of competence.

Beware of conservators or conservation businesses that advertise aggressively. The AIC Code of Ethics recommends discreet announcements of services only. Never entrust your artworks to a group practice without knowing precisely who will be treating your pieces. Often, work is subcontracted out to conservators other than those in the group named in your contract, and your artworks may also be removed from the premises of the group you contract with. Be especially wary of conservators who claim to restore everything from your prints and drawings to your paintings and teapots. One person is rarely qualified to treat everything in a collection.

To find a qualified conservator of prints and drawings, try at least two of the following suggestions.

Get in touch with a major museum that has a collection similar to your own. Ask for a conservator in the conservation laboratory, if there is one. If not, speak to a curator in the department of prints and drawings. Either individual should be able to refer you to a reputable conservator in private practice or to a regional conservation center.

Get in touch with a regional center. Regional centers are nonprofit conservation facilities established to provide conservation services for museums and a small percentage of private collectors. They usually operate on a membership basis; a yearly fee entitles your institution to lower hourly rates than those charged nonmembers. Regional centers are staffed by highly trained professional conservators. A list of these centers appears at the end of this chapter.

Get in touch with the AIC. While the AIC can provide you with the names of members in your area and their level of membership, it does not vouch for any single individual's competence. (The address of the AIC appears above, in the section entitled *The Qualified Professional.*)

Get in touch with administrators of conservation training programs. Most administrators of conservation training programs are interested in hearing about suitable projects for their advanced students. Many have summer internships, funded by government agencies, for which your institution might qualify. If not, conservation training programs are usually glad to recommend graduates, whose work they know, who are in your area. A list of training programs appears at the end of this chapter.

Once you have decided on a conservator, ask questions—and continue asking. A true professional should gladly provide any requested information concerning schooling and experience and should supply references, if asked to do so. Talk to the conservator directly, never through another individual acting as a spokesperson. It is absolutely necessary to establish a good working relationship with your chosen conservator, if you are going to entrust to his or her care the objects in your collection. If the conservator you select seems unwilling to talk to you freely about conservation procedures or to discuss aesthetic issues, take your business elsewhere: a satisfying relationship with a conservator requires trust on both sides. The conservator will appreciate your frankness about your concerns; and you, in turn, should be willing to modify your expectations in deference to the conservator's expertise and advice.

The AIC Code of Ethics and Standards of Practice to which the conservator has agreed also serves the interests of the guardian of a collection of works of art. Once a work of art has been left with the conservator, you are entitled to an examination report, followed by a treatment proposal. The examination report will most likely be a detailed extension of your own, if you provide one. The treatment proposal should include an outline of the proposed treatment, the defects that it is intended to correct, and an estimate of the cost for treatment. You may be asked to initial a statement allowing the conservator to modify the proposed treatment if unforeseen developments make that advisable. Often, in the course of treatment, it is necessary to resort to procedures not specified in the proposal, to rectify unexpected complications. The cost estimate is usually based on an hourly rate, plus materials. The complexity of treatment involved, the rarity of the item being treated, and the deadline for treatment are sometimes taken into account, as well. The proposal should clearly state exactly what will be provided, in return for these charges. Conservators do not ordinarily mat and frame prints and drawings, but may be willing to do so for an additional fee, if asked. Costs for photography and insurance should be itemized. Acquaint yourself thoroughly with the limits of your insurance coverage, before letting a work of art leave the collection for treatment. Your written permission is required before treatment is begun.

Both parties should discuss the treatment and its possible outcome, *before* misunderstandings arise. If you are not pleased with the results of the treatment or if you are confused by terminology used in the report, talk it over with the conservator, immediately. Expectations are sometimes too high. Then, too, the artwork sometimes does not respond well to treatment. Only through honest communication can a satisfactory working relationship between conservator and caretaker/owner/curator be maintained.

When treatment is completed, the conservator should provide a report for your records. It should describe the procedures that were carried out, as well as the result of the treatment. The report may contain recommendations for exhibition and framing or for storage restrictions. Before-and-after photographs of the art treated should be included and should be filed, together with the report, for future reference.

Regional Conservation Centers:
A Partial Listing

Balboa Art Conservation Guild
P.O. Box 3755
San Diego, California 92103
Telephone: (714) 236–9702

Center for Conservation and Technical Studies
Harvard University Art Museums
Harvard University
32 Quincy Street
Cambridge, Massachusetts 02138
Telephone: (617) 495–2392

Conservation Center for Art and Historic Artifacts
264 South 23rd Street
Philadelphia, Pennsylvania 19103
Telephone: (215) 545–0613

Intermuseum Conservation Association
Allen Art Building
Oberlin, Ohio 44074
Telephone: (216) 775–7331

Maine State Museum Regional Conservation Center
State House
Augusta, Maine 04330
Telephone: (207) 289–2301

Northeast Document Conservation Center
Abbot Hall
School Street
Andover, Massachusetts 01810
Telephone: (617) 470–1010

New York State Office of Parks and Recreation
  Bureau of Historic Sites
  Collections Care Center
  Peebles Island
  Waterford, New York 12188
  Telephone: (518) 237–8090
Pacific Regional Conservation Center
  Bishop Museum
  P.O. Box 19000–A
  Honolulu, Hawaii 96818
  Telephone: (808) 847–3511
Rocky Mountain Regional Conservation Center
  University of Denver
  2420 South University Boulevard
  Denver, Colorado 80208
  Telephone: (303) 753–3218
Williamstown Regional Art Conservation Laboratory, Inc.
  Clark Art Institute
  225 South Street
  Williamstown, Massachusetts 01267
  Telephone: (413) 458–8109, Ext. 34
Upper Midwest Conservation Association
  The Minneapolis Institute of Arts
  2400 Third Avenue, South
  Minneapolis, Minnesota 55404
  Telephone: (612) 870–3046

Conservation Training Programs

The Conservation Center of the Institute of Fine Arts
  New York University, Chan House
  14 East 78th Street
  New York, New York 10021
State University College at Buffalo
  Rockwell Hall
  1300 Elmwood Avenue
  Buffalo, New York 14222
Winterthur/University of Delaware Art Conservation Program
  301 Old College
  University of Delaware
  Newark, Delaware 19711

Conservation Programme
  Queen's University
  Kingston, Ontario K7L 3N6, Canada

Library Conservation

School of Library Service
  Conservation Program
  516 Butler Library
  Columbia University
  New York, New York 10027

Advanced-Level Training in Conservation

Center for Conservation and Technical Studies
  Harvard University Art Museums
  Harvard University
  Cambridge, Massachusetts 02138

NOTES

1. A sample examination form is included in the Smithsonian Institution's *The Curatorial Examination of Paper Objects*. One also appears in Anne F. Clapp's *Curatorial Care of Works of Art on Paper*, as figure 6. See "Further Reading."

2. Three articles describing photodocumentation equipment and procedures are recommended: William Leisher and Richard Amt, "Required Photographic Documentation Equipment" (Paper presented at the Eighth Annual Meeting of the American Institute for Conservation, San Francisco, May 1980); Dan Kushel, "Photodocumentation for Conservation: Procedural Concepts and Techniques" (Paper presented at the Eighth Annual Meeting of the American Institute for Conservation, San Francisco, May 1980); and Peter Waters, "Photodocumentation for the Conservation of Books and Related Materials: Suggested Approaches for the Establishment of a Basic System," Library of Congress Conservation Workshop Notes, ser. 800, no. 1 (Paper presented at the Eighth Annual Meeting of the American Institute for Conservation, San Francisco, May 1980).

3. Eastman Kodak Company, *B/W Processing for Permanence*, Publication J–19, (Rochester, N.Y., n.d.); Laurence E. Keefe, Jr., and Dennis Inch, *The Life of a Photograph: Archival Processing, Matting, Framing, and Storage* (London: Butterworth, 1983); "Processing for Permanence," in *Caring for Photographs: Display, Storage, Restoration* (New York: Time–Life Books, 1972), pp. 69–96; Conservation Committee of the Society of Mississippi Archivists, *Pictures that Last: Archival Processing Techniques for Black-and-White Materials*, Leaflet 8 (Jackson, Miss.: May 1984).

4. Further discussion of alterations that can occur in works of art on paper when they undergo deacidification appears in Vincent Daniels's "Color Changes of Watercolor Pig-

ments during Deacidification," *Science and Technology in the Service of Conservation* (Preprints of papers presented at the Tenth Annual Meeting of the International Institute for Conservation of Historic and Artistic Works, Washington, D.C., 1982), pp. 66–70.

5. At this writing, I know of two organizations that have been funded to provide on-site conservation surveys. Consultants from the Northeast Document Conservation Center will visit repositories in New England, New York, and New Jersey, for a modest fee. The American Association for State and Local History will also advise on collections care.

FURTHER READING

American Institute for Conservation of Historic and Artistic Works. *Guidelines for Selecting a Conservator.* Rev. ed. Washington, D.C.: AIC, 1987.

Clapp, Anne F. *Curatorial Care of Works of Art on Paper.* 3d ed. rev. Oberlin: Intermuseum Conservation Association, 1978.

The Cleaning of Prints, Drawings, and Manuscripts: Dry Methods. CPS-4. Washington, D.C.: Smithsonian Institution, Office of Museum Programs Audiovisual Program Coordinator, n.d. [54 slides, script, bibliography, sources of supply].

Collins, Sheldan. *How to Photograph Works of Art.* Nashville: The American Association for State and Local History, 1986.

The Curatorial Examination of Paper Objects. EPS-5. Washington, D.C.: Smithsonian Institution, Office of Museum Programs Audiovisual Program Coordinator, n.d. [154 slides, script, bibliography, sources of supply, glossary, condition report]

McAusland, Jane. "Conservation and Storage: Prints, Drawings, and Water-Colours." In *Manual of Curatorship,* edited by John M. A. Thompson, pp. 245–262. London: Butterworth, 1984.

Orraca, José. "Shopping for a Conservator." *Museum News* 59:4 (January–February 1981):60–66.

Shelley, Marjorie. *Warning Signs: When Works on Paper Require Conservation.* Bulletin 11. New York: New York Conservation Consultancy, 1984.

Walsh, Judith C. "Special Conservation Problems: Basic Conservation Terminology." *Drawing* 5:3 (September–October 1983):55–57.

———. "Special Conservation Problems for Collectors: Choosing a Conservator." *Drawing* 5:6 (March–April 1984):129–130.

Disaster Planning

Ballard, Mary W. *Disaster Planning.* Bulletin 3. New York: New York State Conservation Consultancy, 1983.

Barton, John, and Joanna Weyheiser, eds. *The Disaster Contingency Planning Handbook.* Toronto: Toronto Archivists Group, 1985.

Hunter, John E. *Emergency Preparedness for Museums, Historic Sites, and Archives: An Annotated Bibliography.* Technical Leaflet 114. Nashville: American Association for State and Local History, 1979.

Murray, Toby Kemp. "Bibliography on Disasters, Disaster Preparedness, and Disaster Recovery." Tulsa: McFarlin Library, Archivist Preservation Officer, 1982.

Myers, James N., and Denise D. Bedford, eds. *Disasters: Prevention and Coping.* Stanford: Stanford University, 1981.

The Society of American Archivists. *Pak X: Disaster Prevention and Preparedness, Problems in Archives Kits.* Contents include:

Bohem, Hilda. *Disaster Prevention and Disaster Preparedness.* Los Angeles: University of California, Task Group on the Preservation of Library Materials, 1977.

Michigan Archival Association. *A Program for Disaster Response in Michigan.* Ann Arbor: Michigan Archival Association, 1981.

Fortson-Jones, Judith. *Disaster Prevention and Recovery Plan.* Lincoln: Nebraska State Historical Society, 1980.

Waters, Peter. *Procedures for Salvage of Water-Damaged Library Materials.* Washington, D.C.: Library of Congress, 1979.

Long, Margery S. *Disaster Prevention and Preparedness: A Selected Bibliography.* Detroit: Wayne State University, 1982.

APPENDIX 1

Sources of Supplies

More and more companies have been created or have expanded their inventories to accommodate the needs of archivists, curators, registrars, conservators, framers, and individual collectors in caring for prints and drawings. All major suppliers of paper and board and conservation supplies included in the short reference list immediately below have catalogues and samples available, usually free of charge. Since many offer similar or identical wares, the prudent buyer can save by careful comparison of prices and shipping charges. It is suggested that up-to-date catalogues of many of these companies be kept handy.

An itemized listing arranged alphabetically by product follows the list of major suppliers.

Please note: *exclusion* of a major supplier from the *itemized* list does not mean that the organization does not carry the item in question; consult their catalogue. *Inclusion* in the list does not constitute a blanket endorsement of every product offered by a major supplier.

For our neighbors in Canada, help in the search for supplies may be found in *Museum and Archival Supplies Handbook,* 3rd ed., rev. (Toronto: Ontario Museum Association and Toronto Area Archives Group, 1985).

Paper and Board: Major Manufacturers and Distributors

Mat boards (100 percent rag, 100 percent buffered rag, conservation), acid-free papers, interleaving papers, tissues, acid-free corrugated cardboard, blotting paper, bristol board, folder stock. Some of the following manufacturers and distributors now carry a variety of conservation tools and equipment.

209

Andrew/Nelson/Whitehead
   31–10 48th Avenue
   Long Island City, New York 11101

Charles T. Bainbridge & Sons, Incorporated
   50 Northfield Avenue
   Raritan Center
   Edison, New Jersey 08817

Crestwood Paper Company, Incorporated
   315 Hudson Street
   New York, New York 10013

Hollinger Corporation
   P.O. Box 6185
   3810 South Four-Mile-Run Drive
   Arlington, Virginia 22206

Process Materials Corporation
   301 Veterans Boulevard
   Rutherford, New Jersey 07070

Rising Paper Company
   Housatonic, Massachusetts 02136

University Products, Incorporated
   P.O. Box 101
   Holyoke, Massachusetts 01041

Conservation Materials:
Major Manufacturers and Distributors

Conservation and archival tools, equipment, and materials. Many can also supply mat board and other archival framing and storage papers.

Conservation Materials, Limited
   340 Freeport Boulevard
   P.O. Box 2884
   Sparks, Nevada 89431

Conservation Resources International, Incorporated
   8000 H Forbes
   Springfield, Virginia 22151

Light Impressions Corporation
   439 Monroe Avenue
   Rochester, New York 14603

TALAS (Technical Library Service)
   213 West 35th Street, 7th Floor
   New York, New York 10001

Following are types of supplies, arranged alphabetically, with sources where they may be obtained.

Acrylic Sheet, Clear, Nonfiltering
Plexiglas:
Rohm and Haas
Independence Mall West
Philadelphia, Pennsylvania 19105

Acrylite:
Cyro Industries
697 Route 46
Clifton, New Jersey 07015

Acrylic Sheet, Clear, UV-Filtering
Plexiglas UF-3, UF-4:
Rohm and Haas
Independence Mall West
Philadelphia, Pennsylvania 19105

Acrylite OP-2:
Cyro Industries
P.O. Box 8588
Woodcliff Lake, New Jersey 07675

Adhesives, PVA Emulsion
Jade #403:
TALAS (Technical Library Service)
213 West 35th Street, 7th Floor
New York, New York 10001

Aabitt Adhesives, Incorporated
2403 North Oakley Avenue
Chicago, Illinois 60647

Adhesives, Starch
See above listing, Conservation Materials: Major Manufacturers and Distributors. Also available at health and specialty food stores.

Aerosol Dusters
Dust-Off:
Light Impressions Corporation
439 Monroe Avenue
Rochester, New York 14603
Available also at photographic equipment stores.

Air Compressors
Art and drafting supply stores.

Air Conditioners
See *Environmental Control Equipment*

Air Filters
See *Environmental Control Equipment*

Antistatic Solution
Like Magic:
Lea Manufacturing Company
Waterbury, Connecticut 06720
See also *Framing Hardware and Tools*

Archivists' Pens and Pencils
Micro Essential Laboratory
4224 Avenue H
Brooklyn, New York 11210
See also Conservation Materials: Major Manufacturers and Distributors.

Art-Sorb
Conservation Materials, Limited
340 Freeport Boulevard
P.O. Box 2884
Sparks, Nevada 89431
See also *Desiccants, Silica Gel*

Blades, Scalpel
Fisher Scientific Company International Headquarters
52 Fadem Road
Springfield, New Jersey 07081

Blades, Utility
Local hardware and housewares stores; art supply stores; see also *Framing Hardware and Tools*

Blotting Paper
Alling & Cory
30–35 Thomson Avenue
Long Island City, New York 00010
See also Paper and Board: Major Manufacturers and Distributors; Conservation Materials: Major Manufacturers and Distributors.

Blue-Wool Fading Strips
TALAS (Technical Library Service)
213 West 35th Street, 7th Floor
New York, New York 10001
See also Conservation Materials: Major Manufacturers and Distributors.

Bone Folders
See *Burnishers*

Boxes, Storage
See *Storage Boxes*

Brad-Fitting Tools
See *Framing Hardware and Tools*

Brass Molding Hooks
See *Framing Hardware and Tools.*

Bristol Board (.008 to .012 Cal.), Acid-Free Rag
See Paper and Board: Major Manufacturers and Distributors.

Brushes, Artists'
Available at art and drafting supply stores.

Brushes, Drafting
Available at art and drafting supply stores.

Brushes, Japanese
TALAS (Technical Library Service)
213 West 35th Street, 7th Floor
New York, New York 10001

Conservation Materials, Limited
340 Freeport Boulevard
P.O. Box 2884
Sparks, Nevada 89431

Aiko's Art Materials Import, Incorporated
714 North Wabash Avenue
Chicago, Illinois 60611

Bumpons
See *Framing Hardware and Tools*

Burnishers
TALAS (Technical Library Service)
213 West 35th Street, 7th Floor
New York, New York 10001

Conservation Materials, Limited
340 Freeport Boulevard
P.O. Box 2884
Sparks, Nevada 89431

Light Impressions Corporation
439 Monroe Avenue
Rochester, New York 14603

See also *Framing Hardware and Tools*

Color Control Patches
Eastman Kodak Company
Rochester, New York 14650

Also available at photographic equipment stores.

Conservation Board
See Paper and Board: Major Manufacturers and Distributors.

Contact Paper, Clear
Hardware and housewares stores.

Corner Rounder
See *Encapsulation: Materials and Tools*

Corrugated Cardboard, Acid-Free
See Paper and Board: Major Manufacturers and Distributors;
Conservation Materials: Major Manufacturers and Distributors.

Cotton Applicators
Caligor's
1226 Lexington Avenue
New York, New York 10028
Also available at hospital supply and drugstores.

Denglas
See *Glass, Nonreflective*

Desiccants, Silica Gel
Multiform Desiccant Products, Inc.
1418 Niagara Street
Buffalo, New York 14213

Also available at scientific supply companies. See also
Conservation Materials: Major Manufacturers and Distributors.
Art-Sorb:
Conservation Materials, Limited
340 Freeport Boulevard
P.O. Box 2884
Sparks, Nevada 89431
Dri-Can:
Light Impressions Corporation
439 Monroe Avenue
Rochester, New York 14603

Multiform Desiccant Products, Inc. (address above)
Natrasorb SG 145:
Multiform Desiccant Products, Inc. (address above)

Drafting Powder
Available at art and drafting supply stores. See also Conservation
Materials: Major Manufacturers and Distributors.

Dehumidifiers
See *Environmental Control Equipment*

Dowicide A
See *Fungicides, Sodium O-Phenol Phenate*

Dowicide 1
See *Fungicides, O-Phenyl Phenol*

Dri-Can
See *Desiccants, Silica Gel*

Dry-Cleaning Pad
See *Erasers, Powdered*

Dusting Brush
Art and drafting supply stores.

Dust Cloths
One-Wipe, Stretch 'n' Dust:
Available at hardware and houseware stores.

Dust Off
See *Aerosal Dusters*

Easels, Viewing Stands
Art and drafting supply stores.

Emery Paper
3M Company
3M Center
Building 220–7E
Saint Paul, Minnesota 55144
Also available at hardware stores.

Encapsulation: Materials and Tools
Hollinger Corporation
P.O. Box 6185
3810 South Four-Mile-Run Drive
Arlington, Virginia 22206

Process Materials Corporation
301 Veterans Boulevard
Rutherford, New Jersey 07070

Pohlig Brothers
2419 East Franklin Street
P.O. Box 8609
Richmond, Virginia 23223

University Products, Incorporated
P.O. Box 101
Holyoke, Massachusetts 01041

See also Conservation Materials: Major Manufacturers and
Distributors.

Environmental Control Equipment
*Air conditioners, air filters, dehumidifiers, humidifiers, humidistats,
thermostats:*

Abbeon Cal, Inc.
123 Gray Avenue
Santa Barbara, California 93101

American Air Filter Company
215 Central Avenue
P.O. Box 35530
Louisville, Kentucky 40232

Carrier Air Conditioning
P.O. Box 4808
Syracuse, New York 13221

Honeywell, Commercial Division
Honeywell Plaza, West
Minneapolis, Minnesota 55417

Humid-Aire Corp.
156 North Jefferson
Chicago, Illinois 60606

Johnson Controls, Inc.
507 East Michigan Street
P.O. Box 423
Milwaukee, Wisconsin 53201

Lennox Industries, Inc.
P.O. Box 400450
Dallas, Texas 75240

Nortec Industries, Inc.
P.O. Box 698
Ogdensburg, New York 13669

Erasers, Powdered
Opaline, Skum-X:
Available at art and drafting supply stores. See also Conservation
Materials: Major Manufacturers and Distributors.

Erasers, White Vinyl
Magic Rub:
Available at art and drafting supply stores. See also Conservation
Materials: Major Manufacturers and Distributors.

Ethanol (Ethyl Alcohol)
Reagent Grade, Denatured:
Fisher Scientific Company
52 Fadem Road
Springfield, New Jersey 07081
Also available at other scientific supply companies.

Ethylene Oxide Detectors
Personnel Badges:
3M Company
3M Center
St. Paul, Minnesota 55144
Instruments;
AMSCO, American Sterilizer Company
2425 West 23rd Street
Erie, Pennsylvania 16514

Fading Strips
TALAS (Technical Library Service)
213 West 35th Street, 7th Floor
New York, New York 10001

See also Conservation Materials: Major Manufacturers and Distributors.

Felts
Continental Felt Company
22 West 15th Street
New York, New York 10011

Also available at printing equipment suppliers.

Files, Flat Storage
Gaylord Brothers
Box 4901
Syracuse, New York 13221

Mayline Company
Sheboygan, Wisconsin 53081

Interior Steel Equipment Company
2352 East 69th Street
Cleveland, Ohio 44104

Also available at art and drafting supply stores.

Fillets
See *Framespace*

Film, Ultraviolet Light-Filtering
Solar Protection Systems
176 Hempstead Avenue
West Hempstead, New York 11552

Plastic View
Van Nuys, California 91408

General Electric Company
Plastics Operation
One Plastics Avenue
Pittsfield, Massachusetts 01201

Weather Shield Manufacturing, Inc.
P.O. Box 309
Medford, Wisconsin 54451

Solor Screen Company
53–11 105th Street
Corona, New York 11368

Filmoplast SH
See *Tapes, Linen*

Filters: For Fluorescent Tubes
See *Filters: Ultraviolet Light-Filtering Sleeves*

Filters: Ultraviolet Light-Filtering Sleeves
Solor Screen Company
53–11 105th Street
Corona, New York 11368

Filter Light Corporation
1910 East Wenclover Avenue
P.O. Box 6292
Greensboro, North Carolina 27405

J. Freeman, Inc.
65 Tenean Street
Dorchester, Massachusetts 02122

See also Conservation Materials: Major Manufacturers and Distributors.

Filters, Water
Culligan
2047 Route 22 West
P.O. Box 551
Union, New Jersey 07083

Culligan
1 Culligan Parkway
Northbrook, Illinois 60062

Foam Boards
Fome-Cor
Monsanto Company
800 North Lindbergh Street
St. Louis, Missouri 63167

Folder Stock (.020 Cal.), Acid-free
Hollinger Corporation
P.O. Box 6185
3810 South Four-Mile-Run Drive
Arlington, Virginia 22206

B. W. Wilson Paper Company, Inc.
P.O. Box 11246
2501 Brittons Hill Road
Richmond, Virginia 23230

TALAS (Technical Library Service)
213 West 35th Street, 7th Floor
New York, New York 10001

Fome-Cor
See *Foam Boards*

Forceps
Fisher Scientific Company
52 Fadem Road
Springfield, New Jersey 07081

SPI Supplies
535 East Gay Street
West Chester, Pennsylvania 19380

Also available at other scientific supply companies.

Frame Hanger Hooks
Available at art and drafting supply stores. See also *Framing Hardware and Tools*

Framespace
FrameTek
2134 Old Middlefield Way
Mountain View, California 94043

See also *Framing Hardware and Tools*

Frames, Ready-Made
Light Impressions Corporation
439 Monroe Avenue
Rochester, New York 14603

Graphik Dimensions, Ltd.
41−23 Haight Street
Flushing, New York 11355

Charrette Corporation
31 Olympia Avenue
P.O. Box 4010
Woburn, Massachusetts 01888−4010

A.I. Friedman
25 West 45th Street
New York, New York 10036

Also available at art and drafting supply stores.

Framing Hardware and Tools
S &W Framing Supplies, Inc.
120 Broadway
Garden City Park, New York 11040
United Manufacturers Supplies, Inc.
Box 731
Hicksville, New York 11802
Also available at art and drafting supply stores.

Fumigant Gas Detectors
AMSCO/American Sterilizer Company
2425 West 23rd Street
Erie, Pennsylvania 16514

The Foxboro Company
Foxboro, Massachusetts 02035

Vacudyne Altair
375 East Joe Orr Road
Chicago Heights, Illinois 60411

Fumigation Chambers
Environmental Techtonics Corporation
County Line Industrial Park
Southampton, Pennsylvania 18966

Vacudyne Altair
375 East Joe Orr Road
Chicago Heights, Illinois 60411

Fungicides, O̲ -Phenyl Phenol
Fisher Scientific Company
52 Fadem Road
Springfield, New Jersey 07081

Dowicide 1:
Dow Chemical U.S.A.
Park 80 Plaza East
Saddle Brook, New Jersey 07662
Also available at other scientific supply companies.

Fungicides, Sodium O̲ -Phenol Phenate
Dowicide A:
Dow Chemical U.S.A.
Park 80 Plaza East
Saddle Brook, New Jersey 07662

Fungicides, Thymol
Fisher Scientific Company
52 Fadem Road
Springfield, New Jersey 07081
Also available at other scientific supply companies.

Glass
Beveled Squares, Plate:
Action Glass
572 Albany Avenue
Brooklyn, New York 11203

All-Boro Glass
53 Avenue D
New York, New York 10009

Also available at mirror and glass stores.

Glass-Cleaning Solutions
Light Impressions Corporation
439 Monroe Avenue
Rochester, New York 14603

See also *Framing Hardware and Tools;* also available at hardware and houseware stores.

Super Cote Lens Cleaner:
Denton Vacuum, Inc.
8 Springdale Road
Cherry Hill, New Jersey 08003

Glass Cutters
See *Framing Hardware and Tools.* Also available at hardware and houseware stores.

Glass, Nonreflective
Denglas:
Denton Vacuum, Inc.
8 Springdale Road
Cherry Hill, New Jersey 08003

Glassine, Neutral
See Paper and Board: Major Manufacturers and Distributors; also Conservation Materials: Major Manufacturers and Distributors.

Glazing Points
See *Framing Hardware and Tools*

Glue, PVA
See *Adhesives, PVA Emulsion*

Gossen Panlux Electronic Footcandle Meter
See *Lightmeters, Footcandles*

Gray Scale
Eastman Kodak Company
Rochester, New York 14650

Also available at photographic equipment stores.

Hinging Tissue
   See *Tissue, Japanese*

Hook-and-Loop Cloth and Fasteners
   See *Velcro Fasteners*

Humidity-Indicator Cards
   Multiform Disiccant Products, Inc.
   1418 Niagara Street
   Buffalo, New York 14213

   Micro Essential Laboratory
   4224 Avenue H.
   Brooklyn, New York 11210

   See also Conservation Materials: Major Manufacturers and
   Distributors.

Humidifiers
   See *Environmental Control Equipment*

Humidistats
   See *Environmental Control Equipment*

Hygrometers, Hygrothermographs
   Pastorelli and Rapkin
   287 Green Lane
   London N13 4XS, England

   Science Associates
   31 Airpark Road
   Box 230
   Princeton, New Jersey 08542

   Watrous and Company
   172 Euston Road
   Garden City, New York 11530

   Conservation Materials, Limited
   340 Freeport Boulevard
   P.O. Box 2884
   Sparks, Nevada 89431

   TALAS (Technical Library Service)
   213 West 35th Street, 7th Floor
   New York, New York 10001

   Also available at other scientific supply houses and at hardware
   and houseware stores.

Indicator Strips
   See *pH Measurement*

Ink, Stamping
Library of Congress
Preservation Office
Washington, D.C. 20540

Insta-Check-Surface pH Pencil
See *pH Measurement*

Interleaving Papers
See *Papers, Interleaving*

Jars, Glass, Storage
See *Storage, Glass Jars*

Jade #403
See *Adhesives, PVA Emulsion*

Lead Weights
Conservation Materials, Ltd.
340 Freeport Boulevard
P.O. Box 2884
Sparks, Nevada 89431
Also available at hardware and houseware stores.

Lens Cleaner
See *Glass-Cleaning Solutions*

Light Meters, Footcandle
Gossen Panlux Electronic Footcandle Meter:
Berkey Marketing Company, Inc.
Gossen Division
25–20 Brooklyn-Queens Expressway
Woodside, New York 11377

Weston Electric Instrument Company
P.O. Box 6292
Greensboro, North Carolina 27405
Also available at photographic equipment stores.

Light Meter, Ultraviolet
Littlemore UV light Monitor, Type 760:
Littlemore Scientific Engineering Company
Railway Lane
Littlemore, Oxford OX4 2PZ, England

Science Associates
31 Airpark Road
Box 230
Princeton, New Jersey 08542

TALAS (Technical Library Service)
213 West 35th Street, 7th Floor
New York, New York 10001

Light Impressions Corporation
439 Monroe Avenue
Rochester, New York 14603

Magnifiers, Loupes
TALAS (Technical Library Service)
213 West 35th Street, 7th Floor
New York, New York 10001

Conservation Materials, Ltd.
340 Freeport Boulevard
P.O. Box 2884
Sparks, Nevada 89431

Mat Board, 100 Percent Rag, 100 Percent Rag-Buffered, Conservation
See Paper and Board: Major Manufacturers and Distributors.

Mat Cutters
Keeton Kutter, Dexter Mat Cutter
S & W Framing Supplies, Incorporated
120 Broadway
Garden City Park, New York 11040

United Manufacturing Supplies, Incorporated
P.O. Box 731
Hicksville, New York 11802

Art Brown and Brothers, Inc.
2 West 46th Street
New York, New York 10036

Microspatulas
Fisher Scientific Company
52 Fadem Road
Springfield, New Jersey 07081

Conservation Materials, Ltd.
340 Freeport Boulevard
P.O. Box 2884
Sparks, Nevada 89431

Also available at other scientific supply houses.

Mirror Plates
See *Framing Hardware and Tools*

Mounting Corners
See *Photo Corners*

Museum Board
See Paper and Board: Major Manufacturers and Distributors

Museum Cases
See *Storage Boxes*

Mylar Polyester Type D Film
See *Polyester Film, Clear*

Naphthalene
Fisher Scientific Company
52 Fadem Road
Springfield, New Jersey 07081
Also available at other scientific supply houses and at hardware and houseware stores.

Natrasorb SG145
See *Desiccants, Silica Gel*

Opaline Dry-Cleaning Pad
See *Erasers, Powdered*

Optivisor
See *Magnifiers, Loupes*

Paper Cutters
See *Framing Hardware and Tools*

Paper, PermaLife
B. W. Wilson Paper Company, Inc.
P.O. Box 11246
2501 Brittons Hill Road
Richmond, Virginia 23230

Howard Paper Mill
P.O. Box 982
Dayton, Ohio 45401

Hollinger Corporation
P.O. Box 6185
3810 South Four-Mile-Run Drive
Arlington, Virginia 22206

Light Impressions Corporation
439 Monroe Avenue
Rochester, New York 14603

TALAS (Technical Library Service)
213 West 35th Street, 7th Floor
New York, New York 10001

Papers, Interleaving
Pohlig Brothers
2419 East Franklin Street
P.O. Box 8609
Richmond, Virginia 23223

Reflex Matte:
Process Materials Corporation
301 Veterans Boulevard
Rutherford, New Jersey 07070
See also Paper and Board: Major Manufacturers and Distributors;
Conservation Materials: Major Manufacturers and Distributors.

pH Measurement
Indicator Strips, Archivists' Pens and Pencils:
Micro Essential Laboratory
4224 Avenue H
Brooklyn, New York 11210
See also Conservation Materials: Major Manufacturers and
Distributors.

Photo Corners
Light Impressions Corporation
439 Monroe Avenue
Rochester, New York 14603

University Products, Incorporated
P.O. Box 101
Holyoke, Massachusetts 01041

pHydrion Jumbo Pencil
See *pH Measurement*

Picture-Hanger Hooks
See *Framing Hardware and Tools*

Plexiglas
See *Acrylic Sheet, Clear, Nonfiltering*

Plexiglas UF–3, UF–4
See *Acrylic Sheet, Clear, UV-Filtering*

Polyster Film, Clear
Mylar, Type D:
E. I. DuPont de Nemours and Company, Inc.
1107 North Market Street
Wilmington, Delaware 19898

Transilwrap Company
2615 North Paulina Street
Chicago, Illinois 60614

Hollinger Corporation
P.O. Box 6185
3810 South Four-Mile-Run Drive
Arlington, Virginia 22206
See also Conservation Materials: Major Manufacturers and
Distributors.

Polyester Web
See Conservation Materials: Major Manufacturers and Distributors.

Polystyrene Board
See *Foam Boards*

Propellants
Spra-Tool:
Crown Industrial Products Company
Hebron, Illinois 60034

Also available at hardware and houseware stores, art and drafting supply stores. See also Conservation Materials: Major Manufacturers and Distributors.

Psychrometers, Aspirating
The Bendix Corporation
Friez instrument Division
1400 Taylor Avenue
Baltimore, Maryland 21204

Belfort Instrument Company
1600 South Clinton Street
Baltimore, Maryland 21224

See also Conservation Materials: Major Manufacturers and Distributors.

Psychrometers, Sling
Bacharach Instruments
301 Alpha Drive
Pittsburgh, Pennsylvania 15238

Weathertronics
Division of Qualimatrics, Ins.
P.O. Box 41039

Watrous and Company
172 Euston Road
Garden City, New York 11530

Science Associates
31 Airpark Road
Princeton, New Jersey 08542

See also Conservation Materials: Major Manufacturers and Distributors.

PVA Emulsion
See *Adhesives, PVA Emulsion*

Rag Board
See Paper and Board: Major Manufacturers and Distributors.

Reagent Stains, Tri-Test
  Applied Science Laboratories, Inc.
  218 North Adams Street
  Richmond, Virginia 23220
  See also Conservation Materials: Major Manufacturers and Distributors.

Reflex Matte
  See *Papers, Interleaving*

Respirators with Organic Vapor Cartridges
  Directo Safety Company
  7815 South 46th Street
  Phoenix, Arizona 85040

  Fisher Scientific Company
  52 Fadem Road
  Springfield, New Jersey 07081
  Also available at other scientific supply houses.

Rice Starch
  Available at health food stores and specialty food stores; See also Conservation Materials: Major Manufacturers and Distributors.

Rulers, Straight-Edge
  See *Framing Hardware and Tools*

Scalpels
  Fisher Scientific Company
  52 Fadem Road
  Springfield, New Jersey 07081
  Also available at other scientific supply houses.

Silica Gel
  See *Desiccants, Silica Gel*

Silk Tissue
  See *Papers, Interleaving*

Skum-X
  See *Erasers, Powdered*

Slip Sheets
  See *Papers, Interleaving*
Solander Boxes
  See *Storage Boxes*

Spra-Tool
  See *Propellants*

Storage, Glass Jars
Fisher Scientific Company
52 Fadem Road
Springfield, New Jersey 07081

Also available at scientific supply companies, hardware and houseware stores.

Storage Boxes
Pohlig Brothers
2419 East Franklin Street
P.O. Box 8609
Richmond, Virginia 23223

Spink & Gaborc, Inc.
11 Troast Court
Clifton, New Jersey 07011

University Products Incorporated
P.O. Box 101
Holyoke, Massachusetts 01041

Museum Box Company
28 Graystone Street
Warwick, Rhode Island 02886

Hollinger Corporation
P.O. Box 6185
3810 South Four-Mile-Run Drive
Arlington, Virginia 22206

Process Materials Corporation
301 Veterans Boulevard
Rutherford, New Jersey 07070

TALAS (Technical Library Service)
213 West 35th Street, 7th Floor
New York, New York 10001

Conservation Materials, Limited
340 Freeport Boulevard
P.O. Box 2884
Sparks, Nevada 89431

Storage Tubes, Acid-Free
Pohlig Brothers, Incorporated
2419 East Franklin Street
P.O. Box 8069
Richmond, Virginia 23223

See also Paper and Board: Major Manufacturers and Distributors; Conservation Materials: Major Manufacturers and Distributors.

Swabs
See *Cotton Applicators*

Tapes, Encapsulation
3M Double-Sided Tape #415:
3M Company
3M Center
St. Paul, Minnesota 55144
See also Conservation Materials: Major Manufacturers and Distributors.

Tapes, Linen
Pressure-Sensitive Filmoplast SH:
Hans Neschen, Incorporated
D-3962 Buckeburg
West Germany
Filmolux of Canada
115 Eleta Drive
Scarborough, Ontario M1k 3G8, Canada
See also Conservation Materials: Major Manufacturers and Distributors.

Tapes, Linen (Holland)
Water-Based:
Available at art and drafting supply stores. See also Conservation Materials: Major Manufacturers and Distributors.

Thermometers
Conservation Materials, Limited
340 Freeport Boulevard
P.O. Box 2884
Sparks, Nevada 89431
Fisher Scientific Company
52 Fadem Road
Springfield, New Jersey 07081
Also available at hardware and houseware stores and other scientific supply houses.

Thermostats
See *Environmental Control Equipment*

Thymol
See *Fungicides, Thymol*

Tissue, Buffered
See Paper and Board: Major Manufacturers and Distributors.

Tissue, Japanese
Aiko's Art Materials Import
714 North Wabash Avenue
Chicago, Illinois 60611
Washi No Mise
Road #2
Kennett Square, Pennsylvania 19348
Kalamazoo Handmade Papers
5947 North 25th Street
Kalamazoo, Michigan 49004
New York Central Supply
62 Third Avenue
New York, New York 10003
See also Conservation Materials: Major Manufacturers and Distributors.

Tubes, Storage, Acid-Free
See *Storage Tubes, Acid-Free*

Turn-Buttons
See *Framing Hardware and Tools*

Tweezers
Fisher Scientific Company
52 Fadem Road
Springfield, New Jersey 07081
SPI Supplies
535 East Gay Street
West Chester, Pennsylvania 19380
Also available at other scientific supply houses.

Utility Knives
See *Framing Hardware and Tools*

Ultraviolet Light-Filtering Acrylic Sheet
See *Acrylic Sheet, Clear, UV-Filtering*

Ultraviolet Light-Filtering Film
See *Film, Ultraviolet Light-Filtering*

Ultraviolet Light-Filtering Sleeves
See *Filters: Ultraviolet Light-Filtering Sleeves*

Ultraviolet Light Monitor
See *Light Meter, Ultraviolet*

Velcro Fasteners
Velcro U.S.A.
88 Park Avenue
Nutley, New Jersey 07110

Conservation Materials, Limited
340 Freeport Boulevard
P.O. Box 2884
Sparks, Nevada 89431

Also available at art and drafting supply stores and office supply stores.

Water, Distilled

Hardware and houseware stores.

Water Filters

Culligan
2047 Route 22 West
P.O. Box 551
Union, New Jersey 07083

Culligan
1 Culligan Parkway
Northbrook, Illinois 60062

Weights, Lead

Conservation Materials, Limited
340 Freeport Boulevard
P.O. Box 2884
Sparks, Nevada 89431

Instruments for Research and Industry
108 Franklin Avenue
Cheltenham, Pennsylvania 19012

Also available at hardware and houseware stores.

Wheat Starch

Available at health food stores and specialty food stores. See also Conservation Materials: Major Manufacturers and Distributors.

Wrapping Paper, Acid-Free

See Paper and Board: Major Manufacturers and Distributors.

APPENDIX 2

How To Make Paste

Everyone has a favorite paste recipe, and no doubt the reader will adjust this one, as he or she becomes more familiar with the working properties of the paste these directions will produce.

Most formulas for paste call for a basic starch-to-water ratio of 1:7—weight-to-volume ratio, that is: one gram of starch mixed with seventy milliliters of water, or the nonmetric equivalents of each. In conservation laboratories, other ingredients may be added, to produce increased tackiness or alkalinity, or to increase or decrease the mixture's strength. For general purposes, however, starch and water are the only ingredients needed. For readers working without access to scales, I have provided volume measurements for the starch. Since starches vary in fluffiness, however, these "ready-made" volume measurements are approximate. Ounce equivalents are given, as well.

The difference between paste made with wheat starch and that made with rice starch has long been debated. For general purposes, such as tear repair and hinging, either type of starch can be used, provided that it is of food quality (safe enough to eat, though not intended as a foodstuff) and that it contain no impurities. Both wheat and rice starch can be obtained at conservation supply houses.

The following formula yields a small quantity of paste—about one-third of a cup, which should be enough for routine hinging or tear repair. Paste without preservatives lasts several days. *With* preservatives, paste can last for several weeks. Paste does not have to be refrigerated, but it should be discarded as soon as it sours or separates.

Paste Ingredients and Supplies:

Wheat or rice starch, food grade
Water—distilled, de-ionized, or filtered
Scale for measurement (or teaspoons, if no scale
    is available)
Graduated cylinder or measuring cup, to measure
    milliliters or ounces
Glass jar or beaker
Stove or electric hot plate
Double boiler made of glass or enamel
Wooden spoon
Ceramic or glass storage container with
    nonmetallic lid
Strainer made of cheesecloth or nonmetallic mesh

If preservative is wanted:

Thymol or o-phenyl phenol
Ethanol (ethyl alcohol), reagent grade, denatured

Directions

Weigh out 10 grams (⅓ ounce) of starch. This will be approximately 4½ to 5¼ teaspoons, depending upon the fluffiness of the starch. Mix starch with 70 milliliters (approximately ⅓ cup) of filtered or distilled water. Stir to dissolve any lumps. Let stand for half an hour.

Meantime, fill the bottom of a double boiler with water and bring it to a boil. Reduce heat to low. Pour starch-and-water mixture into the top container of the double boiler and place that over the simmering water in the bottom pan. Stir the starch-and-water mixture continuously with a wooden spoon. The mixture will thicken and then stiffen and turn almost translucent. Continue stirring for a total cooking time of about ten to fifteen minutes. Larger quantites of paste will take longer to cook.

If a preservative is to be added, prepare the solution for it before-hand. Dissolve crystals of thymol or o-phenyl phenol in ethanol until the solution is saturated—that is, until no more will dissolve. O- phenyl phenol is preferable, because it is less toxic than thymol. Stir *only a few drops* of whichever preservative is used into the paste while the mixture is still hot. *If thymol is used, do not add it to the paste without providing adequate ventilation, and* DO NOT BREATHE THE FUMES.

Spoon the cooked paste into a storage container and allow it to cool. When cool, the paste will be quite stiff.

Paste Storage

Glass jars with metal screw tops should not be used for paste storage, because the metal lids will rust easily. Use instead food storage containers with plastic snap-on tops, or glass jars with plastic screw tops. Store the capped containers in a cool, dark place.

To Use Stored Paste

To use stored paste, take a small amount of it out of the container and force it through a strainer of nonmetallic mesh with the back of a spoon once or twice. This will make the mixture much easier to thin with water. Without this step, lumps will form in the paste when water is added to it. Using a short, stiff-bristled brush, mix in distilled, de-ionized, or filtered water, until the paste is of the consistency of heavy cream or yogurt. It is now ready to use.

APPENDIX 3

A Thymol Cabinet and Instructions for Its Use

Probably the most important single essential fact about mold control is this: mold cannot be sustained on prints and drawings kept in an environment of 45 to 55 percent RH. In most instances, when mold is encountered, the only treatment required is that the artwork be moved to a drier environment. In some instances, it should be unframed and any damp materials with which it may be in contact should be removed. Many conservators have stopped using thymol altogether, because they have concluded that it is not necessary, in the first place, or even effective when it is used.

The information that follows, therefore, is provided for two reasons: to persuade those presently using thymol and convinced of the need for it to recognize the need for using it correctly, in terms of its adverse health implications; and to describe the method for using thymol safely when appropriate situations do arise.

The fumes of thymol (isopropyl-meta-cresol) and o-phenyl phenol (Dowicide 1) have been found effective in deactivating a variety of fungi that attack paper fibers and additives commonly found in paper. Traditionally, thymol has been used in airtight cabinets to disinfect moldy papers. While o-phenyl phenol is recommended for use in pastes and humidity chambers, because of its lower toxicity, I have found no guidelines on its use in fumigation chambers—that is, recommended quantities per cubic foot, time of exposure, and so on.

Exposure of a work of art to thymol fumes will not prevent recurrence of mold growth if the art is returned to a humid environment. It will only retard mold growth under humid conditions. Even then, as Haines and Kohler suggest, thymol may not be as effective as it was previously believed to be. Invisible mold spores are virtually everywhere;

new ones will soon settle on the art and grow if conditions permit. Exposure to a fungicide will not alter the appearance of actual mold growth; once there, it will not lessen or disappear.

When to fumigate. Fumigation is not necessary for art on paper under normal circumstances. If mold growth has occurred at some time in the artwork's past, the actual mold spores are long dead and won't cause further problems. New mold spores, present in the air everywhere— even in polar regions—cannot grow under conditions recommended for prints and drawings. Generally speaking, fumigation is undertaken when it is known that a work of art has recently been exposed to high humidity levels for several days, especially if it has come from a dark area with little ventilation. Often, no actual mold growth is visible, but a musty odor will indicate some fungal activity. Mold growth can appear as a sprinkling of tiny dark pinpoints, or as blotchy areas of discoloration, or as feathery wisps. The mold growth may be visible on the glass used in framing a print or drawing rather than on the object itself. Similarly, mold may appear on the backboard or other papers within the frame. If items have been rescued from a high-humidity situation and the paper feels damp, it would be wise to expose such pieces to thymol. Fumigation is more readily undertaken when pastels are involved, because of the greater susceptibility to mold growth of items done in that medium. Since pastels are normally kept framed, some institutions routinely expose pastel works to fumigants whenever they are occasionally unframed for any reason.

When NOT to fumigate. Thymol softens varnishes and some resins. Oil paintings on paper or prints done with inks that look particularly oily or resinous should not be put into thymol cabinets. Parchment may be embrittled by exposure to thymol, and the heat involved in fumigating can cause parchment to buckle excessively. Generally speaking, photographs are not exposed to thymol unless the work is done under the direction of a photographic conservator. Information on the effects of o-phenyl phenol on varnishes and proteinacious material is not available.

Prints and drawings should not be fumigated for mold growth when the precautions below cannot be followed. The reader should be aware that, because of the health risks involved, many conservators have stopped using thymol cabinets entirely and have removed them from the premises.

Precautions to be taken. Thymol is now considered to be a potential carcinogen. Overexposure to the chemical can cause irritation of the eyes, nose, and upper respiratory system. The central nervous system, circulatory system, liver, and kidneys can likewise be affected with prolonged exposure. Extreme care, therefore, must be taken when handling thymol crystals or breathing thymol fumes, since the chemical is toxic via skin absorption, inhalation, and ingestion.

To avoid absorption of the chemical through the skin, always wear neoprene or butyl rubber gloves when measuring out thymol crystals. If thymol does come into contact with skin, wash the affected area immediately with water; if thymol powder or crystals touch the eyes, rinse with running water for fifteen minutes and call a doctor. Wear a respirator fitted with organic vapor cartridges when opening the thymol cabinet or pouring out quantities of crystals. When the door to the thymol cabinet is open, ask everyone not wearing a respirator to leave the room. Guidelines for selecting a respirator are found in Michael McCann's article listed under "Further Reading." Close the door as promptly as possible; never leave a thymol cabinet open for longer than necessary. Do not eat around open containers of thymol crystals or use utensils involved in their handling for any other purpose. After use, clean all tools that have come into contact with thymol.

Do not immediately handle an artwork after it has been removed from a thymol cabinet; allow the fumes it has absorbed to dissipate. Never use the thymol cabinet for any other purpose than disinfecting prints and drawings showing evidence of actual or possible mold growth.

The fumes of thymol are very pungent and quite distinctive, which helps one to be aware of their presence. In addition to its irritating odor, thymol announces itself to the individual entering the early stage of overexposure by inducing headache and respiratory irritation. Of course, it is best not to allow even these early symptoms to develop. Gastric pain, nausea and vomiting, or impaired motor-nerve reactions indicate a situation so dangerous that anyone so affected must be removed from the area immediately.

To avoid the health risks associated with use of thymol, a thymol cabinet should be constructed according to the following specifications.

Design and construction of a thymol cabinet. The diagram shown in figure App. 3.1 was provided by the Center for Occupational Hazards, New York. The center's four-page information and data sheet is highly recommended for anyone working with thymol; it contains the most up-to-date information available on health hazards related to thymol. The cabinet shown in figure App. 3.1 is representative of all thymol cabinets in general. The cabinet should be large enough to accommodate a variety of sizes of prints and drawings, usually up to 30 inches by 40 inches, with plenty of air space around the art objects to allow for circulation of the fumigant. The shelves are made of slatted wood or stretched screening,

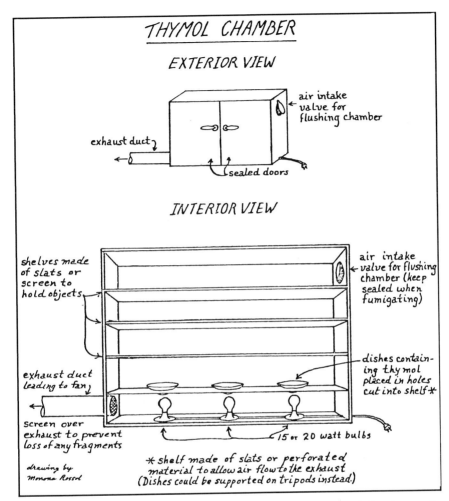

THYMOL CHAMBER

EXTERIOR VIEW

air intake valve for flushing chamber

exhaust duct

sealed doors

INTERIOR VIEW

shelves made of slats or screen to hold objects

air intake valve for flushing chamber (keep sealed when fumigating)

dishes containing thymol placed in holes cut into shelf *

exhaust duct leading to fan

screen over exhaust to prevent loss of any fragments

15 or 20 watt bulbs

* shelf made of slats or perforated material to allow air flow to the exhaust (Dishes could be supported on tripods instead.)

drawing by Monona Rossol

Fig. App. 3.1. This drawing by Monona Rossol, president of the Center for Occupational Hazards, shows both exterior and interior views of a thymol cabinet. The drawing is reprinted, by permission of the artist, from the data sheet "Thymol and O-Phenyl Phenol: Safe Work Practices," by Deborah Nagin and Michael McCann. Copyright © 1982 by the Center for Occupational Hazards.

to allow for overall exposure. Opinions differ on the finish of the interior of the cabinet. Usually, the inside of a wooden cabinet is left unfinished, since some paints are softened by thymol fumes. Deborah Nagin and Michael McCann, in *Thymol and O-Phenyl Phenol: Safe Work Practices*, however, suggest that the inside of the cabinet be painted with an epoxy paint so that the wood does not absorb and then release excess fumes. In either situation, care must be taken to insure that it is only the art itself that is exposed to thymol fumes, and not the people handling it.

For that reason, the cabinet must be as airtight as possible. All joints should be sealed and a rubber gasket should be installed around the doors to guarantee a tight fit. If glass panels are inserted into the doors, these panels should be sealed around all edges.

The Center for Occupational Hazards recommends that the cabinet be equipped with an exhaust fan and an outside vent (see diagram). After fumigation is completed and before the doors are opened, the cabinet is flushed for one hour with fresh air entering an intake vent located in the upper corner of the cabinet. This vent is kept tightly closed at all other times. An outlet vent leads to an exhaust fan located in a window or outside duct. The exhaust fan should have the least rate of air flow possible and should be a forward-curved, centrifugal "squirrel cage" type. For a chamber measuring 30 by 40 by 36 inches, a flow rate of ten cubic feet per minute is sufficient. The air flow within the chamber should not be so vigorous as to disturb thin papers. The motor of the fan should be a nonsparking, brushless-induction type.

For a cabinet having approximately 25 cubic feet of interior space, one shallow glass dish is suspended no less than one inch above each of three 15- or 20-watt light bulbs secured in outlets on the bottom of the cabinet. Barry Byers, in "A Simple and Practical Fumigation System," has recommended that one light bulb and one glass dish be provided for every 9 cubic feet of interior space. That can be done by using small bunson burner tripods available from scientific supply companies or by placing the dishes on a low, slatted wooden or perforated metal shelf. The heat from the light bulbs causes the thymol crystals to sublime— that is, to change directly from a solid state into a gas. It is important that the light bulbs not be stronger than 15 to 20 watts. Too much heat will cause the thymol crystals to overheat and possibly cause deposits of precipitated crystals to form on the inside walls of the cabinet or on the art objects themselves.

Other features of the thymol cabinet should include an on/off switch mounted on the outside of the chamber, and possibly an automatic timer.

Instructions for use. The artwork to be fumigated is placed in the cabinet. Usually it is supported by a thin sheet of paper, measuring only slightly larger than the artwork, for overall support. Books should be open, with their pages separated at various places with folded blotter strips, to aid penetration. Anne F. Clapp, in *Curatorial Care of Works of Art on Paper,* suggests inserting plastic drinking straws to help spread book pages apart. One ounce of thymol for every 16 cubic feet of interior space is divided among the shallow glass dishes. A cabinet measuring 30 by 40 by 36 inches has almost 25 cubic feet of interior space. In this instance, approximately 1½ ounces of thymol would be used. The lights are turned on for one to two hours once a day for three consecutive days. During that time, the cabinet is kept closed, unless the art being fumigated needs more frequent examination. At the end of three days, the cabinet, still closed, is flushed with fresh air entering through the intake vent and exhausted directly outside. If no exhaust system is available, the art should be quickly removed and the cabinet doors shut immediately. The art should be taken into another room or at least put into an area of the fumigation room not frequented by people. The person actually handling the artwork should wear a respirator fitted with cartridges suitable for filtering organic vapors. The art should be handled again only when no thymol odors are detectable.

FOR FURTHER READING

Byers, Barry. "A Simple and Practical Fumigation System." *The Abbey Newsletter* 7, No. 4 Supplement (September 1983): 1–4.

Clapp, Anne F. *Curatorial Care of Works of Art on Paper.* 3rd ed. rev. Oberlin: Intermuseum Conservation Association, 1978.

Clark, Nancy, Thomas Cutter, and Jean-Ann McGrane. *Ventilation: A Practical Guide.* New York: Center for Occupational Hazards, 1984.

Haines, John H., and Stuart A. Kohler. "An Evaluation of Ortho-Phenyl Phenol as a Fungicidal Fumigant for Archives and Libraries." *Journal of the American Institute for Conservation of Historic and Artistic Works* 25 (1986): 49-55.

McCann, Michael. *Respirator Use in Conservation Laboratories.* New York: Center for Occupational Hazards, 1986.

Nagin, Deborah, and Michael McCann. *Thymol and O-Phenyl Phenol: Safe Work Practices.* New York: Center for Occupational Hazards, 1982.

Petherbridge, Guy, and J. Malcolm Harrington. "Safety and Health in the Paper Conservation Laboratory." *The Paper Conservator* 5, 6 (1980, 1981).

An Annotated Bibliography

More specialized references are listed in "Further Reading" at the end of each chapter.

Books

Banks, Paul N. *Matting and Framing Documents and Art Objects on Paper.* Rev. ed. Chicago: Newberry Library, 1973.

This technical leaflet discusses in simple, straightforward terms the general causes of paper deterioration and the proper procedures for matting, hinging, glazing, and framing.

Clapp, Anne F. *Curatorial Care of Works of Art on Paper.* 3d rev. ed. Oberlin: Intermuseum Conservation Association, 1978.

The Bible of conservation literature, this book addresses everyday problems of dampness, dryness, heat, acidity, light, mold, and insects; basic conservation procedures; and the mechanics of matting, framing, encapsulating, and storing art on paper. Clapp specifies sources for materials and equipment and includes a sample examination form and diagrams of storage boxes, a fumigation chamber, and matted and framed works of art.

Dolloff, Francis W., and Roy L. Perkinson. *How to Care for Works of Art on Paper.* Boston: Museum of Fine Arts, 1971.

This small handbook summarizes the history of papermaking and describes inherent faults of paper, as well as its enemies—careless handling, humidity, light, heat, air pollution, and insects. Dolloff and Perkinson outline proper procedures for matting and framing and provide a useful guide to materials and sources and a selected bibliography.

Glaser, Mary Todd. *Framing and Preserving Works of Art on Paper.* New York: Sotheby Parke Bernet, 1972.

This excellent pamphlet considers the various aspects of framing, including matting, hinging, glazing, and sealing of frames.

Hauser, Robert. *Paper: Its History and Conservation.* Housatonic, Mass.: Rising Paper, 1980.

This book addresses the history of papyrus, parchment, and paper, and the technology that produces them, with some attention to the permanence of paper in general and the properties of high-quality papers.

Kenyon, Douglas. *Framing and Conservation of Works of Art on Paper.* New York: Crestwood Paper, 1980.

This seven-page booklet considers the common enemies of paper and the proper procedures for matting and framing. I strongly disagree with the author's opinion that unvarnished wooden cabinets are optimal storage furniture.

Plenderleith, H.J., and A. E. A. Werner. *The Conservation of Antiquities and Works of Art.* 2d rev. ed. London: Oxford University Press, 1971.

This book, long considered the authority in its field, remains invaluable, today, for its consideration of artistic materials other than paper. The reader would, however, be ill-advised to follow procedures recommended in chapters 2 and 3 for restoration of papyrus, parchment, and paper.

Rogers, Madeline. "Framing Works of Art on Paper." *Art and Antiques* 3, no. 2 (March–April 1980): 50ff.

Rogers's interview with two New York conservators covers various problems and includes instructions for the use of archival materials and procedures.

Schonberg, Jeanne. *Questions to Ask Your Framer and Answers You Should Get.* Los Angeles: Tamarind, n.d.

The eighteen questions and answers concern aesthetic aspects of framing and the instructions that could reasonably be given to a framer.

Shelley, Marjorie. *The Care and Handling of Art Objects.* New York: The Metropolitan Museum of Art, forthcoming.

A handbook setting forth guidelines for the proper care of museum objects, including prints and drawings.

Zigrosser, C., and C.M. Gaehde. *A Guide to the Collecting and Care of Original Prints*. New York: Print Council of America, 1965.

This ever-popular book discusses prints and the market for them, including such controversial issues as dealers' qualifications and codes of ethics. A section on the care and conservation of fine prints addresses the causes of common problems and provides instructions on proper matting, hinging, and framing. Advice is also given on the selection of a paper conservator.

Periodicals

History News. The American Association for State and Local History, Nashville, Tennessee.

Includes technical leaflets that are especially informative.

Museum News. The American Association of Museums, Washington, D.C.

Concerned with general curatorial conservation subjects.

Technology and Conservation of Art, Architecture, and Antiques. Technology Organization, Boston.

Read by conservators and preservationists and has reader-service cards useful for obtaining suppliers' information.

Journal of the American Institute for Conservation. The American Institute for Conservation of Historic and Artistic Works, Washington, D.C.

Addresses conservators and conservation scientists and reports on recent developments in conservation. The AIC *Newsletter* comments on current events in conservation on a bimonthly basis.

Studies in Conservation. International Institute for Conservation of Historic and Artistic Works, London.

Addresses conservators and conservation scientists.

Journal of the IIC.-CG. The International Institute for Conservation of Historic and Artistic Works, Canadian Group, Ottawa.

Addresses conservators and conservation scientists.

The Paper Conservator. Institute of Paper Conservation, London.

> Contains highly technical information specifically for paper conservators.

Restaurator: International Journal for the Preservation of Library and Archival Material. Munksgaard International, Copenhagen.

> Published irregularly, but contains articles of interest to paper and book conservators.

Art and Archaeology Technical Abstracts. International Institute for Conservation of Historic and Artistic Works, the Getty Conservation Institute, Santa Monica, California.

> Contains abstracts of articles concerning all aspects of the conservation profession.

The Abbey Newsletter. Ellen McCrady, Preservation Department, Brigham Young University, Provo, Utah.

> Chiefly addresses bookbinders, but often discusses recent developments in paper conservation.

Index

lems, 96; and glazing material, 131
Temperature; levels ideal for paper and parchment, 14, 25; practical range, 25; fluctuations in, 25-26, 159-160; windows and temperature control, 163; effects of high temperatures, 167
Tengujo, 121, 188. *See also* Tissues, Japanese
Tetrapanax papyriferus ("rice paper"), 4, 8
Thymol: to combat mold growth, 45, 85, 165-166; thymol and photographs, 45; harmful to some art materials, 45, 165-166; thymol strips in storage containers, 166; as preservative for paste, 234; adverse health implications, 237-238
—Thymol cabinet: and safety precautions, 236-241
"Tide lines": on grounded papers, 100
"Time toning," 27
Tissues: for repairing artworks, 79, 187-188; in lining, 141; in hinging, 120-121, 125; and slipsheets, 151; and storage mats, 151-152
—Japanese tissues: and early wood engravings, 62; names and characteristics of, 120-121
"Traveling" artworks: packing safely, 90; with glass in frames, 90, 135-137; and flaking, 96; glazing materials for, 131
Trimming artworks, 113, 143*n3*

Ukiyo-e prints: and light sensitivity, 75
Unframing prints and drawings, 137-139
Ultraviolet light: and daylight, 91; effects on paper and pigments, 91; measures to lessen effects, 167-170

—Filtering agents: ultraviolet-resistant glazing materials, 131, 168

Velcro cloth, 183
Vellum, 10, 165
Visitors' rules: for handling prints and drawings, 155-156

Wallpaper, 140, 155. *See also* Oversized artworks
Water: potential source of damage, 145, 147, 180
Water-based paints, 91
Watercolors: categorized among prints and drawings, 5; in colored prints, 75; supports and light reflection, 90; durability, 91; light sensitivity, 91, 92, 131
Water-sensitive media: testing for, 195-196
Water sensitivity: spot-testing, 192-193
Waxy crayons, 101, 102
Whatman paper, 17, 18
White lead pigment: and air pollution, 95, 96, 157
Window opening, 115-119 *passim*
Wire screens, 147. *See also* Storage
Woodblock prints, 75
Woodcuts, 62, 64
Wood engravings, 62, 63, 64
Wooden storage equipment: files, cabinets, 147-148; shelving, 149
Wood pulp: in papermaking, 17, 19, 24, 28-29, 37; and mat board, 110, 111; in short-fibered papers, 195; and deacidification, 199